BEST ADVICE ON WRITING *INSPIRATIONAL* FICTION...

A NOV

STARTS NOW. . . . .

VEL
IDEA

>

ChiLibris

 TYNDALE HOUSE PUBLISHERS, INC.,
CAROL STREAM, ILLINOIS

Visit Tyndale's exciting Web site at www.tyndale.com

TYNDALE and Tyndale's quill logo are registered trademarks of Tyndale House Publishers, Inc.

A Novel Idea: Best Advice on Writing Inspirational Fiction

Copyright © 2009 by ChiLibris. All rights reserved.

Cover photo copyright © by Julie Chen. All rights reserved.

Cover designed by Julie Chen

Interior designed by Dean H. Renninger

Edited by Kathryn S. Olson, Caleb Sjogren, and Erin E. Smith

Published in association with the literary agency Books & Such, Inc., Janet Kobobel Grant, 4788 Carrisa Ave., Santa Rosa, CA 95405.

Library of Congress Cataloging-in-Publication Data

A novel idea : best advice on writing inspirational fiction / [edited by Kathryn S. Olson, Caleb Sjogren, and Erin E. Smith].
  p. cm.
  ISBN 978-1-4143-2994-9 (sc)
1. Christian fiction—Authorship. 2. Christian fiction—Technique. I. Olson, Kathryn S. II. Sjogren, Caleb. III. Smith, Erin E.
  PN3377.5.C47N68 2009
  808.3—dc22   2009022882

Printed in the United States of America

15 14 13 12 11 10 09
 7   6   5   4   3   2   1

CONTENTS

Foreword
  Angela Hunt and Robin Jones Gunn xi

Introduction:
  Why Fiction? *Sharon Hinck xv*
  Nothing Is Wasted *Amy Wallace xvii*
  To Write *Karen Kingsbury xviii*

PART ONE: THE FUNDAMENTALS OF FICTION

Chapter 1: Plot
  The Plot Skeleton *Angela Hunt 3*
  Essentials of Fiction: Generate Conflict *Randy Alcorn 12*
  The Sagging Middle *Gail Gaymer Martin 13*
  Planning Your Series *Sandra Byrd 18*
  Essentials of Fiction: Keep It Credible *Randy Alcorn 23*
  Nine Steps to a Moving Story Arc *Gayle Roper 24*
  Red Herrings, Clues, and Other Plot Devices *Robin Caroll 25*
  Let's Do the Twist *Brandilyn Collins 29*

Chapter 2: Characters
  Up Close and Personal: Getting on Intimate Terms with Your
      Characters *Susan Meissner 35*
  The Muscles of Storytelling *Jill Elizabeth Nelson 42*
  Essentials of Fiction: Unforgettable *Randy Alcorn 42*
  Crafting Real-Life Characters *Tamera Alexander 47*

Essentials of Fiction: Write in Three Dimensions
  Randy Alcorn 47
Essentials of Fiction: Don't Construct, Create *Randy Alcorn* 51
Wrestling Through the Issues with Your Characters
  Lisa Tawn Bergren 52
Birth of a Character *Jerry B. Jenkins* 52

Chapter 3: Dialogue
Dialogue as Action *James Scott Bell* 57
Essentials of Fiction: Write Authentic Conversations
  Randy Alcorn 60
The Dollhouse Syndrome *Donita K. Paul* 63

Chapter 4: Point of View
Everything You Wanted to Know about POV . . . but Were
  Embarrassed to Ask *Robin Jones Gunn with Angela Hunt* 65
Point of View: Connect with Your Characters
  Carol Umberger 72

Chapter 5: Pacing
Pacing on Purpose *Brad Whittington* 77
Creating Page-Turning Chapter Endings *Sharon Dunn* 82
Essentials of Fiction: Make It Compelling *Randy Alcorn* 86

Chapter 6: Setting
Bringing Setting to Life *Patti Hill* 89
Protagonist, Antagonist . . . Setagonist *Nancy Rue* 93

Chapter 7: Descriptions
The Power of the Right Word *Deborah Raney* 97
Essentials of Fiction: Resist the Urge to Explain *Randy Alcorn* 102
The Building Blocks of a Scene *Jill Elizabeth Nelson* 104

CONTENTS

Essentials of Fiction: Specify *Randy Alcorn* *105*

PART TWO: DEVELOPING YOUR CRAFT

Chapter 8: Preparation

How to Read Novels like a Writer *Linda Hall* *111*
The Work before the Work *Jane Kirkpatrick* *116*
An Interview with Francine Rivers: Preparation *119*
Research: Immersing Yourself in History *Cara Putman* *121*
Essentials of Fiction: Don't Skimp on Research *Randy Alcorn* *124*
Interviewing the Others *Anne de Graaf* *125*

Chapter 9: The Discipline of Writing

Staying Organized in the Writing Process *Elizabeth White* *129*
Doing a Fast First Draft *Linda Ford* *134*
Tunnel Vision—a Writer's Friend *Carolyne Aarsen* *139*
Essentials of Fiction: Work Hard *Randy Alcorn* *140*
Conquering the Block *Janelle Clare Schneider* *142*
Finding a Twenty-Fifth Hour in Your Day *Rick Acker* *145*
Essentials of Fiction: Rewrite It *Randy Alcorn* *146*

Chapter 10: Finding Your Voice

The Rules, Voice, and When to Deviate *Mary DeMuth* *151*
Essentials of Fiction: Stay Invisible *Randy Alcorn* *156*
Finding and Honing Your Writer's Voice *Camy Tang* *157*
An Interview with Francine Rivers: Voice *163*

Chapter 11: Writing with Expression

Writing to Change Lives *Karen Kingsbury* *165*
Writing Novels from the Inside Out *Mary DeMuth* *173*

Essentials of Fiction: Create an "Aha" Moment
Randy Alcorn 176

Chapter 12: Handling Rejection
The Power of Humility *Hannah Alexander* 179
When God Says Wait *Janelle Clare Schneider* 183
Rethinking Rejection *Kim Vogel Sawyer* 184

PART THREE: WRITING CHRISTIAN FICTION

Chapter 13: Discerning Your Calling
How I Felt God Calling Me to Write for Him
Robin Lee Hatcher 189
An Interview with Francine Rivers: Calling 190
Writing: Ministry or Profession? *Rene Gutteridge* 193

Chapter 14: Distinctives of Christian Fiction
What Makes Christian Fiction Christian? *Ron Benrey* 199
Avoiding Preachy Fiction *Virginia Smith* 204
Writing the Nuances of Christian Content in Fiction
Randy Singer 207
An Interview with Francine Rivers: Distinctives 210
Closing the Bedroom Door *Terri Blackstock* 212
Evil in Fiction *Athol Dickson* 220

PART FOUR: NETWORKING AND MARKETING

Chapter 15: Soliciting Feedback
Confessions of a Critique Groupie *Virginia Smith* 229
Developing a Critique Partner Relationship *Tamera Alexander and Deborah Raney* 233

CONTENTS

Beware of CGD: Critique Group Dependency *Angela Hunt* 238

Chapter 16: Breaking into Publishing
How to Write a Proposal *Mindy Starns Clark* 243
How to Write a Compelling Synopsis *Nancy Mehl* 253
Formatting Your Manuscript *Siri Mitchell* 257
What to Expect from a Writers' Conference *Deborah Raney* 258
Top Writers' Conferences *Deborah Raney* 262
What to Expect from an Editor *Colleen Coble* 264

Chapter 17: Marketing
Promoting Your Novel *Melanie Dobson* 269
Shameless Self-Promotion *Patricia Hickman* 276
Blogging! Who, Me? *Maureen Lang* 279
The Value of Online Social Networks *Rachel Hauck* 286

Appendix:
The Writer's Indispensable Bookshelf *Tamara Leigh* 289

Contributors 293

FOREWORD

Angela Hunt and Robin Jones Gunn

Spiritual serendipity is a wonderful thing. The book you hold in your hand was birthed on the way to a Five Guys hamburger restaurant because one of us (Robin) just happened to have a long-lost relative in the other's (Angela's) neighborhood, so we just happened to carpool home after a convention, and we just happened to go out for a bite to eat, and we just happened to discuss how a group of novelists could help writers throughout the world by pulling together and donating some time and effort. . . .

The group of novelists in question was the group known as ChiLibris, which began on a hot Sunday afternoon in July 1999. Twenty-five novelists gathered for lunch during a Christian booksellers' convention and had such a grand time together they decided to keep in touch via the Internet. Since that quiet beginning, the group has grown to nearly three hundred Christian novelists, all of whom are multipublished. So what might this group have to share with aspiring writers? Plenty, we thought. And the idea for this book was born.

But we know things don't "just happen." The God who directs our steps and has already recorded all of our days planned that moment of epiphany. He fired up Robin's tender heart for missions and combined it with Angela's penchant for organizing projects; he energized agent Janet Grant with enthusiasm and spurred Tyndale House Publishers to catch the vision. He gifted editor Jan Stob with patience and wisdom, and most of all, he inspired dozens of willing writers to give of themselves and their experience to help you . . . and, in so doing, to aid writers around the world who seek to share the gospel of Jesus Christ with others.

We're wondering if the fact that you are now holding this book might be a "God thing" as well. Have you long sensed an urge to tell stories? Do you delight in capturing words and turning them into images on a blank page? Have others often told you, "You should be a writer"? When given the opportunity, do your thoughts and feelings come together to weave stories that stay tucked away inside? You may well be a novelist, and now may well be the time to pursue that possibility.

Listen to this portion of Galatians 6 from *The Message*. These verses make a fitting exhortation for all writers:

> Make a careful exploration of who you are and the work you have been given, and then sink yourself into that. Don't be impressed with yourself. Don't compare yourself with others. Each of you must take responsibility for doing the creative best you can with your own life.

There's nothing quite like the thrill of seeing the body of Christ in action. It is our hope and prayer that the articles in this book will help you learn to better communicate stories that can reach hearts and change lives. And by purchasing this book, know that you are furthering the work of Media Associates International, an organization dedicated to training Christian publishers and writers in difficult places around the globe. All those who contributed to this book have agreed that the entire proceeds from sales will go to MAI to provide international training. You can check out what MAI is doing to further the gospel through Christian publishing by visiting www.littworld.org.

What do you think? Are you ready to take responsibility for doing your creative best? May the spiritual serendipity in your writing life begin!

INTRODUCTION

¶

Why Fiction?
Sharon Hinck

Sweat prickled on Nathan's forehead and ran down toward his beard. The shade of the palace throne room did little to ease the Mediterranean heat. His knees trembled with age and fear, yet his voice rang clear as he addressed the king. "There were two men in a certain town . . . but the poor man had nothing except one little ewe lamb."

God sent a prophet as his vehicle to convict King David of his sin. Nathan told a story, and David's heart was pierced.

Now that was a good day for fiction.

We spend most of our hours using direct, specific, nonfiction words. We ask our children to do their chores, tell our friends about the things we saw yesterday, and go about the business of life in the commonsense place of literal conversation. Pastors and teachers communicate effectively in sermons and lessons. Christian writers share principles to help us walk the path of following Christ.

So why has God called so many of his children today to write fiction? Why did Jesus augment his teaching and preaching with storytelling? Can a novel be a vibrant and valuable art form for the Christian writer?

As Christians, we constantly struggle to utter the unutterable. We long to share concepts beyond our human ability to understand—the transcendence of God's holiness, the potency of forgiveness, the depth of God's love for us. Fiction helps us find ways to express those truths of magnitude because it is relatable, symbolic, and engages the emotion—unique qualities that make it a vital art form.

FICTION IS RELATABLE

Fiction weaves truth into slice-of-life depictions to which readers can relate. It provides a touchstone to common experiences of humanity and a way to examine those experiences. When Jesus sat on a grassy slope surrounded by the hurting, he painted word pictures—salt, lamps, bread, rusting treasure.

One time he told a simple story: "A woman has ten silver coins and loses one. Does she not light a lamp, sweep the house, and search carefully?" The women sitting at his feet smiled and nodded. They understood that experience. They'd felt it. Jesus built on that connection. "In the same way, I tell you, there is rejoicing in the presence of the angels of God over one sinner who repents." The story helped the listeners understand how much God valued them.

FICTION USES THE POWER OF SYMBOL AND METAPHOR

The harsh sound of fabric ripping punctuated the words of the prophet Ahijah as he stood alone on a dusty road with Jeroboam. "This is what the Lord, the God of Israel, says: 'See, I am going to tear the kingdom out of Solomon's hand.'" Old Testament prophets often used dramatic re-creation and shared the metaphors that God gave them to speak. Scarlet sin turned white as snow. An unfaithful wife bought back. A golden statue with feet of clay.

When Jesus stood on the wet and rocking planks of a boat on the Sea of Galilee, he also used the poetic language of symbols. "A sower went out to sow his seed. . . ." Gathered in a crowded home, he leaned back and told stories. "I am the good shepherd." "I will make you fishers of men." "You are the light of the world."

God's use of symbol and metaphor gives us a way to make connections and gain a deeper understanding of his truth. When we write stories, we follow his model.

NOTHING IS WASTED

God never wastes an experience or trial in our lives. Good or bad, easy or painful, he is able to use everything in our lives to grow us and make us more like him. And he gives us the privilege of encouraging others along this same journey.

We simply need eyes to see and the willingness to open our lives. Then we can help others through the power of fiction. My writing mentor calls it "bleeding into your work." It's as if you open yourself up and pour into your work everything that makes you who you are. All the joy. The pain. The questions asked. The lessons learned.

It's not for the faint of heart. Oftentimes it's painful. But it's worth the struggle.

When we as writers take our fears, beliefs, imaginations, and research and offer them up for the Lord to use, we are changed, and our fiction carries the power of truth and the fingerprints of our God on every page.

—Amy Wallace

FICTION ENGAGES EMOTION

Stories also touch the emotions. When God sent Nathan to confront David about his sin, the poignant story of the cruel landowner killing his neighbor's pet lamb broke through David's defenses and stirred his heart—allowing the Holy Spirit to further the work of repentance.

In the farming communities of Galilee, Jesus' story about the sower and the seed stirred a longing to be the good soil that "produced a crop—a hundred, sixty, or thirty times what was sown." What traveler could listen to the tale of the Good Samaritan and not have their emotions engaged by the plight of the man who was beaten and robbed?

God designed us as beings with emotion as well as intellect. A well-crafted novel or short story touches readers on both levels.

Fiction explores the truth of human experience, deepens understanding of life through symbol and metaphor, and touches the heart. In order to provide that powerful experience, it helps to keep in mind a few elements most readers

TO WRITE

You hold the pen of hope and
    healing,
you who tell of fear and feeling.
Power to touch the jaded soul;
power to make the broken whole.
To entertain, to intertwine,
to take us back in tests and time.
Write you must—now go from here;
write and keep the Savior near.
Now, Spirit, lead us every page;
through our words, be center stage.
Give us love for those who read;
give us words so they might see.
Author God, now through your
    power
guide us from this very hour.
Let us tell of love and light
and grant us strength so we might
    write.
—Karen Kingsbury

look for in a novel: entertainment, explanation, encouragement, and experience.

FOUR GIFTS OF FICTION

- **Entertainment.** People turn to stories to relax, to rest, and to shift their minds into a playful place. Reading is a form of recreation that strengthens imagination and empathy. Play is part of a healthy human existence, and entertainment that can bring refreshment in a way that honors God is a precious gift.
- **Explaining our world.** Through recorded history, people have told stories to help make sense of their experiences. It's vital that those of us who know the love of God be among the storytellers in our cultures. As a character grapples with questions, the reader can also explore those themes.
- **Encouragement and connection.** C. S. Lewis said, "We read to know we are not alone." My favorite letters from readers are the ones that say, "That's exactly how I feel, but I didn't know how to put it into words." Whether a mom identifies with the supermom syndrome of *The Secret Life of Becky Miller* or the journey toward emotional health of *Stepping into Sunlight,* fictional characters can reassure us that many of our struggles are universal.
- **Experiencing a new perspective.** When we read a powerfully written novel, we enter the skin of a new person. We feel her struggles and celebrate her triumphs. We watch her grow, and we grow with her. While stories meet our need to feel connected to someone similar to us, they can also help us understand someone who is different. We come out the other side of the book changed.

WRITING FICTION

In a letter to his lifelong friend Arthur Greeves, C.S. Lewis wrote, "I am sure that some are born to write as trees are born to bear leaves: for these, writing is a necessary mode of their own development." For all of you who are "born to write" and might not yet believe that calling, this book is for you. Ask God what he is inviting you to do with all those stories you've kept tucked away inside. Learn all you can about the craft of writing. Take those all-important first steps of trusting God in a new way and see what happens. The published novelists who generously contributed to this project want you to know that we stand with you. Along the way we have learned a thing or two about what works when refining the art of storytelling and what doesn't. On these pages you will find many of those helpful tips along with much thoughtful advice and direction.

Offering the gift of fiction to readers can take as many different forms as there are different writers: humorous voices or melancholy voices; overt themes of faith or subtle hints of spiritual threads; stories to introduce aspects of God to those who don't know him or tales designed to encourage and challenge Christian readers. God is so awesome and so multifaceted that we need a variety of means to communicate about him. Every genre contributes something to the wealth of fiction—literary, mystery, historical, thriller, women's fiction, fantasy, science fiction, contemporary, and more.

Whichever kind of fiction God calls you to write, it can give new glimpses of him and serve his Kingdom on earth, and that makes every day a good day for fiction.

THE FUNDAMENTALS OF FICTION

PART ONE >

CHAPTER 1
PLOT

❡

The Plot Skeleton
Angela Hunt

Imagine, if you will, that you and I are sitting in a room with one hundred other authors. If you were to ask each person present to describe their plotting process, you'd probably get a hundred different answers. Writers' methods vary according to their personalities, and we are all different. Mentally. Emotionally. Physically.

If, however, those one hundred novelists were to pass behind an X-ray machine, you'd discover that we all possess remarkably similar skeletons. Beneath our disguising skin, hair, and clothing, our skeletons are pretty much identical.

In the same way, though writers vary in their methods, good stories are composed of remarkably comparable skeletons. Stories with "good bones" can be found in picture books and novels, plays and films.

Many fine writers tend to carefully outline their plots before they

3

begin the first chapter. On the other hand, some novelists describe themselves as "seat-of-the-pants" writers. But when the story is finished, a seat-of-the-pants novel will (or should!) contain the same elements as a carefully plotted book. Why? Because whether you plan it from the beginning or find it at the end, novels need structure beneath the story.

After mulling several plot designs and boiling them down to their basic elements, I developed what I call the "plot skeleton." It combines the spontaneity of seat-of-the-pants writing with the discipline of an outline. It requires a writer to know where he's going, but it leaves room for lots of discovery on the journey.

When I sit down to plan a new book, the first thing I do is sketch my smiling little skeleton.

To illustrate the plot skeleton in this article, I'm going to refer frequently to *The Wizard of Oz* and a lovely foreign film you may never have seen, *Mostly Martha*.

THE SKULL: A CENTRAL CHARACTER

The skull represents the main character, the protagonist. A lot of beginning novelists have a hard time deciding who the main character is, so settle that question right away. Even in an ensemble cast, one character should be featured more than the others. Your readers want to place themselves into your story world, and it's helpful if you can give them a sympathetic character to whom they can relate. Ask yourself, "Whose story is this?" That is your protagonist.

This main character should have two *needs* or *problems*—one obvious, one hidden—which I represent by two yawning eye sockets.

Here's a tip: Hidden needs, which usually involve basic human emotions, are often solved or met by the end of the story. They are at the center of the protagonist's "inner journey," or character change, while the "outer journey" is concerned with the main events of the plot. Hidden needs often arise from wounds in a character's past.

Consider *The Wizard of Oz*. At the beginning of the film, Dorothy needs to save her dog from Miss Gulch, who has arrived to take Toto because he bit her scrawny leg—a very straightforward and obvious problem. Dorothy's *hidden* need is depicted but not directly emphasized when she stands by the pigpen and sings "Somewhere Over the Rainbow." Do children live with Uncle Henry and Aunt Em if all is fine with Mom and Dad? No. Though we are not told what happened to Dorothy's parents, it's clear that something has splintered her family, and Dorothy's unhappy. Her hidden need, the object of her inner journey, is to find a place to call home.

Mostly Martha opens with the title character lying on her therapist's couch and talking about all that is required to cook the perfect pigeon. Since she's in a therapist's office, we assume she has a problem, and the therapist addresses this directly: "Martha, why are you here?"

"Because," she answers, "my boss will fire me if I don't go to therapy." Ah—obvious problem at work with the boss. Immediately we also know that Martha is high-strung. She is precise and politely controlling in her kitchen. This woman lives for food, but though she assures us in a voice-over that all a cook needs for a perfectly lovely dinner is "fish and sauce," we see her venture downstairs to ask her new neighbor if he'd like to join her for dinner. He can't, but we become aware that Martha needs company. She needs love in her life.

CONNECT THE SKULL TO THE BODY: INCITING ACTION

Usually the first few chapters of a novel are involved with the business of establishing the protagonist in a specific time and place, his world, his needs, and his personality. The story doesn't kick into gear, though, until you move from the skull to the spine, a connection known as the *inciting incident*.

Writers are often told to begin the story *in medias res*, or in the middle of the action. This is not the same as the Big Incident. Save the big event for a few chapters in, after you've given us some time to know and understand your character's needs. Begin your story with an obvious problem—some action that shows how your character copes. In the first fifth of the story we learn that Dorothy loves Toto passionately and that Martha is a perfectionist chef. Yes, start in the middle of something active, but hold off on the big event for a while. Let us get to know your character first . . . because we won't gasp about their dilemma until we know them.

In a picture book, the inciting incident is often signaled by two words: *One day* . . . Those two words are a natural way to move from setting the stage to the action. As you plot your novel, ask yourself, "One day, what happens to move my main character into the action of the story?" Your answer will be your inciting incident, the key that turns your story engine.

After Dorothy ran away, if she'd made it home to Uncle Henry and Aunt Em without incident, there would have been no story. The inciting incident? When the tornado picks Dorothy up and drops her, with her house, in the land of Oz.

The inciting incident in *Mostly Martha* is signaled by a ringing telephone. When Martha takes the call, she learns that her sister, who was a single mother to an eight-year-old girl, has been killed in an auto accident.

Think of your favorite stories—how many feature a hero who's reluctant to enter the special world? Often—but not always—your protagonist doesn't want to go where the inciting incident is pushing him or her. Obviously, Martha doesn't want to hear that her sister is dead, and she certainly doesn't want to be a mother. She takes Lina, her niece, and offers to cook for her (her way of showing love), but Lina wants her mother, not gourmet food.

Even if your protagonist has actively pursued a change, he or she may have moments of doubt as the entrance to the special world looms ahead. When your character retreats or doubts or refuses to leave the ordinary world, another character should step in to provide encouragement, advice, information, or a special tool. This will help your main character overcome those last-minute doubts and establish the next part of the skeleton: the goal.

THE END OF THE SPINE: THE GOAL

At some point after the inciting incident, your character will establish and state a goal. Shortly after stepping out of her transplanted house, Dorothy looks around Oz and wails, "I want to go back to Kansas!" She's been transported over the rainbow, but she prefers the tried and true to the unfamiliar and strange. In order to go home, she'll have to visit the wizard in the Emerald City. As she tries to meet an ever-shifting set of subordinate goals (follow the yellow brick road; overcome the poppies; get in to see the wizard; bring back a broomstick), her main goal keeps viewers glued to the screen.

This overriding concern—will she or won't she make it home?—is known as the *dramatic question*. The dramatic question in every murder mystery is, *Who committed the crime*? The dramatic question in nearly every thriller is, *Who will win the inevitable showdown between the hero and the villain*? Along the way readers will worry about the subgoals (*Will the villain kill his hostage? Will the hero figure out the clues?*), but the dramatic question keeps them reading until the last page.

Tip: To keep the reader involved, the dramatic question should be directly related to the character's ultimate goal. Martha finds herself trying to care for a grieving eight-year-old who doesn't want another mother. So Martha promises to track down the girl's father, who lives in Italy. She knows only that his name is Giuseppe, but she's determined to find him.

THE RIB CAGE: COMPLICATIONS

Even my youngest students understand that a protagonist who accomplishes everything he or she attempts is a colorless character. As another friend of mine is fond of pointing out, as we tackle the mountain of life, it's the bumps we climb on! If you're diagramming, sketch at least three curving ribs over your spine. These represent the *complications* that must arise to prevent your protagonist from reaching his goal.

Why at least three ribs? Because even in the shortest of stories—in a picture book, for instance—three complications work better than two or four. I don't know why three gives us such a feeling of completion, but it does. Maybe it's because God is a Trinity and we're hardwired to appreciate that number.

While a short story will have only three complications, a movie or novel may have hundreds. Complications can range from the mundane—John can't find a pencil to write down Sarah's number—to life-shattering. As you write down possible complications that could stand between your character and his ultimate goal, place the more serious problems at the bottom of the list.

The *stakes*—what your protagonist is risking—should increase in significance as the story progresses. In *Mostly Martha*, the complications center on this uptight woman's ability to care for a child. Lina hates her babysitter, so Martha has to take Lina to work with her. But the late hours take their toll, and Lina is often late for school. Furthermore, Lina keeps refusing to eat anything Martha cooks for her.

I asked you to make the ribs curve because any character that runs into complication after complication without any breathing space is going to be a weary character . . . and you'll weary your reader with this frenetic pace. One of the keys to good pacing is to alternate your plot complications with rewards. Like a pendulum that swings on an arc, let your character relax, if only briefly, between disasters.

Along the spiraling yellow brick road, Dorothy soon reaches an intersection (a complication). Fortunately, a friendly scarecrow is willing to help (a reward). They haven't gone far before Dorothy becomes hungry (a complication). The scarecrow spots an apple orchard ahead (a reward). These apple trees, however, resent being picked (a complication), but the clever scarecrow taunts them until they begin to throw fruit at the hungry travelers (a reward).

See how it works? Every problem is followed by a reward that matches the seriousness of the complication. Let's fast-forward to the scene where the balloon takes off without Dorothy. This is a *severe* complication—so severe it deserves a title of its own: *the bleakest moment*. This is the final rib in the rib cage, the moment when all hope is lost for your protagonist.

THE THIGHBONE: SEND IN THE CAVALRY

At the bleakest moment, your character needs *help*, but be careful how you deliver it. The ancient Greek playwrights had actors representing the Greek gods literally descend from the structure above to bring their complicated plot knots to a satisfying conclusion. This sort of resolution is frowned upon in modern literature. Called *deus ex machina* (literally *"god from the machine"*), this device employs some unexpected and improbable incident to bring victory or success. If you find yourself whipping up a coincidence or a miracle after the bleakest moment, chances are you've employed deus ex machina. Back up and try again, please.

Avoid using deus ex machina by sending two types of help: external and internal. Your character obviously needs help from outside; if he could solve the problem alone, he would have done it long before the bleakest moment. Having him conveniently remember something or stumble across a hidden resource smacks of coincidence and will leave your reader feeling resentful and cheated.

So send in the cavalry, but remember that *they can't solve the protagonist's problem.* They can give the protagonist a push in the right direction; they can nudge; they can remind; they can inspire. But they shouldn't wave a magic wand and make everything all right.

For Dorothy, help comes in the form of Glinda the Good Witch, who reveals a secret: The ruby slippers have the power to carry her back to Kansas. All Dorothy has to do is say, "There's no place like home"—with feeling, mind you—and she'll be back on the farm with Uncle Henry and Auntie Em. Dorothy's problem isn't resolved, however, until she applies this information internally. At the beginning of the story, she wanted to be anywhere *but* on the farm. Now she has to affirm that the farm is where she wants to be. Her hidden need—to find a place to call home—has been met.

In *Mostly Martha*, the bleakest moment arrives with Lina's father, Giuseppe. He is a good man, and Lina seems to accept him. But after waving good-bye, Martha goes home to an empty apartment and realizes that she is not happy with her controlled, childless life. She goes to Marlo, the Italian chef she has also begun to love, and asks for his help.

THE KNEECAP AND LOWER LEG: MAKE A DECISION, LEARN A LESSON

Martha realizes that her old life was empty—she needs Lina in her life, and she needs Marlo. So she and Marlo drive from Germany to Italy to fetch Lina and bring her home.

You may be hard-pressed to cite the lesson you learned from the last novel you read, but your protagonist needs to learn something. This lesson is the *epiphany*, a sudden insight that speaks volumes to your character and brings them to the conclusion of their inner journey.

James Joyce popularized the word *epiphany*, literally the manifestation of a divine being. (Churches celebrate the festival of Epiphany on January 6 to commemorate the meeting of the Magi and the Christ child.) After receiving help from an outside source, your character should see something—a person, a situation, or an object—in a new light.

When the scarecrow asks why Glinda waited to explain the ruby slippers, the good witch smiles and says, "Because she wouldn't have believed me. She had to learn it for herself." The scarecrow then asks, "What'd you learn, Dorothy?" Without hesitation, Dorothy announces that she's learned a lesson: "The next time I go looking for my heart's desire, I won't look any farther than my own backyard." She has learned to appreciate her home, so even though she is surrounded by loving friends and an emerald city, Dorothy chooses to return to colorless Kansas. She hugs her friends once more, then grips Toto and clicks her heels.

THE FOOT: THE RESOLUTION

Every story needs the fairy-tale equivalent of "and they lived happily ever after." Not every story ends happily, of course, though happy endings are undoubtedly popular. Some protagonists are sadder and wiser after the course of their adventure. But a novel should at least leave the reader with hope.

The resolution to *Mostly Martha* is portrayed during the closing of the film. As the credits roll, we see Marlo and Martha meeting Lina in Italy; we see Martha in a wedding gown (with her hair down!) and Marlo in a tuxedo; we see a wedding feast with Giuseppe, his family, and Martha's German friends; we see Martha and Marlo and Lina exploring an abandoned restaurant—clearly, they are going to settle in Italy so Lina can be a part of both families. In the delightful final scene, we see Martha with her therapist again, but this time he has cooked for her and she is advising him.

Many movies end with a simple visual image—we see a couple walking away hand in hand, a mother cradling her long-lost son.

ESSENTIALS OF FICTION: GENERATE CONFLICT

Fill your novel with conflict.

If there's no conflict, there's no plot. No one wants to read about flawless, blissful people whose lives are just peachy. It's not real. Great fiction raises moral dilemmas, good versus evil, where the character goes through gut-wrenching setbacks before victory. For example, consider J. R. R. Tolkien's Lord of the Rings trilogy. The all-time best seller is the Bible; it's full of conflict, failure, and truth—the tragedy of Christ's death followed by his resurrection victory and awaited triumphant return.   —*Randy Alcorn*

That's all we need to realize that our main character has struggled, learned, and come away a better (or wiser) person. As a writer, you'll have to use words, but you can paint the same sort of reassuring picture without resorting to "and they lived happily ever after."

Your story should end with a *changed* protagonist—he or she has gone through a profound experience and is different for it, hopefully for the better. Your protagonist has completed an outer journey (experienced the major plot events) and an inner journey that address some hurt from the past and result in a changed character.

WHAT NEXT?

Now that we've reached the foot of our story skeleton, we're finished outlining the basic structure. Take those major points and write them up in paragraph form. Once you've outlined your plot and written your synopsis, you're ready to begin writing scenes. Take a deep breath, glance over your skeleton, and jump in.

¶

The Sagging Middle
Gail Gaymer Martin

Most writers have ideas about the opening and ending of their novels. They know how to grab readers with goals, conflicts, and believable motivation. But what about the long, long middle? Here are some proven techniques for keeping the reader turning those pages from start to finish.

STRATEGIC PLOTTING AND PACING

The plot is the journey. Pacing is the rate at which problems affect the journey. Think of climbing into a canoe and heading down an unfamiliar river (the journey). The river holds unexpected hazards and dangers (the problems). Between occasional calm stretches of water, the canoe encounters tree branches, rocks, the difficult flow of a whirlpool, the current caused by a towering boulder, and dangerous white water. When the destination is within reach, a waterfall roars ahead of the canoe, its current dragging the canoe forward. One small bypass appears to reach dry land, and the final battle begins.

Good plotting also includes:

- A strong need or goal that can change or destroy the character or his purpose
- Powerful opposition—either external or internal—that deepens conflict
- A compelling situation or duty that binds characters in their struggle
- More than one possible solution to a character's dilemma, forcing a choice
- Effective backstory used on a need-to-know basis

SUBPLOTS

Subplots must be connected to the original journey. Internal subplots involve a character dealing with an issue that's part of his personal life. An external subplot is a force from outside the character. An internal subplot might be a man who is caught in a web of lies he has created, while an external subplot could be a man destroyed by another person's lie.

Subplots should not overwhelm the original plot but enhance it by adding conflicts and tension. The number of subplots depends on the genre and book length. Normally a shorter novel will have fewer subplots. Typical subplots might include:

- A suspense element
- A friend whose problem parallels a main character's and provides a different angle
- A friend or roommate whose problems complicate the main character's life
- Career issues such as constant traveling or loss of position
- A proposition that affects the main story
- Information that threatens the main character
- A romantic element of falling in or out of love

SECRETS

Secrets affect people's lives by holding them back from success or happiness and creating feelings of guilt or fear of discovery. Avoid disclosing the secret too early in the story. Instead use the techniques of hints, clues, or foreshadowing, or give the same secret to another character and show the main character's reaction. Reveal the secret only after readers care about the character. This allows the revelation to create reader empathy.

INTERRUPTED SCENES

This technique works well during scenes where something or someone is in jeopardy. End a scene in the middle of the action—the phone rings and the reader knows it could be the killer; the heroine finds a musty box in the basement and opens the lid hoping to find a clue that will make a difference in her life.

EVOLVING MOTIVATION

Characters are motivated by something that creates a need. You might be motivated to attend a conference for the purpose of networking and learning the craft, but your motivation will change if you learn that an agent or editor is interested in your manuscript. What was a general purpose now becomes specific and more personal. A subplot for a novel might be: A woman confides to a social worker that she suspects her husband is having an affair. The social worker offers the woman help, but when the social worker begins to see the same symptoms in her own husband, the problem becomes personal, and therefore her motivation changes, as does her perspective on the problem.

RAISING THE STAKES

This is similar to evolving motivation, but it adds an element of danger. Imagine Julie works at an abuse clinic as a counselor. She was motivated toward this career because her mother had been abused by her father. But the motivation shifts when Julie's husband begins to abuse her. Now the stakes deepen when Julie threatens to report the abuse. Her husband threatens to kill her, then vanishes. This creates an exciting life-and-death situation.

Raising the stakes can be used in any genre and with a variety of possibilities. Bring in death as an intimate possibility. Make a trustworthy character untrustworthy, or turn a friend into an enemy. Or add time pressure to the situation: the ticking clock or bomb under the table.

ASKING "WHAT IF"

Ask "what if . . . ," and then state a possible event. This technique changes a character's situation by adding complications or by twisting fate, causing the story to take a new turn. For example:

- What if the main character's home burns down?
- What if he misses the train and loses the account?
- What if a neighbor moves in and causes problems for the main character?
- What if the accused is proven innocent?
- What if attempts to help only make the situation worse?
- What if it rains the day of the community picnic?

ADDING A CHARACTER

When the story begins to bog down, bring someone new to town. A new character can stir up plot elements by adding more responsibility or more tension to a character's life. The character might be:

- An ex-boyfriend or fiancé who plays havoc with the romantic elements in the story
- An ailing or a meddling parent who creates a time factor and obligations
- A neighbor who causes confusion by gossiping or needing help

REMOVING A CHARACTER

Characters play specific roles. They add motivation, information, or conflict to the story. When a character is cut, another way must be found to replace the role he or she played in the book. If this role is added to one of the main characters, it can add a twist to the plot; bring greater tension, emotion, or conflict; and deepen characterization. For example, Julie hires a caregiver for her ailing mother with whom she has conflict. The caregiver requests a higher salary. Julie can't afford to pay more, so she must become her mother's caregiver. This provides more drama and opportunity for Julie and her mother to heal their relationship.

IMPOSSIBLE SITUATIONS

Impossible situations add levels of complication to a plotline. Put the character at a fork in the road with neither choice offering a positive option. These are common occurrences in life and can provide dynamic plot elements. For example, to remain in his position at the firm, a character must do something illegal. Or to remain with the woman he loves, the hero must reveal his father's crime. In these situations, both choices set up further problems.

¶

Planning Your Series
Sandra Byrd

It's no secret that series books are favorites among both readers and writers. Readers anticipate spending more time with people and places they've grown to love, eagerly awaiting the newest installment of a beloved series. Midnight release parties and advance sales herald these new editions. Writers enjoy developing deeper story lines for their characters and turning what might have been an 80,000-word book into a fuller, meatier, 250,000-plus-word story arc. For the author, signing a contract for multiple books offers a sense of career security—you know what you'll be working on for at least a few years. But planning a series that satisfies publishers, readers, and writers takes a little extra forethought. Ready to write? Here are a few considerations to keep in mind.

TYPES OF SERIES

It's helpful, first, to define what a series is. Fiction books are commonly referred to as either "stand-alone"—books that have no relation to other books by the same author—or "series"—books that *are* related in some way to other titles. What ties series books together can vary, but there are several common approaches.

Most series have the same character as the protagonist in each book. While every title in the series reveals something new and different about his or her journey through life, the focus is on one person. Because of that, we grow closest to, and cheer on, the main character even as we also enjoy the minor characters. It's important, then, that you take a lot of time crafting this character because he or she will be carrying not only one book but many.

Other series have the same cast of characters, with each book in the series focusing on a different point-of-view character. This approach allows the reader to learn more about several people over the course of the pages. Oftentimes readers quickly grow attached to the point-of-view character in book one. If you hope to have each book focus on a different person, you'll have to effectively set up those secondary characters who will become central characters in future installments. If you make them likable and vulnerable when they are introduced as supporting cast members and hint at problems we want to see them overcome, we'll look forward to seeing the spotlight on them in future books.

Sometimes series are tied together not by the same characters but by a theme, locale, or period of time. Themes might include a focus on people getting through hard times, with each book showcasing a new set of characters with different problems, or a focus on different sets of friends enjoying adventures and life together.

Sometimes themes focus on Scripture—for example, showing different sets of people illustrating the concept "to save your life you must lose it."

NUMBER OF BOOKS IN A SERIES

Traditionally, literary series take one of two forms—one preplanned, one more free-form and market-responsive. Usually when the author and publisher agree to work together on a series, they establish in advance how many books will be in that series. For adult books, it's often a trilogy. For young adult and teen/tween series, more books are often planned from the get-go as the books are shorter and kids are even more loyal series fans than adults. When you know in advance how many books you'll be writing, it's easier to plot out a story arc for the series, and then develop a story question for each book.

Remember, each new book must carefully weave in any threads necessary to get the readers up to speed without seeming as though they're reading through a synopsis.

Sometimes series are unexpectedly popular, and neither reader, writer, nor publisher is ready to let the story end. In that case, the author and the publisher may contract to produce future installments of a book or books that are already published or under way. While each book still must satisfy its story question within the confines of the cover, the smart writer will realize that future books may lie ahead. When plotting a series, it's good to consider what kind of character growth, spiritual growth, and complicating situations the characters may find themselves in should the series be extended due to healthy sales.

ASKING THE RIGHT QUESTIONS

Fiction plots are really about questions: posing them, complicating them, delaying the answer, and then arriving at a satisfactory resolution. For the series author, two sets of questions must be considered.

Series Question

First, the overall series arc will have a question. To make sure individual books in a series feel like parts of a whole, it's important for the author to think through what the overall series question will be before beginning. This question will be posed, either expressly or implicitly, at the outset of the series.

For example, in a series about a twentysomething woman who is finding herself, the series question might be, Will she find the satisfying life that God has planned for her, is she missing it, or has she been forgotten? Book one might detail how she comes to understand God's love for her and risk leaving behind what she thought she knew to test what is unknown. Book two might show the resolution of her professional life, while leaving an unanswered question about her romantic life. Book three would wrap it up, showing that yes, as she learned to trust God, her faith life, her professional life, and her romantic life all came together. In each book, we see her grow, and of course, threads of each plotline will be woven into each book.

A historical series may show different people, either common or well-known, living out their faith through difficult times. The series question would be, Are people called to live their Christian lives today the same as they were yesterday? Each book would then aptly explore that question through its characters and the situations they find themselves working through.

Story Questions

Even though series books will be episodes of a larger story, it's important to make each book a self-contained whole. When readers buy a book they expect to feel satisfied with the journey as they finish the last page. It's not "playing fair" with readers to lead them through an entire book only to be told, in one way or another, that they must "stay tuned" for the next book to have all questions resolved.

Does this mean that there are no unanswered questions in a series? Of course not. What it does mean is that each book will have a story question of its own that will be answered by the end of the book. However, the overall series question will still be outstanding, and readers will want to follow the series to have that question answered, as well as to join the characters for the next installment in the adventure. You can play fair with readers by asking a series question at the outset of a series—and stringing along the final answer till the end of the last book—while opening a story question at the beginning of each book and resolving that by that book's last chapter.

For example, in a young adult series about a teenager who moves to London with her family, the series question may be, Will she find a new, fulfilling life in London, trusting that God has had his hand in the move? Or will she have abandoned everything at home for nothing and end up lonely, unfulfilled, and out of place? The story question of the first book then, would ask, Will God provide her with a new sense of well-being? The second book would address whether she will find friends who care for her. The third book could introduce a romantic element. The story question of the fourth book would be, How can she serve God in her new town? While the overall series question is being answered bit by bit, each book has a story question that is answered within its own pages. That way, the author both satisfies and tantalizes the reader.

CLOSING A SERIES

If you're writing a preplanned trilogy, you'll know exactly how many words you need to get your series finished, perhaps three books of 75,000 to 100,000 words. That makes it easier to plan. Don't give all the good stuff away in book one; make sure you save enough plot and character meat to end strongly.

If you don't know in advance how many books your series will have, planning can be a bit more difficult. If you're writing a historical series or one based on a theme, you can simply continue to add characters to the time period or theme without sacrificing story line or character growth. If you are using the same beloved ensemble cast, make sure that while your characters do grow in each book, you've left room for them to continue to mature. That way, should you write more books in the series, you will have material to work with.

However, be careful not to dribble the story out, with each successive book getting weaker and weaker. If you've run out of material, it's time to say good-bye. Better to end a series with a strong finish

ESSENTIALS OF FICTION: KEEP IT CREDIBLE

Don't ever let readers see the "strings."

They will if someone acts out of character. Actions must be credible—when you have a surprising dramatic action, make sure you've built a sufficient foundation for it. The surprise must ring true to the whole book. —*Randy Alcorn* and with a loyal, satisfied readership than to draw out a story that has, naturally, already concluded.

While planning a series can take more time and energy up front than planning a stand-alone book, you'll have ready-made characters when it comes time for future books and save on development and plotting time along the way. It will all be worthwhile when it's *your* books that live on in the hearts and minds of the readers.

NINE STEPS TO A MOVING STORY ARC

1. The main character must face an overarching life issue of a moral, ethical, or spiritual nature. He is caught in a situation that requires him to consider issues he would rather avoid, issues that will affect the rest of his life.
2. Our story puts a human face to the overarching issue so that our readers can grasp its practical implications. Discussion of the cost of freedom or the quality of life may be wonderful in a philosophy classroom, but a story is about *specific* people in *specific* situations.
3. In these specific circumstances, the main character must ask hard questions that lead to major choices. Some of the questions and decisions seem small, but together they lay the motivational and circumstantial groundwork for the final big choice. Each small choice takes the character another step along the twists and turns of his or her moral, ethical, or spiritual path.
4. To make the main character's dilemma as intense as possible, an event from the past throws the current situation into high relief. The occurrence in the past that holds such emotional charge may have been done *by* the character or done *to* the character. Either way, memory and fear make the present questions more painful and the choices harder.
5. A moment of high drama forces the protagonist to make the big choice.

¶

Red Herrings, Clues, and Other Plot Devices
Robin Caroll

A plot device is an element an author purposely places in a book to further the plot of the story. Books, movies, and TV shows all incorporate plot devices in one form or another. When used skillfully, plot

All the previous questions and answers, the seemingly little events, have brought the character to the fish-or-cut-bait moment. It's theologian Martin Luther saying, "Here I stand, so help me God." It's right or wrong. Good or bad. Best or merely better.

6. The big choice must have potentially serious consequences—loss of life, loss of love, loss of job, loss of reputation.

7. The choice must be made on selfless moral, ethical, or spiritual grounds.

8. The proper choice makes our main character more worthy than she or he was at the beginning of the story. This choice has the power to redeem those in need of redemption or to bestow greater honor on those of previously high character.

9. In a well-written inspirational story, the choices of the main character challenge the reader to want to be more worthy too. If the main character could do the right thing in a time of adversity, so too can the reader. If the main character can triumph in adversity, so can the reader, no matter how hard the choice, no matter how harsh the consequences, because doing right for the right reasons is a victory in itself. —*Gayle Roper*

devices flow from the story naturally, pushing the characters and plot along toward the big finale and taking the readers along with them. Here are some of the most common plot devices.

RED HERRING

Smoked herring has a very strong odor and was once used to distract hunting dogs, causing them to lose the scent they were supposed to be tracking. Writers use red herrings in much the same way—to distract the reader. This device is used in all fiction genres, but predominantly by mystery and suspense authors.

A red herring is most commonly used to make a certain character appear to be guilty when he really isn't. The writer creates these characters to look as if they have motive, means, and opportunity to be the villain. These characters, while legitimately having a vested interest in the crime, are in the story only to cause the reader to doubt the identity of the actual villain. The use of red herrings maintains tension and uncertainty.

CLUES

Almost every genre uses clues of some sort—hints about a character's motivation, suggestions of "whodunit" in a mystery novel, even the mention of a character having a secret in a romance novel. Clues help writers create or build upon already established tension to keep the story moving. These clues about a character or a plot draw the reader deeper into the book.

FALSE CLUES

Similar to red herrings, false clues are intended to distract the reader from the true meaning or motivation. For instance, if an author wants the reader to believe falsely that a certain character is the antagonist, the writer could have someone observe that character having an argument with the victim on the day of the murder. This would lead the reader to believe the character had motive. Yet the truth might be that the arguing couple was simply practicing for a play they were going to do together. The witness was right, but also wrong at the same time. A great false clue will distract the reader from the truth, but remember that the clue must be plausible or the reader will feel cheated.

THE TWIST

Almost every genre in fiction today uses the twist. A twist is an unanticipated turn of a story that gives the reader a new view. For example, in a contemporary romance, a couple has overcome misunderstandings, missteps, and various other complications to profess their love to one another. The reader believes this man and woman will get their "happily ever after." But suddenly, a woman appears onstage who claims to be the man's wife. The author has thrown the reader a twist and complicated the plot in an unexpected manner.

FLASHBACKS

A flashback is a narrative segment of a book that takes the reader back to an earlier part of a character's life. This is normally done to introduce the reader to the character's background. Flashbacks are usually kept very short—just long enough to provide the key information.

FORESHADOWING

With foreshadowing, the reader is given a hint about the future, often in a symbolic way. For example, if a character is a high school principal who is forced to interrupt a fistfight between two teens, this event could symbolically foreshadow the marital arguments that will later become the main conflict of the book.

CHASE SCENES

Chase scenes are found not only in books but also in almost every action/adventure script in Hollywood. This device is a scene written between main plot points that doesn't further the plot. Its main purpose, in fact its only purpose, is to heighten tension and compound conflict—no actual automobiles required.

DEADLOCK

In a deadlock, two or more characters are at an impasse in which neither can win. Use of this device can rev up tension and lead the characters and plot in a totally new direction. For example, if two men are in love with the same woman and are at each other's throats, but she's in love with a third, the first two men are in a deadlock—even if they come to blows, neither can win since the woman is in love with another.

PYRRHIC VICTORY

This is a plot device in which there is a victory, but with a devastating cost to the winner. The term is aptly named after King Pyrrhus. He was victorious in his battles against his foes, but his army suffered irreplaceable casualties. Use of this device can alter characters' motivation and/or goals, which can take the plot in a different direction.

THE MACGUFFIN

This device was made popular by Alfred Hitchcock. It consists of an object that motivates the forward action of the characters but in itself isn't important. For example, in a mystery novel, the MacGuffin could be a missing earring or a lost key. In a contemporary novel, the object could be a photograph of the heroine's father or a cameo that belonged to the heroine's mother.

¶

Let's Do the Twist
Brandilyn Collins

What is a story twist? Most will identify it as a *surprise,* something that keeps your novel from being predictable. A twist is an assumption—or subconscious belief—turned on its head. Let me share what I've discovered about coming up with twists for a story and then using them effectively.

TWO STEPS FOR PLOTTING THE TWIST

Step 1: List All the Assumptions Inherent in Your Premise
Every premise is loaded with assumptions. Your job is to find them. But remember, assumptions are subconscious—even to you. You'll have to dig deep within your mind to find them. Think of the times in real life you've been tripped up by a wrong assumption. "Oh, wow, what a surprise! I just assumed . . ." You fill in the blank. Why were you so surprised to learn your assumption wasn't true? Because

you never thought about it consciously. The assumption was deeply embedded in your thinking. As you think of assumptions inherent in your novel's premise, write them down. It doesn't matter how outlandish they are. This is not the time to edit yourself. The longer your list of assumptions, the more you'll have to choose from for step 2.

Here's an example: In a novel's opening scene, John and Lisa, a married couple, are in their kitchen. The scene is told from Lisa's point of view. The phone rings and Lisa answers. It's her ob-gyn, saying, "Congratulations! The test is positive—you're pregnant!" Lisa is thrilled. She and John have been trying for years to have a baby, and they've been anxiously awaiting this phone call. Lisa hangs up the phone, tells her husband the news (which he already apparently guesses, since he's heard her side of the conversation), and they fall into each other's arms and weep.

What are the assumptions inherent in this premise? Here's a hint: Read the premise again carefully. If I've told you something is true, you can know it is. But if something's *perceived* by a character, that perception may or may not be true. Within that perception may lie an assumption or two. Write your own list of assumptions first to see how many you come up with. Then read mine.

The baby was formed from John's sperm and Lisa's egg; Lisa is really pregnant; John's weeping is joyful; the child will be born healthy and without handicaps; the call is genuine; the voice of her doctor is not being faked by a demented liar; John and Lisa are both physically able to produce this child; both truly desire this child; the person running the test didn't mix up patient labels; the ob-gyn called the right number; Lisa and John have been sexually intimate recently; there is just one baby; John doesn't already have a child he doesn't know about; John has not had a vasectomy; Lisa will remain healthy enough to bear the child; John doesn't have a mistress or Lisa a boyfriend; their friends and family will be happy for them; Lisa is a woman; John is a man; the doctor is telling the truth about the positive test; the test is not a false positive; the gestation period will be nine months; Lisa and John want the baby for normal parenting purposes; they will still be married when the baby is born; John will be alive when the baby is born; Lisa will be alive when the baby is born; the baby will be either a boy or a girl; the baby is human.

Some of these assumptions—the ones embedded most deeply in our subconscious mind—seem rather bizarre. The assumption, for example, that the baby will be human lies so deep within our subconscious most of us can't find it even when we're looking for it. But *the deeper in the subconscious mind an assumption lies, the greater the possibility of the twist.* Makes sense, right? The more deeply embedded your belief in something, the more surprised you'll be when you find it ain't so.

Step 2: Choose a Few Assumptions and Turn 'Em on Their Heads
Once you have as many assumptions as possible listed, choose one or two (or more) to twist. A couple of notes here:
  1. Twists are relative. Your genre will have a lot to do with determining how surprising a twist you want. If Lisa and John's story is a women's fiction novel, the baby isn't going to end up an alien. However . . .

2. Don't be too quick to discount an assumption twist that seems too bizarre. Assumptions don't always have to be completely turned on their heads. Tilting them just a little often works just as well. For example, of course Lisa and John's baby will be human. But what if he is born with an uncanny, almost inhuman ability to do something? Or maybe the child is born with some unusual and indefinable personality defect that sets him apart. Either one of those scenarios could be used in a women's fiction novel. These examples probably wouldn't be the ultimate twist in the story. But they may provide a major surprise in the middle of the book or at the end of the first act.

When I plot my suspense novels, I ask myself, "What would be the most gut-punching twist to this story?" The answer is an event or revelation that turns one of the most deeply embedded assumptions on its head. After I figure out this major twist, I'll come up with numerous smaller ones to build tension along the way to that final revelation.

MAKING THE TWISTS WORK IN YOUR STORY

The key to effectively using the twists you've come up with is "writing to the twist" by *strengthening its foundational assumption in the mind of the reader.* When you "write to the twist," everything leads the reader to continue in the assumption while in truth the story is moving toward the twist. In a sense you're writing *two* stories—the one you want the reader to believe and the story of what really happened. Every plot point, every tiny detail, has to fit both scenarios.

Take, for example, Agatha Christie's classic novel *Murder on the Orient Express.* Hercule Poirot boards the Orient Express to Istanbul along with more than a dozen other passengers. Mr. Ratchett, an American, is soon murdered—stabbed twelve times. Agatha Christie bases the book's twist on a deeply embedded assumption inherent in every mystery novel: There are many suspects, but *only one* of them did it. Poirot gathers clues and slowly discovers that everyone else on the train had the means and the motive to commit the murder. Christie "writes to the twist" by reinforcing the one-culprit assumption in the reader's mind. Page after page she layers onto that assumption through Poirot's struggles to discover the murderer. The final twist reveals that *twelve* passengers committed the murder, each stabbing Mr. Ratchett one time. Once the reader knows the twist, the clues leading up to it become obvious. But with the protagonist so focused on finding one culprit, the reader is led to believe there *is* only one—until Poirot finally puts it all together.

Writing to the twist is painstaking work. There are rules to follow. First, you're not allowed to cheat the reader. You can't show a character thinking, *I am innocent of this crime* only to reveal later that he's guilty. (Unless—*aha!*—this character turns out to be an unreliable narrator. Assumptions upon which these twists are built: *I can believe what the character tells me. The character is in his right mind.*) But a character can certainly perceive things wrongly. She can spend the entire story chasing wrong perceptions with every thought and every action based upon those misconceptions. The more a character acts upon wrong assumptions, the more a reader is swept along in them.

A second rule is that you must sprinkle legitimate clues throughout the story. Most writers know this. What trips them up is how liberally to sprinkle them. Here's an important guideline: *Write for the smartest reader.*

In my suspense novels I'm writing to a vast audience of possible readers—from those who have never read suspense before to voracious suspense readers well experienced in discovering embedded clues. If I wrote to the inexperienced suspense reader, I'd include far too many clues. Result: all the other readers wouldn't be surprised by the twist. If I wrote even to the middle of the spectrum of readers, I'd still bore those who are my strongest target audience—avid suspense fans. Besides, avid suspense fans are the folks who'll most keep me on my toes. If I can come up with a twist to surprise them and write it effectively, I'll have a good story. Too many authors write to the middle of the spectrum. Don't do that. Regardless of your genre, when writing to the twist, write for your smartest reader.

Afraid your plot is predictable? Remember: *a twist is an assumption turned on its head.* Find those assumptions in your premise. Then go out and do the twist.

CHAPTER 2

CHARACTERS

¶

Up Close and Personal: Getting on Intimate Terms with Your Characters
Susan Meissner

Great stories always hinge on great characters. Without Scarlett O'Hara, *Gone with the Wind* would be just another docudrama on the Civil War. Without Captain Ahab, *Moby Dick* is just a tale about whaling. Without Christine, *The Phantom of the Opera* is just a meddling spirit ticked off by an uncaring world.

Characters drive the plot of any great story. A stellar setting, a riveting premise, and an emotionally weighted conflict are as essential as a car's engine, wheels, and fuel. But if there's no one we care about behind the steering wheel driving the details, the story will go nowhere. Without convincing, compelling, conflicted characters, the story stalls.

Memorable characters are those that force us to care about them;

that's what keeps us turning the pages. Even characters we are meant to dislike give a story color and personality when they are richly drawn. Crafting characters that your readers can care about begins where all caring begins: at the point of knowledge.

WHAT MAKES A GOOD CHARACTER?

Think of all the people you know really well. Your parents. Your siblings. Your spouse. Your best friend. Most of the time, the people we know really well are also the people we care about. If pressed, most of us could make a detailed list of the personality traits of our closest friends and family. We know these people. We've spent time with them. We know their history. We know what they are afraid of, what they dream of, what motivates them, what annoys them, what makes them sad, what makes them angry, what entertains them, what infuriates them. We know their pet peeves, their quirks, their habits, their preferences, their accomplishments, and their misfortunes. We've seen them at their worst and at their best. We know whom they admire, whom they despise, whom they respect. We know what they value and what they don't.

This long list of attributes is what gives a friend or family member dimension and depth, not just to you but to everyone else as well. When you have the benefit of this kind of knowledge about a person, you can anticipate what they will say and do when trouble falls on them. Knowledge in this sense is power. It is the power to logically anticipate a believable reaction because of the depth of your familiarity with a person.

Novel writing is all about putting a make-believe person who wants something into a make-believe situation that thwarts him and then making him respond. The more we know about this make-believe person, the more we can craft responses and actions and dialogue that seem real. The more real these responses seem, the more real the make-believe person seems. And when a character seems *real*, readers make an emotional connection to the fictitious person that keeps them turning pages, keeps them invested.

For a recent project, I spent a month getting to know my protagonist, a twenty-year-old college student, the only daughter of affluent parents, before I wrote a word of her narrative. I created a biographical sketch of this young woman, who thinks she has risen above stereotypical judgments. I did this because I needed to know how she *thinks*, not just how she looks or what kind of clothes she wears.

I began by making a list of her fears, dreams, hopes, peeves, passions, strengths, and weaknesses. I interviewed her as if she were sitting right across from me, imagining what her answers would be. I asked her what she wanted most at that moment and what would happen if she failed to get it. I asked what stood in her way. I asked her how she planned to succeed. I endowed her with flaws and virtues, habits and quirks, some of which never showed up in the book. I gave her a childhood history—much of it known only to me—that shaped her into the adult she is now. Knowing all these intimate details about her made her seem real to me, even as I wrote her into existence. There were many times when I had to ponder what her answer would be to a question. Sometimes I would craft an answer and then immediately delete it. It didn't ring true. I'd try again. And again. Eventually I would land on the response that seemed to gel with what I already knew about her.

To keep her from sounding like me with every answer, I thought of the real people I know or characters in movies and books that she resembles. If I asked them these same questions, what would they say? And since my characters are usually amalgams of people and other characters I know or am intrigued by, I was able to give her her own distinct persona.

There were many times, during scenes of dialogue especially, when the writing simply flowed because I knew exactly what she would say or do. We had spent time together. She was no stranger to me.

CREATE YOUR CHARACTERS' ATTRIBUTES

To get at this level of intimacy with your characters, you need to invest in prewriting time. Much of what you write in prewriting won't show up in the story itself. What it will do is *empower* you to write the story. Here's one way to get the job done:

- Start with your character's name and age and construct his or her family tree. Include parents, in-laws, siblings, and grandparents if they play into the persona of your character. Decide where your character grew up, where he went to school, if he had enabling parents or authoritative parents or absent parents. What effect did siblings have on the person he became as an adult?

- Make a list of his preferences, everything from food to music to clothes. Describe his physical appearance. How does he feel about the way he looks?

- Decide whether your character is dominant or submissive. Pessimist or optimist. Extrovert or introvert. Forgiving or unforgiving. Loud or quiet. Certain or unsure. Hopeful or hopeless. Organized or disorganized. Cautious or a risk taker. Does your character have a relationship with God? Consider having your character take a personality test like the Myers-Briggs Type Indicator.

- Make a list of your character's hopes and dreams and fears. What is she motivated by? What stands in her way? Who will help her?
- Make a list of your character's abilities, talents, and habits. How can she use these abilities to reach her goal?
- Make a list of her flaws. How will these affect her in her quest? Who will thwart her?

INTERVIEW YOUR CHARACTERS

Once you have a thorough background like this, it is much easier to envision an imaginary conversation with your character about how he or she thinks. I interview my characters, even those who have little stage time. If their presence matters to my protagonist, I need to know why.

Here's an excerpt from a character interview from one of my recent books. This character, Bart, barely shows up in the story, but he is my young protagonist's father and has a huge influence on her. And because of that I needed to know him well.

> **What are you afraid of?**
> I'm afraid of missing out on things because I wasn't paying attention and missed an opportunity. You have to take some risks if you want to make it in this life. You can't sit around and expect things to just come your way.

> **How do you handle frustration?**
> Well, see, if you just calm down and wait, one of two things will happen. One, you will figure out what to do to make things right. Two, it will begin not to matter.

Are you an extrovert or an introvert?
I'm an outside kind of guy. I don't have any trouble talking to people, and I don't have any trouble telling people like it is.

Pessimist or optimist?
Life is too short to be ticked all the time.

How easy is it for you to trust people?
I can trust people. I can also read people. I don't reward my trust to people I don't enjoy reading.

Do you tend to keep things or get rid of them?
I like to go through life without a lot of stuff. Stuff just weighs you down. I mean, do you really need a closet?

Do you have any secrets?
Well, I don't talk about it, so maybe it's not a secret, but I still love Janet. I probably always will. I would have married her. But I don't want Tally to start missing what she didn't have, so I just keep that quiet.

Do you like taking risks?
Of course.

What stands in the way of your happiness right now?
I can be happy right now. But I'd like to find the jewelry and stuff. I think Tally might want a closet. And she wants to go to college.

How will you get past what stands in your way?
I'm going to find it. If it's there, I'll find it.

What will happen if you fail?
Well, we'll just go back to doing what we were doing—living without it.

If you could change one thing about your past, what would it be?
I would have married Janet.

After I had this imaginary conversation with Tally's father, Bart, I came to understand her motivations in fresh ways and I was better able to imagine how a sixteen-year-old girl with this man for a father would think. If I posed a question to Bart that I didn't think I knew the answer to, I approached that question as an information void that needed to be filled.

Interviewing all the main characters in this way and sketching out their quirks, strengths, and flaws not only prepared me to write their story but also shortened the overall writing time—I spent fewer hours staring at the computer screen. It also decreased the amount of editing I had to do when the story was done because characters tend to stay consistent when you are intensely familiar with them from the get-go.

If you're not sure how to clothe your character with layers of personality *before* you begin writing about her, then begin by writing her biography, for no other reason than to create for her a past from which you can draw. Keep in mind that you are not writing backstory that you'll have to find a way to integrate into your story arc; you are prewriting information that will become a resource center, a bank to withdraw from or a grocery store to shop from as you write your story.

And yes, your characters will change and evolve and perhaps surprise you along the way, and you may find that you are suddenly working with people you only thought you knew. Unforeseen plot developments are part of the wonder and thrill of novel writing. Developing intimacy with your characters doesn't prevent your story from taking new directions you hadn't planned on, but it does help you create richly drawn characters your reader will care about, no matter which direction your story goes.

¶

The Muscles of Storytelling
Jill Elizabeth Nelson

The familiar phrase "put some muscle into it" applies to storytelling as much as to manual labor. The goals, motivations, and conflicts (GMC) of the characters propel a story along, much like the muscles

ESSENTIALS OF FICTION: UNFORGETTABLE

Create at least one unforgettable character.

Forgettable characters make forgettable stories. Plot, setting, and characterization are the greatest elements of fiction, but the most important is characterization. While most plots aren't remembered in detail, great characters are—Huckleberry Finn, Sherlock Holmes, even Darth Vader.

—*Randy Alcorn*

that move the human body, sometimes in vigorous action, sometimes in slight but significant gestures.

To establish GMC, we must ask and answer the following questions in clearly defined terms:

- What does the character want? (goal)
- Why does the character desire this goal? (motivation)
- What stands between the character and achieving the goal? (conflict)

A *goal* can be something as insignificant as finding the missing grocery list, as long as that goal contributes to the forward momentum of the overall story. Or a goal may be as enormous as thwarting a nuclear attack. The grocery list goal might be appropriate to flesh out a scene, and the nuclear disaster goal more functional as the main character's central focus for an entire novel.

A goal need not be noble, particularly in the case of the antagonist; however, it must be believable and measurable. In other words, a character's goal must be consistent with his personality and situation, and the achievement or nonachievement of the goal should have identifiable effects upon the character's life.

For instance, in Brandilyn Collins's powerful novel *Color the Sidewalk for Me*, the main character's goal is to earn her mother's love and forgiveness. This objective is consistent with the character's background and situation. Progress toward or away from the goal is measured by interaction between the characters in any given scene. During the story, the protagonist does many things out of bitterness and frustration that work contrary to the goal, yet the acceptance of her mother remains her heart's desire. Unless she can achieve this goal, she will spend the rest of her life in alienation—an identifiable effect on her future.

The importance the character attaches to the goal defines his or her *motivation*. The more clearly we can demonstrate for the reader why a character wishes to achieve a particular goal, the more readers will care whether or not the goal is achieved. Motivation is a huge factor in enticing readers to invest their emotions in the story. Without a compelling motivation driving a character toward a goal, why should the character—much less the reader—care if the goal is reached?

In Sharon Hinck's *Stepping into Sunlight*, a young mother struggles to overcome posttraumatic stress disorder brought on by witnessing a violent crime. Her situation is aggravated by her isolation in a new community while her naval chaplain husband is deployed at sea. Why shouldn't she simply give in to the dark depression and hide in her home? Because she has a young son depending on her to be a normal mommy. Now that's a motivation readers will find relatable and compelling.

The more obstacles we can place between a character and his deeply motivated goal, the more readers will feel the need to turn the pages and find out what happens next. *Conflict* can arise from other characters, circumstances, forces of nature, or from within the character himself.

Other characters' goals and motivations provide the bedrock conflict for most stories. For example, if character A is determined to win the race and character B is equally determined that character A will not even enter the race, the two are set on a collision course that can provide an engrossing tale.

Circumstances may also block the achievement of a goal. For instance, if a character is without insurance, he may have difficulty finding the means to pay for a necessary surgery. Such a story setup contains inherent conflict between the character and a largely impersonal obstacle to his well-being. How the character overcomes the obstacle—or not—fills out the plot of the story.

Forces of nature can also provide wonderful conflicts. If a character's child is lost in the woods but a forest fire is compelling evacuation of the area, tension escalates in a situation that is already serious.

However, inner conflict provides one of the most difficult obstacles for a character to overcome, as well as a heart-twister for readers, because the character is in opposition to himself. How touching might a story be about a woman who must choose between her baby's death and letting another woman of despicable nature raise him? Such a novelization of the biblical tale of Solomon's wisdom would be permeated with this type of inner conflict.

A story plot flows when GMC is incorporated into scenes, whole chapters, and the entire novel in escalating degrees. Consider the following points and examples:

Every scene should contain a specific, miniature GMC that plays out to either resolution or frustration (or a combination of the two) by the end of the scene. In *Gone with the Wind,* Margaret Mitchell's classic set in the Civil War South, Scarlett O'Hara plots to steal Ashley Wilkes, the man she loves, away from his fiancée. Her flirtations with other men to make him jealous, followed by her passionate declaration of love, end in complete rejection by Ashley. Worse, Scarlett's resulting fit of temper is witnessed by an infuriating rogue, Rhett Butler. Humiliation upon humiliation for Scarlett, and a marvelous example of goal, motivation, and conflict played out to delicious frustration by the end of a scene.

Every chapter should be guided by a larger GMC that does not result in final resolution but in more and greater problems. In one of my own novels, museum security expert Desiree Jacobs battles throughout the first chapter to shield her father from what she sees as a wrongful FBI investigation and to protect his precarious health by removing some of the burden of running the company. By the end of the chapter, her father is dead and the FBI investigation is intensified. Total disaster! Yet the rest of the book proceeds at a frantic pace as Desi scrambles to defend her father's good name and preserve the business he built. Disaster has complicated and escalated the GMC, not eliminated it.

The overall story arc should be driven by a major GMC that is related to the theme of the book. John Steinbeck's masterpiece *The Grapes of Wrath* paints a powerful word picture on the theme of ordinary people struggling to preserve dignity and worth in the face of devastation. Steinbeck's story arc delves deeper than mere physical survival; it goes to the heart of the survival of the human spirit. The lesser GMCs of every scene and every chapter reinforce the central GMC of the entire novel. Such cohesive focus is a hallmark of books that survive the test of time to become classics.

Here are two exercises that will help develop recognition of GMC in a story and the use of GMC to develop a plot.

1. Choose a favorite book and read the first scene. List the characters and each of their goals, motivations, and conflicts. Identify how the GMCs intertwine, hook the reader, and propel the story forward.

2. Create a goal, motivation, and conflict for each of the following characters: a farmer, his wife, and the couple's grown son. At least part of the conflict must be due to clashing goals and motivations between the characters. Observe! Once the GMC for each character is set up, a story is ready to be told.

Without GMC, we writers have no story to tell, but once we set up the GMC for each character, we have the power necessary to move the story forward. And the same way that muscles propel the body, powerfully structured GMC moves the story from the mundane to the marvelous.

§

Crafting Real-Life Characters
Tamera Alexander

The primary reason readers read is to be moved, to be changed, to live the experiences of the characters themselves. They want to turn that last page and be different for having taken that journey with those characters they've lived with—they've *become*—over the past

ESSENTIALS OF FICTION: WRITE IN THREE DIMENSIONS

Make sure your central characters are three-dimensional—round, not flat.

Characters shouldn't disappear when they turn sideways. In a short story, you can show just one side of a character, like his anger or determination or fear. In a novel, you have to show (not tell) his intellectual, emotional, social, and spiritual sides, including his fatal flaws. Characters shouldn't be props or puppets or robots. Three-dimensional characters don't just serve the plot, they *drive* the plot—e.g., Captain Ahab and Scarlett O'Hara. Ask yourself, "Is my main character someone I'd want to spend three hundred pages with?" If readers don't care about the character, they don't care what happens to her—so plot no longer matters. —*Randy Alcorn*

350 pages. This happens when readers connect with characters who are real, who make mistakes (oftentimes repeatedly), and who not only encounter obstacles but battle through one after another to reach their goals. But how do writers craft compelling, "real" characters? By making them identifiable.

When's the last time you finished a book and you not only wished the story hadn't ended, but you also thought about the book's characters long after you turned the final page? The characters in that story became real to you. They took on lives of their own.

Characters come alive when authors:

1. Give them a past hurt or wound
2. Make them likable
3. Make them fallible
4. Make them good at what they do
5. Put them in jeopardy

WOUNDED HEROES

We've all been hurt in some way or another. Woundedness makes a character approachable, and we are naturally drawn to people (and characters) with whom we feel we have something in common. Your protagonist must have suffered some kind of wound when the story begins—an unhealed source of continuing pain.

A character's woundedness often stems from something that happened in their adolescence. It could be from a single event or from an ongoing situation or stigma they endured. This hurt can manifest itself in a fear in the character's current life that the reader glimpses at the start of the story but that the author doesn't completely reveal until much later in the book, because facing this fear is part of the character's growth—often referred to as the character's *arc*—and will be woven throughout the story.

A character's woundedness must be healed in some way by the end of the book. This doesn't mean that it goes away completely or that the hero or heroine acts as if that event never happened. But they are no longer enslaved by fear as they once were. They have grown in their journey and, hopefully, so has the reader.

LIKABLE CHARACTERS

We relate to characters we like. Characters who have a sense of humor and the ability to make others laugh, and who can laugh at themselves. We are drawn to characters who are compassionate and who put others' good before their own. This is where secondary characters really come in handy.

Secondary characters are great vehicles for showing the likability of our protagonists and for reflecting their positive attributes (as well as negative). If you have secondary characters who admire the hero and heroine, or who find them funny or interesting, or who are grateful to the protagonists for helping them, chances are good that your readers will feel that same "likability" in them too.

FALLIBLE CHARACTERS

Characters don't always make right choices because people don't always make right choices. Characters who do the exact opposite of what they know is best to do—due to stress or a situation they've gotten themselves into—raise the interest level of readers. First, because we've all been there before. But second, because we're invested to read on and find out what's going to happen to the character now that they've lied, or cheated, or stolen something.

We empathize with characters who don't always feel appropriate emotions, or who battle emotions that they shouldn't feel. This can be especially effective in romance or romantic suspense. The hero is attracted to the heroine and yet knows they shouldn't be together because of their different stations in life or because it wouldn't be best for the other person, etc.

TALENTED CHARACTERS

We're drawn to characters who are talented and powerful, who are good at what they do; characters who can do something better than anyone else. We empathize with people when we greatly admire their skill.

Someone who is especially talented or skilled is often singled out to use that special skill. But intervening often comes at a cost. The character with special skills—who is talented and powerful—must be willing to sacrifice something to help with his or her skill.

CHARACTERS IN PERIL

We identify with characters who are facing imminent danger or who are undergoing unfair treatment or facing undeserved misfortune. The danger can be physical or emotional, but it must threaten the protagonist's well-being somehow.

Many novels begin with a character in a perilous situation, either of their own volition or one that's been forced onto them. They may be hanging off the side of a building or a mountain, or they may have a stalker after them or be facing unexpected news that is going to change their world forever. Or perhaps the carriage they're riding in crashes and nearly takes them over the cliff with it.

Beginning with a character in peril makes them more empathetic to the reader.

Creating identifiable characters makes all the difference in writing a story that readers enjoy and remember for years to come. You might be asking yourself, "Do I have to give my protagonists *all* of these distinguishing traits?" Not at all. But you must give them at least one (if not more) in the first few pages of your book to hook readers, to make them feel invested in your characters in such a way that they want to keep reading, keep turning those pages.

When readers are committed to the characters, the story will take on a life of its own and will draw them in from the very first page. Ultimately, we want to write novels that not only elicit emotion but also take readers on a journey with our characters and leave them changed forever.

ESSENTIALS OF FICTION: DON'T CONSTRUCT, CREATE

Don't just *construct* characters; *create* them.

As we are created by God as whole and unique human beings, a character is a living whole, not just a collection of traits. Our characters must be more than the sum of their parts. Characters are real—they have backstories, histories, childhoods, and events that have shaped them. The writer must know all the details even though he won't pass them all on. If our characters are not real to the author, they'll never be real to the reader. Try to create memorable "tags" for your characters. Fred Holevas, former vice president of the high school I attended, was described in the *Oregonian* as "Dirty Harry with the heart of Mother Teresa." Perfect. —*Randy Alcorn*

¶

Wrestling Through the Issues with Your Characters
Lisa Tawn Bergren

Some of the most powerful Christian fiction I've read has impacted me on an emotional, mental, and theological level, and I strive to do the same with my own writing by getting nose to nose and not

BIRTH OF A CHARACTER

One of my favorite memories is of a woman seeking me out in my office in Chicago. She was in her seventies, clad in black, way overdressed for the weather, bent, and dragging one foot.

"You the writer Jenkins?" she said.

"I am."

"Reader," she said. "Fan."

"Thanks."

"One question. Where do you get your ideas for characters?"

What could I say—"From people like you"?

I said, "I make 'em up."

"Figured as much. Good day."

While many ideas come from seeing people like her and imagining what their lives must be like, characters appear in my mind's eye as I'm writing. The more vital the character is to the story, the more clearly I see him.

In one novel, my lead buys a gun on the black market in South America from a national wearing thick, black, horn-rimmed glasses. That's all we know about him. My guess is you already have a picture of him in your mind. You can probably even hear his accent.

backing down from my characters' heart and mind issues—issues like love, anger, fear, pain, desire, temptation, or separation.

The best letters I receive say, "It sounds like you've experienced this." That's when I know that I've hit the mark—especially if I *haven't* personally experienced it. In one of my novels, the heroine has serious issues with her mother, who is in the last stages of Alzheimer's. Her mother was a self-centered, abusive woman who would've never been nominated for Mother of the Year. But my character must come to realize that her mother is never going to ask her for forgiveness for her failures—and that it's important to forgive her anyway. Now,

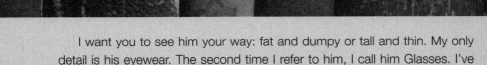

I want you to see him your way: fat and dumpy or tall and thin. My only detail is his eyewear. The second time I refer to him, I call him Glasses. I've referred to others as Big Mouth, Pants, or Shoes. I don't need to get to know them; they're just props. But, I hope, distinctive ones.

Some may disagree with my belief that you don't need to have developed your entire cast when you start a novel. But I think it's far more fun for you and the reader if you put your lead characters together, then see who else shows up at the door.

In one series, I introduced a big detective who proved earthy and likable. Readers (and I) fell in love with him. Eventually he took over the series.

The more important a character, the better you should know his personality. His physical description, however, can be left much to the reader's imagination. I like to offer hints, but that's all. Readers enjoy seeing a character the way he looks in their own minds.

Keep your eyes open. Characters abound everywhere.

—*Jerry B. Jenkins*

I enjoy a pretty healthy relationship with my own mom, so it was a challenge to understand that buildup of frustration and bitterness that plagues so many people . . . for so many justifiable reasons. But once I did, I could feel the walls that kept my character from love on several levels, and I understood, as a novelist, what I would need to tear down for my heroine to find healing. That's the kind of wrestling I'm talking about.

Writers who dare to invest themselves in their characters, feel what they feel, think how they think—*operate out of their particular foundation and understanding of the world*—will create unique characters who change and evolve as they wrestle through their issues. This is the growth, the transformational process that readers seek, because in witnessing it in another, they too may experience growth and transformation. And it has a secondary benefit for a writer: when I force myself into another's head and heart, someone far different from me, I write a new story and have a fresh perspective that leads to new plot possibilities and conclusions. I never want my readers to say, "Well, I liked reading her books, but they all seem the same." Since I'm about to start my sixteenth novel, that forces me to venture farther and farther afield with my characters, writing about people who are not like me and my loved ones—but whom I come to know as family, in time.

The best characters stay with you long after you've turned the last page, right? And the characters that stay with me are those with whom I've been in the ring: Hadassah in Francine Rivers's Mark of the Lion series taught me the cost of standing up for faith in a world that would rather see a person die than profess the truth; the mother—and her son—in Angela Hunt's *The Debt* helped me think through ministry on a personal basis . . . where it is most effective; the possessed man in Tracy Groot's *Madman* brought home demonic possession and insanity, the slow degradation of the mind—and Christ's dominion over all—on a whole new level. These three authors changed me, changed my thinking, changed something in my heart by the power of their work. I would venture to say that each author wrestled through each chapter alongside her characters. And it shows.

Unless our characters are growing, changing, developing, becoming more than they once were, I think we need to go back to the drawing board and give them something bigger to wrestle, a taller Goliath to face . . . and conquer. Nice stories are good, but if we're striving to write life-changing fiction, tales that have an impact for the Kingdom, we have to include such impact for our characters.

So what's happening for your main characters? What's going right for them? More important, what's going wrong? A writing instructor once made me go through an exercise that I find especially powerful:

1. What's the worst thing that could happen for your character? Write that scene now.
2. Got it? Now make it worse.
3. Got that? Now make it worse again.

I groaned through each level of that exercise, actually muttering in alarm, "Oh no! I can't go *there*!" But pushing characters to the worst place—and best place—often gives us the depth of characterization we need in our novels. It forces our characters to reach for everything that God has given them emotionally, physically, relationally, and spiritually, and in that moment, allows an opening for true change and transformation to be portrayed.

Some of those scenes hurt. I've written many scenes with tears streaming down my face because I'm *moved* by what's happening to my characters, and that's when I know God is doing something powerful in me, and hopefully, in my writing. The *best* books move us on a visceral level. We *feel* the characters' pain, rejoice in their glories, ache with them through the hurt, cheer as they gain enlightenment. The best writing is a physical act—*wrestling*—not a passive spectator sport. Dare to suit up and enter the ring, and you'll make it through the rounds to be declared a winner.

CHAPTER 3

DIALOGUE

¶

Dialogue as Action
James Scott Bell

Novelist Elizabeth George has a nice acronym that every writer should memorize: THAD—Talking Head Avoidance Device. What she means is that in every scene that employs dialogue, there must be more going on than mere speech.

And just what is true fictional dialogue? Dialogue is not the exact representation of real-life speech: taking verbal tangents, making small talk, killing time, filling spaces with hesitators. We often talk when there is not much to say. But dialogue in fiction must have a purpose. While it should, in most cases, *give the impression* of real-life speech, it should always be uttered for dramatic reasons.

Such reasons reside in the minds and intentions of the characters.

John Howard Lawson, noted playwright and screenwriter during Hollywood's golden age, said that dialogue ought to be considered a

compression and extension of action. This exceedingly important definition tells us that what a character says is part of his or her objective.
Characters must *want* something. They must come into conflict with
other characters who oppose that want.

So characters use dialogue to help them get their way. If you
remember only this much, it will enrich your dialogue enormously.

AGENDAS

Think of each scene you write as involving characters with agendas.
If characters are not in the scene with purpose, they should be kicked
off the page or reshaped so they do have a reason for being there. You
begin writing dialogue by first being clear about your characters' objectives and making sure there is tension between those objectives.

Here is an example from the classic film *On the Waterfront.* Terry
Malloy is a washed-up boxer who now does the bidding of the local
union boss, Johnny Friendly. At the beginning of the film, Terry has
unwittingly been part of the murder of Joey Doyle, a neighborhood
kid. Joey's sister, Edie, is innocence compared to Terry's street tough-
ness. As they sit down at a table, let's take a look at the characters'
agendas and what they mean in the scene.

> EDIE: Were you really a prizefighter?
>
> TERRY: I used to be.
>
> EDIE: How did you get interested in that?
>
> TERRY: I don't know. I had to scrap all my life; I might
> as well get paid for it. When I was a kid my old
> man got bumped off. Never mind how. Then they
> stuck Charley and me in a dump they call a "chil-
> dren's home." Boy, that was some home. Anyhow, I

ran away from there and fought in the club smokers and peddled papers and Johnny Friendly bought a piece of me.

EDIE: Bought a piece of you?

TERRY: Yes. I was going pretty good there for a while. And after that . . . What do you really care, am I right?

EDIE: Shouldn't everybody care about everybody else?

TERRY: Boy, what a fruitcake you are.*

Edie wants to get to know Terry. Terry is willing to go a little way with this, but ultimately we see he is cynical about her agenda. No one really cares about anybody deeply, he thinks.

But she really does care, and to Terry that means she's a "fruitcake." After the drinks come to the table, Terry reveals what his real view of life is:

TERRY: You wanna hear my philosophy of life? Do it to him before he does it to you.

EDIE: I never met anyone like you. There's not a spark of sentiment, or romance, or human kindness in your whole body.

TERRY: What good does it to you besides get you in trouble?

EDIE: And when things and people get in your way, you just knock them aside, get rid of them. Is that your idea?

---

* *On the Waterfront*, directed by Elia Kazan (1954; Columbia Pictures).

TERRY: Don't look at me when you say that. It wasn't my fault what happened to Joey. Fixing him wasn't my idea.

EDIE: Who said it was?

TERRY: Everybody's putting the needle on me. You and them mugs in the church and Father Barry. I didn't like the way he was looking at me.

EDIE: He was looking at everybody the same way.

Now we have direct conflict over what life should be about. And it's tied to the death of Edie's brother. Terry feels the guilt closing in and wants to avoid it. Edie wants him to face up to it.

Here's the lesson: When you write any scene involving characters talking, be sure you know what each character wants, and put those wants into conflict. This can be done in *any* scene, even those involving characters who are allies.

Let's say you have a scene where the lead is talking over her troubles with her best friend. Instead of having the friend be a simple

ESSENTIALS OF FICTION: WRITE AUTHENTIC CONVERSATIONS

Define your character through dialogue; make your dialogue authentic but concise.

Don't let all your characters sound alike. Unless they're stiff and formal, be sure they use contractions, like real people do—"Let's" not "Let us," "can't" not "cannot." Actual conversation is wordy, repetitive, and boring when reduced to writing, so make sure your dialogue *sounds* true to life, but make it more concise than real speech. Don't bootleg into your dialogue information that you want the reader to know but characters wouldn't ever say.

—*Randy Alcorn*

sounding board, give her an agenda too. Perhaps she's late for picking up her child from school, yet the lead is keeping her from leaving. Or the friend has a subtle feeling that the lead is making up the story, and that is reflected in her reactions and responses.

Knowing the agendas in the scene will go a long way toward strengthening your dialogue.

PERSONAL EQUILIBRIUM

The characters in your stories should be out of equilibrium. They are bothered, challenged, afraid, disoriented—and must fight to achieve a level of inner peace. The biggest fight must be in the heart of the lead character, but all characters should have some sort of disturbance roiling inside them.

And by the way, this applies to any kind of writing you do, from the lightest fare to the deepest tragedy.

In Neal Simon's *The Odd Couple,* for example, Oscar Madison's equilibrium as a happy slob is disturbed when his despondent friend, Felix Unger, moves into his apartment. Felix is a neat freak to the extreme. So neat, in fact, that it ruins Oscar's weekly poker game. The players can't stand Felix puttering around cleaning up and spraying air freshener while they try to win the pots.

So when Oscar and Felix are left alone, Oscar decides it's time to have it out.

> FELIX: But don't you see the irony of it? Don't you see
> it, Oscar?
> OSCAR: Yes, I see it.
> FELIX: No, you don't. I really don't think you do.
> OSCAR: Felix, I'm telling you I see the irony of it.

FELIX: Then tell me. What is it? What's the irony?

OSCAR: The irony is—unless we can come to some other arrangement, I'm gonna kill you. That's the irony.*

Oscar is so wedded to his bliss as a slob that he is about ready to throttle Felix. It's a trivial thing, but in comedy the trivial is elevated to the essential, as it is here.

So dialogue, as an extension or compression of action, becomes a way for characters to get back into a comfort zone. Before you start writing the dialogue in a scene, ask, Why are the characters in a state of discomfort? What is going on in the deep parts of their lives?

This is how you get *subtext* into your dialogue. The words spoken give evidence of something more going on beneath the surface.

DIALOGUE AS WEAPON

Another way to view dialogue is as a *weapon*. In very intense scenes it becomes an implement for battle, both defensive and offensive.

In the Warner Bros. classic *Casablanca*, the newly arrived Nazi major, Strasser, wants to assert his power and authority in front of Rick Blaine, the American who runs a saloon and keeps out of politics.

STRASSER: Do you mind if I ask you a few questions? Unofficially, of course.

RICK: Make it official if you like.

STRASSER: What is your nationality?

RICK: I'm a drunkard.**

---

* Neil Simon, *The Collected Plays of Neil Simon*, Vol. 1 (New York: Plume, 1986), 258–259.
** *Casablanca*, directed by Michael Curtiz (1942; Warner Bros. Pictures).

The first volley in this little battle of wits comes from Rick. He shows, in his answer, both subtle contempt and a complete disregard for the man's authority. A few lines later, Strasser lobs a grenade:

STRASSER: We have a complete dossier on you. "Richard Blaine, American. Age thirty-seven. Cannot return

THE DOLLHOUSE SYNDROME

A phenomenon occurs when a little girl is playing with dolls and a dollhouse. She elaborately sets up the room where her play is to take place. She puts the dollies in the dollhouse room. Then when she is ready for the play to proceed, she picks up two dolls and holds them in her hands. Usually when one doll speaks the little girl wiggles or bounces that doll while she provides the "talk." Then she wiggles or bounces the other doll and provides the answering "talk." When the talking is done, she puts them back in her dollhouse.

An author can be guilty of a similar character extraction if he doesn't keep his characters connected to the scene. Here are some fixes for the dollhouse syndrome:

- Action tags. (Sandra screamed as she fell off the cliff. "Help!")
- Reaction to outside stimulus. (With his hand, Joe shaded his eyes against the glare of the sun. "Sandra, are you hurt?") Anchors speaker to setting.
- Reaction to inside stimulus. (The disgust Sandra felt bubbling up against her erstwhile lover nearly burst through her lips. "I suggest you get an ambulance.") Anchors speaker to emotion.
- A personal gesture, characteristic action, or movement. (Joe scratched his neck and whistled. "I may need one myself.") Reveals the speaker's frame of mind.

Keep your characters anchored in their setting and circumstances, and watch them come to life. —*Donita K. Paul* to his country." The reason is a little vague. We also know what you did in Paris. Also, Herr Blaine, we know why you left Paris.

At this point Rick takes the dossier from Strasser's hand.

STRASSER: Don't worry. We are not going to broadcast it.
RICK: Are my eyes really brown?

Here, Rick's weapon is facetiousness. He is fighting back against the authority he finds contemptible.

When you read a novel or watch a movie, notice how many times dialogue is used as a weapon, especially in scenes of high conflict. Try to imagine the characters using words as bullets, clubs, and bazookas. And when you consider your dialogue, look for those opportunities to "pour it on."

These three areas of fictional dialogue—agendas, equilibrium, and weaponry—hang together. The stronger the agenda, the more it shows lack of equilibrium, and the more likely the character is to use dialogue as a weapon.

Seek, then, to know your characters deeply, and place them in situations of direct conflict with other characters. Do so, and you'll never have the problem of mere "talking heads."

CHAPTER 4

POINT OF VIEW

❡

Everything You Wanted to Know about POV . . . but Were Embarrassed to Ask

Robin Jones Gunn with Angela Hunt

The conference room buzzed with hushed conversations. Professional editors and hopeful first-time authors lined up like speed-daters. The opinion of the publishing professionals might well determine the future of the novices who came and went every fifteen minutes.

I fidgeted as my assigned editor skimmed my first chapter. The seat felt warm from the previous prospective author.

Looking at me over the top of his glasses, the editor said, "Your POV is all over the place. You need to stay in one head. Third-person limited works best for beginning writers like you. Keep working on it."

I thanked him and stood, feeling too embarrassed to admit that I had no idea what a POV was, let alone a third person limited. All I knew was that I had come to the writers' conference because I loved to tell stories. I knew I had a lot to learn, but how could I have spent so many years working on a novel and have no clue what these basic insider terms meant? I was ready to pack up my rejected little first chapter and go home.

But I didn't. I kept asking questions, and I kept writing. I hope you'll do the same. With some valuable input from my novelist friend Angela Hunt, here is everything you wanted to know about POV . . . but were embarrassed to ask.

TYPES OF POV

Point of view (POV) refers to the perspective from which a story is told, and like ice cream, it comes in many flavors and varieties: first person, second person, third person. Third-person limited, third-person distant, third-person close. And the granddaddy of them all, omniscient.

Let's begin with third person. In this POV a narrator—the author—stands outside of the character and relays information.

When Mary woke up, she noticed it was raining.

If you describe the scene only through Mary's eyes and thoughts you will be using third-person limited, meaning you are limited to revealing only what Mary sees, hears, feels, smells, or thinks. The editor I met at the conference was right when he said that this point of view works best for beginning writers. Novelist Jefferson Scott, aka Jeff Gerke, tells writers to get a short piece of two-inch PVC pipe. Hold it up to your eye and peer through it. If you think of yourself as the POV character, in that scene you can only write what the character is thinking, seeing, hearing, and sensing.

If you want to write something from another character's POV, you need to begin a new scene. Only one POV character per scene. And be careful with how many POV characters you have in a book, or you may stretch your readers too thin and prevent them from bonding with your characters.

The third-person limited POV can be close or distant. Close means that you tell a great deal about what Mary's thinking and feeling. You can even express indirect thoughts without having to italicize them or write, "she thought," since we're already in her head.

> When Mary woke up and looked out the window, she saw raindrops like tears upon the glass. She should have known the day would be as gray as her mood. Why did George have to leave her now?

If you want the reader to assume or guess, make the POV distant so readers have no idea what Mary's feeling or thinking:

> When Mary woke up, she saw rain pelting the window. She got out of bed and dressed quickly.

If anyone else enters the scene, we must not have access to that character's thoughts or feelings because this scene is in Mary's POV. Look at these two examples:

> Mary lowered her feet to the floor when Mother came into the room. "Why are you sleeping so late?" Mother

said, wondering why her daughter looked so pale. A bruise marked Mary's forehead.

Mary lowered her feet to the floor when Mother came into the room. "Why are you sleeping so late?" Mother asked. "You don't look well . . . and how did you get that bruise on your forehead?"

Do you see why the first example is wrong and the second one is right? If we're in Mary's POV, we shouldn't know what Mother is thinking or wondering. Her thoughts will have to be revealed in gestures, words, or tone of voice.

Perhaps you'd rather have Mary tell her story using first-person perspective. In this point of view, a character speaks in his or her own words.

When I woke up I noticed it was raining. Rivulets streaked the windowpanes like tears, and the sky was as gray as my mood. Why did George have to leave me now?

Though it is rarely used, let's take a look at second person, in which the reader becomes a character in the story:

You woke up to rain this morning. Water streaked your windowpanes like tears, and your heart felt as gray as the sky outside. Why did George have to get all freaky and leave you now? Because he was a jerk, that's why. Or maybe he just didn't like you.

Finally, there's omniscient POV, often called the "God view" because the unseen narrator knows all:

> In the house on Forty-second Street, at six fifteen in the morning, Mary Jones opened her eyes and thought the raindrops on her window looked like tears. Why had George chosen to leave her now? He had his reasons, of course, none of which were known to Mary. But in his heart of hearts, he knew he would never be the man she needed. Or wanted. Because she could never accept his secret. And secrets, as the sages say, have a way of bubbling to the surface.

Some writers commit what we call "head-hopping"—one minute they're in Mary's head, and a moment later, in the same scene, they're in George's. They might try to tell you that they're simply using omniscient POV, but they're not. In true omniscient POV, the narrator has a unique voice, and it's consistent throughout the story. Omniscient POV was popular in Dickens's era; it's not employed as often today.

HOW DO I DECIDE WHICH POV TO USE?

As the writer of a third-person story, try to picture yourself as a theater director who sits right up front and makes sure each character takes his or her cue and gives the right inflection to each line. Every look and gesture means something. Each scene builds on the next. Every prop has a purpose. You direct the story in such a way that your audience connects with the characters, enters in at an emotional level, and believes the ending when it comes (hopefully) all too soon.

Third person works well for building multilayered stories. There's room for setting the tone of the story and giving descriptive views of the surroundings. The characters show their emotions through actions and inflections. Dialogue helps move the story along and builds an understanding of the relationship between the characters.

Third person can also be quite intimate if you "zoom in" as we did in the example with Mary. Notice that the narration is like a camera. First we see Mary waking up in her bed. Then we zoom into her head and gain access to her thoughts.

Third person is also useful if you're writing a mystery or thriller and you don't want to reveal clues to the reader too soon. If you're writing first person, the reader expects to have complete access to the protagonist's thoughts, feelings, and memories. In third person, it's permissible to withhold certain thoughts, feelings, and memories if it serves your plot. In the Sherlock Holmes stories, for instance, the story is told not by Holmes, but by Watson . . . because Sir Arthur Conan Doyle didn't want the reader to be privy to Holmes's deductive reasoning. It's much more fun to leave the reader in suspense until the ending, when the detective explains everything.

Now, as the writer of a first-person story, try to picture yourself as that same theater director. Only this time, instead of staying in your seat, you take to the stage in the role of the lead character. The play relies heavily on dialogue and the main character's thoughts and actions to carry the story to a satisfying conclusion.

First person works well for stories where the main character needs to give readers a diary sort of transparency. Readers "shadow" the main character throughout the story and are given immediate access to his or her thoughts and feelings. Some genres rely heavily upon first-person POV: chick lit, young adult fiction, and other stories where the reader yearns to spend a lot of time in the protagonist's head.

The weakness of first-person POV is that the writer can get so caught up in the character's stream of consciousness (writing every thought that pops into the character's head) that the pace becomes sluggish and the story becomes crowded with ruminations that don't really matter. If something does not advance plot or deepen character, hit the Delete key.

If you want to use omniscient point of view, you'll need a very good reason for doing so. It's perfectly permissible for an omniscient story to open with a "wide-angle lens" and then zoom in on one character, but the technique can be difficult and you'll need to maintain the narrator's voice throughout the story.

Can you mix points of view in a novel? Can you, for instance, write all the protagonist's scenes in first person and everyone else's in third person? Yes—it's been done. But you'd better be able to justify your reasoning to an editor, because it is unusual. To avoid disrupting the flow of the narrative, most editors prefer that the POV be consistent throughout the book—which can make it difficult if you've chosen to write first person and need to include a scene in which your protagonist does not appear.

GIVE YOUR FAVORITE POVS A TRY

Here's a writing exercise that will help if you're not sure which POV to choose. Pick a scene from your story and write out that scene from a third-person POV. Pay attention to your pronouns. Make sure you don't jump into any other character's head. Imagine that you're holding that piece of PVC pipe. You can see inside your character's head as well as what he can see in front of him. That's all. You cannot see someone making a face behind him.

After writing the scene in third person, start again, writing the same scene in first person. Make sure you now use "I" pronouns. You are taking on the voice of that main character and helping your readers come alongside the story by inviting them to see and think and feel everything the main character is experiencing. The reader hears the POV character's frustration in his dialogue and sees the scene through his eyes—up close and personal.

If you're brave, have a go at omniscient or second person POV. But be warned—unless you are amazingly brilliant, you are courting rejection simply by bucking current trends.

Have a look at all versions of your scene. Which one gave you the most freedom to keep the scene moving along? Which version sounds truer to the character as you see him or her in your imagination? Most important, which do you like best? Take that one as your strength for this current project. You can always try a different POV for your next project.

Now go write your heart out.

¶

Point of View: Connect with Your Characters
Carol Umberger

People read fiction to be entertained, to escape into another world, to experience another time or place vicariously. However, one can read a nonfiction history book or a book on oceanography or a travel diary if all one wants is to experience a different time and place through a factual recital. What makes fiction different is that the reading experience is an emotional one. This search for feeling is one of the main reasons people read fiction. The technique used to relay those emotions is point of view.

Point of view (POV) isn't just a technique for telling a story. It isn't simply a matter of deciding who will narrate a particular book, chapter, or scene. POV done well adds meaning, subtext, and suspense, and it is essential in the development of character and plot. POV is the foundation for creating an intimate relationship between the reader and the book's focal characters. That intimacy is what makes characters come to life on the page and keeps the reader's interest.

You may have heard the story of the three blind men describing an elephant. One man ran his hands over the leg and said, "This is a tree." The second man explored the trunk and said, "No, this is a snake." The third man grasped the tail and said, "No. You are all wrong. This is a rope." Each man "saw" the elephant in a different way, based upon his experience with it. As we see the world through a given character's eyes, the power of point of view unleashes that character's uniqueness on the written page much as an actor imbues a role with his own idiosyncrasies and worldview.

Readers identify with the character—in essence, become the character. Readers experience the setting, the events, through the perspective of another person, thus broadening their worldview. But readers can't know what to think or how to feel about an event unless the viewpoint character shows them.

You as the writer must decide whose story you are telling—whose viewpoint and perspective, whose feelings and emotions will provide the focus for the action in the book or in a particular scene. Perhaps you will decide that the entire book will be written from one character's POV. Perhaps you want both the protagonist and the antagonist. Maybe three POVs are needed if you want to give a heroine's POV as well. *Who tells the story affects the way your readers experience the story.*

Movies and stage productions have an advantage over books in that they are visual. We can see the characters' facial expressions and body language as well as the surroundings. We can hear the cadences of voices and the musical background. We can literally see the characters' reactions to one another and to events.

How do you do that on the written page? You center your scene on a character who stands to win or lose so your readers can feel for him or against him. To be effective, each scene must possess a viewpoint character through whose eyes we see the story unfold. In effect, we get inside that character's skin, inside his head, as he experiences the story rather than have him simply narrate events.

By staying in one character's skin for an entire scene, you allow your readers to bond with that character. Staying in one point of view, showing how the character sees the world through his reactions, allows your readers to get to know the character and to identify with him, to see that they have emotions and interests in common with the character.

If you think of POV as being a movie camera, visualize a handheld, amateur video in which the camera never stays put long enough for viewers to really see what's happening. This is exactly what happens to your readers when you switch POV constantly. You yank them away from one character and take them into another one's head. But you don't stay with any characters long enough for the reader to identify with them or care about them.

Taking this movie analogy further, you the author are the book's director: You know the story and the characters. You call the shots and place the camera in position. But the reader can only know what the camera records from its perspective, i.e., the point of view that you have chosen. As the author you must get out of your point of view, the perspective from which you view the scene, and be able to see what you write as the reader sees it. All that counts for the reader is what you have written down, not what you *think* you have written down.

A story concerns itself with someone's reaction to what happens—feelings, emotions, impulses, dreams, ambitions, motivations, and inner conflicts. Your character must clue the reader in to those feelings and emotions.

The first sentences of every scene must set the stage and anchor the reader to time and place. As quickly as possible, make it clear which character is telling this part of the story. Use the telling details of time and space and the character's reactions to what he sees, touches, hears, smells, or tastes. In other words, use the five senses so that your reader can experience what the character is experiencing.

> "Wake up, lass," a woman's voice crooned. "Come, 'tis only a bad dream. Ye are safe."
>
> As the nightmare and its terror faded, Gwenyth fearfully opened her eyes to see a woman sitting by her bed. Gwenyth touched the covers, to see if they were real and not straw, to know the dream was truly over. The reality of the warm, soft bed and the sweet-smelling chamber sank in and her sobs quieted.*

---

* Carol Umberger, *Circle of Honor* (Brentwood, TN: Integrity Publishers, 2002), 77–78.

The POV character is Gwenyth, and we know this from her emotional reaction—fear. She sees a woman; she touches the bedding; she smells something pleasant. These sensory details reassure her—and the reader—that the dream and its terror are gone. The fact that we live seven centuries later hasn't changed what it feels like to awaken from a bad dream, and your reader immediately identifies with the character.

Once you have clearly established the POV character, continue the scene using that character's reactions, emotions, and sensory details to remain firmly in his or her head. The reader can only know what this character experiences.

Let's imagine a scene where a husband is waiting for his wife in a restaurant. He is drinking coffee, reading the paper, and wondering if his wife will be late as usual. We are in his POV. He hears the bell over the door and looks up. She comes in, face flushed red from running. Wait, how does he know she was running? Did he see it? Not unless we tell the reader that he saw her through the window. She stands there, doesn't remove her coat. He can see from her expression that something has upset her.

She hasn't said a word, and we only know her through the eyes of the POV character. But we know, as he does, that something upsetting has made her late. What is it? This is the tension an author can build with POV to make the reader want to turn the page. Here we see that POV helps to create suspense by conveying information that only one character knows. We watch the story unfold through the perspective of one character and yet get to know them both.

Point of view is the single most powerful tool in a writer's toolbox. Use it purposefully to fine-tune your story and create an intimate experience that keeps readers turning the pages.

CHAPTER 5

PACING

❡

Pacing on Purpose
Brad Whittington

Back in the eighties, one of my students introduced me to Stephen R. Donaldson's Thomas Covenant chronicles. Early in the first book the protagonist storms out of his attorney's office, is hit by a car, and wakes up at the top of a narrow thousand-foot tower with no walls. Pretty intense. And the intensity doesn't let up for five hundred pages. It was an exhausting read.

You have to give Donaldson credit. It's not easy to redline the intensity meter for five hundred pages. However, it's not necessarily desirable, either. Good writing has ebb and flow. Your pacing choices should be governed by several considerations, including voice, style, context, character, and setting. You can control the pace through thoughtful decisions about word choice, sentence size and structure, use of dialogue and narrative, and even punctuation.

CONTENT

One issue that plagues beginning writers is what to put in and what to leave out. Pacing can help with that decision. When things are moving fast, the character has no chance to observe details of the scenery, and consequently the reader shouldn't be reading about them. When the pace is fast, report only what the point-of-view character will be able to notice, and nothing more.

Think about the last time you were in a fast-paced situation. Maybe a car slammed on its brakes in front of you, forcing you to swerve or skid to avoid a collision. Did you notice the license plate or what song was on the radio? Or maybe you were engrossed in the latest draft of your project and looked up to realize you were late to an important appointment. Did you notice if the bed was made or if the coffee was turned off?

Likewise, when the pace is slow, you can bring depth to the story by including details that reveal character or evoke a sense of place without the constraints of keeping things going at maximum speed.

PUNCTUATION

Punctuation is probably the least used tool for pacing, and for good reason. The rules are pretty rigid. But the judicious use of the semicolon can be employed on occasion. Excessive use can be annoying, but used sparingly, it provides a subtle method for pacing because it suggests a stronger connection between two sentences, and therefore a smaller mental stop.

WORD CHOICE

As Mark Twain said, "The difference between the almost right word and the right word is really a large matter—it's the difference between the lightning bug and the lightning."

It's obvious that longer words take more time to read. It may not be obvious that word length can affect the urgency a reader feels when reading a scene. If a lawyer is arguing a case in court, he might circumnavigate the table while making his opening remarks. Longer words are appropriate not only to give a sense of the environment but also to slow the pace as we see the wheels of justice grinding slowly. But if that same lawyer is trying to outrun an assassin, he will circle the table, or veer around it, or even vault it. Whatever he does, he'll do it with a short word, preferably a one-syllable word.

Word length isn't the only aspect of word choice that affects pacing. If the main character is trying to get over the mountains before freezing to death in the blizzard, he'll find the pass, not the col. Obscure words, no matter how appropriate, or even how short, will slow the pace, perhaps even stop it altogether as the reader either reaches for a dictionary or throws the book across the room.

A draft I submitted to my publisher described the weather-beaten face of an old woman living in a cardboard box like this:

> Peering from behind the leathery skin and craquelure of wrinkles in the warm glow of sunset, I saw an innocent girl of sixteen.

The editor called. I had picked up *craquelure*, the fine pattern of cracks formed on old paintings, from a Robertson Davies novel and thought it was perfect to describe the woman's network of wrinkles.

I chose to keep the reader in the story rather than to keep the word in the manuscript.

WORD COUNT

Consider this excerpt where Mark, the protagonist, is attacked by two guys.

> He toed a pinecone, one that wasn't open, green, dense and spiky as a pineapple. He got his work boot under it and kicked it at my head. As I ducked it the driver rushed me. Before I could react I was pinned to the ground. He grabbed the pinecone in his right hand and slammed it against my head. I felt the thorns tear the flesh on my ear and rip along my cheek, pulling my hair across my face. I rolled my head away before it got to my eye and swung a fist at his head. He rolled off of me and I rolled the other way to get to my feet.
>
> That's when Shotgun kicked me in the stomach.
>
> The woods went dark around the edges, telescoping to a pinpoint that receded from me. I curled inward, arms crossed over my gut, fingers clutching at my ribs. My mouth opened, but nothing went in or out. I was caught at the terminus of a long exhale, one that might last a year. I was aware of the pain in my stomach as a detail, noted along with the thin edge of individual pine needles pressed against my right cheek, the tickling crawl of blood seeping down my left cheek, the musky smell of rotting timber, the sound of wind rushing through my head and a pressure against my ears like

I was at the bottom of Toodlum Creek. I gaped like a fish, but it was as if a sock had been stuffed down my throat. I quivered with the spasms in my gut and turned in a small arc as my legs ratcheted back and forth, but the long exhale would not end.*

Notice that the second paragraph is a single sentence, only eight words long. The paragraph break and the single simple, short sentence highlight the importance of this action. Separating it from the other actions with a paragraph break emphasizes it more than anything else could—more than an exclamation point or italic or bold or caps. The pace stops with that sentence, just like the world stops for Mark with that kick.

The paragraph that follows describes the next few seconds but takes 165 words to do it. The change is intentional. The few seconds of elapsed time feel like an eternity to Mark. To communicate this experience to the reader, I slow down time by describing minute sensations in detail.

A lot happens in the first paragraph, but it uses fairly long sentences to tell the story. It could be tightened up to increase the pace.

He toed a green pinecone, hard and covered in spikes. With a grunt, he kicked it at my head. I ducked. The driver rushed me and pinned me to the ground. He grabbed the pinecone and slammed it against my head. The thorns ripped my ear and cheek. I rolled my head

---

* Brad Whittington, *Escape from Fred* (Nashville: Broadman & Holman Publishers, 2006), 177–178.

away. It missed my eye. I swung a fist at his head. He rolled off. I rolled the other way.

This version cuts forty-three words. It moves faster but has less detail. Every edit involves trade-offs between sometimes competing goals. In this case it would be voice or style versus pacing.

The next time you sit down to write, whether a first draft or during one of your editing passes, think about the choices you can make to create the pacing (slow or fast) that you want for the scene. You're the driver. You can hit the gas or the brakes simply by the choices you make. Have fun!

¶

Creating Page-Turning Chapter Endings
Sharon Dunn

Discerning how and where to end a chapter is extremely important in structuring a novel. The end of a chapter is the most likely place for a reader to decide the book is not worth reading. The good news is that if a reader's interest in the story has started to wane, the end of a chapter provides a great opportunity to win them back with a strong chapter hook. While there are many methods for ending a chapter, three of the most prominent involve breaking up a scene between chapters, revealing a character's internal struggles, and building suspense about an upcoming event. In addition, even if a chapter has ended in a good place, the hook can often be strengthened through revision.

CUT IN THE MIDDLE OF THE ACTION

Splitting a scene into multiple chapters is one of the most effective ways to hold reader interest. However, you cannot be random about how you break up the scene. Instead, look for the moment in the story when there would be a question planted in the reader's mind.

At the end of chapter 25 in Rene Gutteridge's *Snitch*, one of the female police trainees, Mack, is listening to surveillance. Her supervisor asks Mack if she hears anything. Mack shakes her head, then holds up her hand. "Wait! I've got something."* The chapter ends there. The reader will have to turn the page to find out what Mack heard.

Another strong place to break up a scene is the point at which a reader becomes concerned about the physical or emotional well-being of a character. A character may have just been hit in the head or just been given some bad news. What a perfect place to end a chapter. Put the second half of the scene in the next chapter. The reader will turn the page to see if she is knocked unconscious or to find out how he responds emotionally to the bad news.

Creating a chapter hook by splitting a scene can be used quite a bit in a novel. However, if your novel is written in first person, you have limitations when cutting a scene between chapters. If half of your scene is at the end of chapter 12, the only option is to go immediately to the other half of the scene at the beginning of chapter 13. But if your novel is written in third person, you have a wonderful

---

* Rene Gutteridge, *Snitch* (Colorado Springs, CO: WaterBrook Press, 2007), 195.

opportunity to hold the suspense even longer by inserting a different scene from a different character's point of view between the halves of the split scene.

REVEAL A CHARACTER'S HEART

One of the fiction writer's most important tasks is to create characters readers identify with. When mapping out a plot, a writer must think not only about external action but also about the changes and discoveries that happen inside a character as a result of the action. Often characters will make vows that are tied into their internal struggles. In his book *Plot and Structure*, James Scott Bell points out that ending a chapter with a character making a vow gives the reader a reason to keep reading.

In Siri Mitchell's *The Cubicle Next Door*, a young woman, Jackie, reveals that she was a child of parents who weren't married. Her father went off to war and died, and her mother, faced with raising a child alone, abandoned her. Jackie was raised by her grandmother. Chapter 4 ends with Jackie talking about her background and making the vow not to do what her mother did. Jackie says, "Losing your heart meant losing your mind. So I planned to do whatever it took to stay in control of mine."* Once this internal struggle is revealed through Jackie's vow never to fall in love, Mitchell is able to use that struggle as a chapter hook several times during the novel. Sometimes at the end of a chapter, Jackie opens her heart to the man who is pursuing her, and at the end of the other chapters, the emotional walls go up even stronger than before.

Sometimes what is in a character's heart is evil. He or she may

---

* Siri L. Mitchell, *The Cubicle Next Door* (Eugene, OR: Harvest House Publishers, 2006), 38.

make a vow that could harm another character. Sharyn McCrumb's character Rowan Rover is a tour guide and amateur hit man who has been hired to kill a woman on his tour, Susan Cohen. After a failed attempt at pushing Susan off a precipice and nearly losing his own life, chapter 10 ends in Rowan's point of view: "He closed his eyes and vowed to get safely down from Roche Rock, if only for the pleasure of seeing Susan Cohen dead and silenced."* Because we as readers don't want to see Rowan succeed and because his attempts at bumping Susan off are humorous, we are motivated to keep reading when we see that Rowan has even greater resolve to accomplish his evil task.

MENTION AN UPCOMING EVENT

This technique involves a reference to a future event that is sure to involve all sorts of conflict and entanglements. The event can be anything from a date, to meeting a long-lost friend, to a stakeout on a murder suspect.

In Jan Karon's *At Home in Mitford*, Father Tim, a small-town rector and lifelong bachelor, has made some big changes in his life. Because of health concerns, he is exercising and eating better. At the end of chapter 3, Father Tim decides while he is jogging that with all the changes he has made in his life, he should do something new and exciting. The chapter ends with "The idea came upon him quite suddenly. He would give a dinner party."** Father Tim hardly seems like he would be the host with the most. As readers, we have come to care about Father Tim, and because we know he is an introvert,

---

* Sharyn McCrumb, *Missing Susan* (New York: Ballantine Books, 1991), 163.
** Jan Karon, *At Home in Mitford* (New York: Viking Penguin, 1994), 41.

we would have concerns about his ability to pull a party together. Those concerns compel us into the next chapter to see how the party comes together.

FIND YOUR HOOK WHEN YOU REVISE

Oftentimes a writer has good instincts about where to end a chapter. The chapter has ended in the right place, but the scene just needs a little revision. Making the hook a true page-turner sometimes involves cutting excess weight off the end of a chapter to create a crisper ending. In *Plot and Structure,* James Scott Bell suggests that if a scene fizzles out, often the best thing to do is cut the last paragraph or two. Bell points out that "you don't have to write every scene to its logical conclusion."* A chapter ending is stronger if there is a sense of something left hanging. The editing doesn't always have to be as drastic as cutting whole paragraphs. Sometimes making the hook work involves just cutting a single line.

Here is an example of how cutting a line from one of my own mysteries made the chapter ending stronger. In this example, Tammy,

ESSENTIALS OF FICTION: MAKE IT COMPELLING

Always give readers a compelling reason to keep turning pages.

They have a thousand alternatives—why should they read your book? Give them uncertainty and create anticipation. "What's next?" keeps them turning the pages, but predictability is fatal. Figure out the parts readers will skip over; then cut them out. —*Randy Alcorn*

---

* James Scott Bell, *Write Great Fiction: Plot & Structure* (Cincinnati, OH: Writer's Digest Books, 2004), 125.

a single mom, is struggling to raise her troubled son, who has been missing for several hours.

The original:

> Tammy took in a deep, full breath of air. "You know, Mom, my brain just feels so hammered, I can only focus on the next thing I have to do, which is find my son, make sure he's breathing and not on the way to the police station."
>
> She pushed the door open and stepped outside.

The revision:

> Tammy took a deep breath. "You know, Mom, my brain just feels so hammered. I can only focus on the next thing I have to do, which is find my son, make sure he's breathing and not on the way to the police station again."*

Cutting the last line puts the focus more on the safety of Tammy's son than on the mundane action of stepping outside. Sometimes when we get to an end of a chapter, we overwrite and overexplain. It is better to end a chapter with the sense of things not yet concluded and with questions and concerns planted in the reader's mind.

As you read published fiction and find yourself turning the page at the end of a chapter, stop for a moment. Listen to your own thought

---

* Sharon Dunn, *Death of a Garage Sale Newbie* (Colorado Springs, CO: Multnomah Books, 2007), 111.

patterns. What were you thinking as you turned the page? Were you wondering about the outcome of an event? Were you concerned about the physical or emotional well-being of the characters? Or did you simply have an unanswered question in your head?

As you work on your own writing, take a moment to step out of your writer shoes and into your reader shoes. Try to see what you have written as a reader encountering it for the first time. Ask yourself this question: If I was reading this chapter, would I be motivated to turn the page? Then write the chapter ending that demands such a response.

CHAPTER 6

SETTING

¶

Bringing Setting to Life
Patti Hill

The world I knew changed dramatically when I read The Chronicles of Narnia. A wardrobe became a portal to a wondrous kingdom; my dream of a talking horse became less far-fetched; and I became a Daughter of Eve to be feared in battle, as long as I'm backed by an army of Minotaurs. Unforgettable stories of any genre transport readers like me to places we've never been before, whether the destination is quite familiar or as magical as Narnia. To accomplish this metaphysical marvel, setting must come alive.

Setting moves beyond its generic role as backdrop when a landscape, an attic hideaway, or even a rabbit warren becomes a vehicle of change for the characters. For instance, thanks to vivid writing, a reader might feel compelled to wash the Alabama clay off his feet after reading *To Kill a Mockingbird*; in *The Old Man and the Sea*, he watches

Cuba slip into the horizon and self-doubt taps his shoulder; but in the company of Scarlett O'Hara, he leans back to luxuriate in the "moist hungry earth" of Tara in *Gone with the Wind*. A masterfully built story universe uses the elements of history and culture, geography and climate, and flora and fauna to shape the characters and the stories, and most important, to pull the reader irresistibly in.

History and culture press hard at Jack London's characters in the brittle cold of the Klondike. For London, *The Call of the Wild* was a contemporary story. He lived the history and packaged his story in his intimate understanding of the time and place. The Klondike is an unforgiving landscape during troubled times. Two major financial panics caused massive unemployment in the United States. Men were desperate to feed their families, so they headed north to take risks otherwise considered unreasonable. Buck, the protagonist, is a dog stolen from his master in California to pull sleds in Alaska. The law was survival, and so the culture of the gold rush was brutal and opportunistic. Whips and clubs increased the performance of the dogs, and weak dogs were shot where they fell. In part, it is the pressure of history and culture that transforms Buck from gentleman's companion to alpha dominance of a wolf pack and freedom.

Before you sit down to a blank screen, take the time to immerse yourself in the history and culture of your setting. Start with primary sources—newspapers, archived letters, and memoirs—from an actual location or from a place that approximates your imaginary setting. Primary sources give you an inside-out look at a time and place. Depending on the locale, you'll read about crop failures and beauty pageants and gut-wrenching tragedies, and how a community responds. Learn what the people value through editorials, services rendered, and which stories are reported. Letters, for their intimacy and mundane details, make history especially personal. Glean details that will breathe life into your setting. You'll be tempted, but don't move on to geography and climate, or even develop your characters, until you have saturated yourself with the history and culture of the place, even if, in the case of fantasy or science fiction, you have to create these elements yourself.

When you're steeped in your setting's culture, strengthen the influence of place on your characters by discovering what is unique about the geography and climate, those elements that both challenge and bless. Reading John Krakauer's *Into Thin Air* convinced me that I lack the mettle to be a mountaineer. Krakauer's descriptions made my lungs ache for oxygen and my limbs leaden, and yet I was compelled to follow his ill-fated ascent of Mt. Everest. In the end, he questions the motivations of his fellow climbers along with his own. The mountain changes his perceptions and alters his reality.

Climate and geography will determine how people travel, what kinds of houses they live in, how they dress, what they eat, and how they recreate. Weather caresses and pounces. Include the full spectrum of its personality on your characters. Where sun and heat are relentless, pursuit of water and shade motivates characters to move by night or take circuitous routes to gather water. In the bayou, your character may travel by pirogue. An island dweller will be tied to ferry schedules and battle isolation. Winter travel in the mountains brings danger of blizzards and ice and avalanche. Even the beaches of Southern California impact their players. There's fog to frizz the hair, and sand seeps into every pocket. To portray a setting, I only set my stories in places I know well.

I grew up watching the sun set behind the California Channel Islands. As familiar as the humps of land were, I knew nothing about the flora and fauna that thrived there. Then I read *Island of the Blue Dolphins* by Scott O'Dell, the true story of a Native American girl, Karana, stranded on an island for years. Wild dogs menace her until she abandons cultural norms to protect herself. She paddles toward the eastern horizon, but the canoe leaks and she turns back. Her escort is a pod of dolphins, an omen of good luck that bolsters her spirits. Although strongly tied to her people, Karana uses the flora and fauna of the island to strengthen her independence.

To strengthen the impact of the natural world on your characters, get specific. Don't name every tree in the forest, but your readers carry memories tied to peach, eucalyptus, and aspen trees. They know where they grow and how they smell, if the leaves flutter or twirl, attract bees or ignite on a whim. Connect with that memory. Mood and plot points abound when place intercepts your characters. Think of a pansy growing in a cracked driveway or a rattlesnake coiled across a path. As soon as I've decided on a setting, I splurge on plant, animal, and insect identification books and set out walking. And I always take my camera.

Bringing your setting to life takes deliberate preparation. The payoff is a reader entrenched in your story, because fiction needs to be true. And to be true, fiction must reflect life. Think of all the ways *your* setting, where *you* live, impacts you. I live in the high desert of western Colorado, where summertime highs average near one hundred degrees. To compensate, I rise early to exercise, garden, and run errands. By the time temperatures are pushing into the nineties, I'm ensconced in an air-conditioned office, composing an imaginary universe where my characters are shaped by the setting I've created.

¶

Protagonist, Antagonist . . . *Setagonist*
Nancy Rue

We have been to Mitford and Middle-earth, places we could never have visited had they not been created at the skillful hands of Karon and Tolkien. We return to them not only because they have been vividly painted by the masters but because the places themselves breathe as deeply as Father Tim and Bilbo Baggins.

Yet as authors we often shortchange setting in our own fiction, and we do so to the detriment of our stories. Obviously a well-developed sense of place brings the reader into the environment of the tale and provides natural opportunities for symbolism. But it isn't just the descriptive passages. It is the fact that Middle-earth and all other memorable places in fiction are characters themselves. If we as novelists carve out settings that take their place in our cast, we too can open up worlds that will be lived in and pondered and returned to.

The *place* needs to be developed in the same way that any main character is.

Be as specific with your setting as you are with your protagonist. It isn't a matter of going on for paragraphs to define every nook and cranny, but it does involve specificity in the images that *are* used to establish the place. Michael Connelly's Harry Bosch never simply drives down a street. He's on Sepulveda Boulevard in Van Nuys or Topanga Canyon Boulevard in Chatsworth. He seldom just grabs a bite to eat. He has shrimp fried rice at Chinese Friends on Broadway or stops for coffee at Union Bagel in Union Station. Through those nuggets of detail we come to see the city of Los Angeles as we do Harry: tough, relentless, and infinite in its variety.

What is the specific setting of your story? What details will give it the personality you want it to have?

Decide whether the setting is your protagonist's ally or one of his or her antagonists. I lived in the Reno, Nevada, area for eighteen years and did not consider it my friend. The climate was harsh and the terrain barren and daunting. As soon as I returned to the South, I was at once embraced by the soft lushness that soothed my soul. It must be the same for our protagonists—there must be an attitude, a response, that affects their story.

As your story opens, is the setting an ally to your protagonist or one of his or her antagonists? Write a paragraph in which your protagonist expresses his or her feelings about this place (whether you intend to use this paragraph in your manuscript or not).

Just as an effective character must change as a result of the things that happen, so too must a setting-character. Think of *The Lion King's* Simba coming back to the savanna to find that Scar has allowed it to fall into ruin. The changes in the place spur changes in the character.

Does your setting evolve in any way in the course of the story? How does that affect the development of your protagonist?

To maintain the dynamic nature of character in your setting, the protagonist's feelings toward the setting may also change. If we allow the relationship between the setting-character and the protagonist to remain static, we may miss an opportunity for dramatic growth.

Do your protagonist's feelings toward the setting change in the course of the story? Is any meaning tucked in there?

One of the highest compliments a reader can pay me is to say,

"I was in Port Orchard, and I kept expecting to see Demi and Sully around the next corner." If any of us is to receive such high praise in our ministry of writing, we have to take our readers with us to a place that is itself a living, breathing element of life.

CHAPTER 7

DESCRIPTIONS

§

The Power of the Right Word
Deborah Raney

For a writer, words are like daubs of color on a painter's palette or notes on a musician's staff. The right words, strung together in just the right order, become powerful tools in the hands of a skilled artist. Using a precise word in just the right place can move a reader to tears or to action, and it can make the difference between an interesting article and a call to arms, between a nice story and a life-changing piece of fiction.

Words are amazing things. With a unique combination of a hundred or so characters arranged into words, I can build a captivating set as surely as a Broadway stage crew. A string of carefully chosen words can say so much more than what is actually stated on the paper.

Consider this sentence:

Charles James Stanford IV brushed a freshly manicured hand over the sleek mahogany desktop and depressed the blinking intercom button.

With twenty words, I've not only shown the obvious—well-manicured hand, nice desk, intercom—but I've also implied every-thing those images symbolize: a man wealthy enough and vain enough to afford and desire manicures, a ritzy office, a secretary on the other end of the intercom. Good ol' CJ's multiple names and numeral tell us that he is someone important—or at least he would like us to think he is.

By extrapolating from those few written words, we could deduce more: that the office is located in a large city, probably in an upscale section of town; that Mr. Stanford's office is large. (Doesn't the very word *mahogany* sound imposing? And there's that intercom system.) We could assume that this man is a tad extravagant since he's sprung for a fancy desk . . . and maybe a bit self-absorbed, since he takes time for manicures.

But there's even more. Our man isn't jabbing or punching the buttons on the intercom, but merely depressing them. He's a cool, calm, collected character. We can feel fairly certain that when he picks up that phone, he'll handle with aplomb whatever news is wait-ing on the other end.

Now consider an almost identical scene—man at desk—that sets an entirely different stage with the exact same number of words:

Shorty Stanford shoved aside a jumble of coffee-stained newspapers, raked his palm over the splintered desktop, and grabbed the phone.

First, the obvious: We've got a messy, splintered desk and a man who has to answer his own telephone. A man named Shorty isn't usually putting on airs. And we might wonder about his workload, since he obviously has time to drink coffee over the newspaper. Yet our Shorty is anything but calm. He's shoving and raking and grabbing. We can almost see the sweat beading on his forehead.

A few simple words can create not merely a vivid backdrop for each scene in your book but deep characterization for the people about whom you write—whether they are real or imaginary.

Think of your book as a play. Have you forced your readers to sit in the back row of the theater watching an early rehearsal? The stage is empty, the lights dim. Backcloths and scrims have been rolled up and stored away. The actors wear no costumes or makeup, and their hands and eyes are restrained by the scripts they hold. We may get the gist of the story, and even be enthralled with the dialogue if it's well delivered. But something is missing.

Oh, what a difference if instead, we invite our readers to front-row seats on opening night. Backdrops are beautifully painted and props are in place; our actors are in full costume and makeup, with their hands and eyes free to clarify and embellish the dialogue. The sound and lighting have been carefully orchestrated to set the mood and to spotlight each player's best assets. Now we are not just hearing the story; we are experiencing it.

You can improve your manuscript exponentially by simply reworking the first paragraph or two of each chapter to set the stage as vividly in the reader's mind as if he were watching a scene from a smash hit on Broadway.

Choose your words with care—especially those first words that will serve as a backdrop for your scene. If you make every syllable significant, the payoff will be great, because once you've set the stage properly, without changing another word each paragraph that follows will be more vibrant, more emotional, more real, simply because the reader carries those first impressions with him throughout the scene.

Words truly come to life when they are used to show the reader the senses—not just what was seen or heard, but an almost tangible sense of how it felt, smelled, and tasted.

A good book makes readers envision the actions and understand the emotions of the characters. But a great book allows them to actually feel those emotions—to almost live as the characters even after they've closed the cover of the book.

Here is how each of the senses—and the words that personify them—can enrich your novel.

SIGHT

As we saw in the two scenes with the office desk earlier, the reader needs to be able to envision the setting and characters very early in the scene. But go a step further. What is the lighting in the room like? Sunshine through a sparkling clean window, the purple tinge of fluorescent light, or a dimly lit, shadowed room? Each conveys a very different feeling. Just as on a movie set or in a painting, lighting can help create the mood you want the scene to convey. And it takes precise words to paint the exact image you intend. Purple shadows are different from lavender ones, and dim is a different kind of dark than inky.

SOUND

The most obvious and important use of sound in a novel is voices, dialogue. But using the sense of sound creatively can give each character's voice a distinct quality. And background noises are every bit as important in setting the mood of the scene and in helping the readers feel that they are not just reading your story, but experiencing it. As you rewrite, concentrate on putting yourself into the scene. What sounds would you be hearing in the setting you've created? Then use creative words to express each sound. Instead of saying, "The sound of the boat motor filled the air," say something like "The roar of the boat's engine echoed off the water." Or better yet, use onomatopoeia: "the putt-putt-putt of the boat's motor" or "the plip-plip-plip of raindrops."

SMELL

Any setting you could possibly create will have a distinctive smell. Think how many places you could identify—even wearing a blindfold and earplugs—merely by the smell. Use that fact in creating a believable setting for each scene. And don't just say, "The doctor's office had an antiseptic smell to it." Instead be specific about how the smell affected your character—"The pungent scent of Betadine and rubbing alcohol stung her nostrils." The object is to paint such a vivid picture that you cause the reader's nose to sting. A good thesaurus can be invaluable in helping you find just the right word to express what you wish the reader to feel.

TASTE

Taste can convey not only pleasure—as in the pleasant taste of food or peppermint or a cool drink of water, but it can also express emotion, as in "bitter bile rose in his throat." A kiss has the flavor of peppermint or cinnamon, of lipstick or garlic or rain. Tears licked from lips taste salty. Fear and anger put a metallic tang in one's mouth. Taste is probably one of the most neglected senses in literature, outside of using it to describe food. But it can be employed to great advantage to express emotion. Layer taste into your scenes as you rewrite.

FEEL

Giving your scenes literal texture helps your novel become a figuratively textured piece of work as well. Don't forget that like you, your characters have sensitive skin and fingers that allow them to feel more than mere emotion. The velvety softness of a baby's cheek speaks so much more than just texture. The coarse roughness of a man's cheek does the same. Use those sensations to add depth and "color" to your scenes. Use texture as a metaphor for the emotion you wish to portray: "She flinched at the sensation of his rough hands and jagged fingernails against the delicate skin of her bare arms."

ESSENTIALS OF FICTION: RESIST THE URGE TO EXPLAIN

Resist the urge to explain (RUE).

"Jacob was strong-minded and argumentative; Marguerite was painfully shy." That's laziness. Don't tell it, show it. One of the greatest writing mistakes, especially of beginning fiction writers, is overexplanation. Strive for subtlety. Don't explain everything to readers. Let them figure it out—they want to. Avoid prolonged internal monologue, and don't interrupt dialogue with explanation and commentary. Character and mood are shown in action and conflict and dialogue. Not "'Please be quiet,' he said angrily," but "Shut your mouth or I'll shut it for you." (Now you don't need the adverb *angrily*.) —*Randy Alcorn*

THE "SIXTH SENSE"

The paranormal has become a huge element in literature today, from mystery to romance. The phenomenon may have its disturbing side, but as Christians writing fiction, we have a wonderful opportunity to portray that element of the supernatural from a biblical perspective. God performs miracles; he sends angels to protect and assist us; he continues to speak to his people in that still, small voice; and he has given each of us a conscience, empowered by the Holy Spirit, to show us right from wrong and to help us discern danger and evil. Don't forget to use that most holy "sense" in your stories, for such portrayals are what may draw an unsaved reader into a knowledge of God and turn our simple words into a ministry and a calling.

One caution in using the senses: It is possible to be too obvious—to beat the reader over the head with the fact that we tried to sneak all the senses into each scene. Like seasoning in a stew, too much of one spice might overpower another more important one. So think carefully about which sense, which word, will best bring each particular scene to life and then carefully pinch in just the right amounts of one or two of the other senses.

A good thesaurus is a wonderful tool in helping you come up with creative ways to express the senses. I love *Roget's 21st Century Thesaurus* with its Concept Index that allows you to look up auditory words, olfactory words, etc., and discover wonderfully fresh and expressive phrases to describe and define the senses.

So, here's to putting together a string of perfect words that will become an article, a book, a novel—or even a play—that will bring down the house!

¶

The Building Blocks of a Scene
Jill Elizabeth Nelson

A story involves more than a strong plot, and a reading experience is made of many small components. Even once you have established strong goals, motivations, and conflicts that thrust the plot forward, the minutiae of sentence and phrase construction deserves attention. Phrases and sentences are built from motivation/reaction units (MRUs), which should clearly convey the writer's meaning by maintaining the logical sequence of events.

Merriam Webster's Collegiate Dictionary defines *motive* as "something (as a need or desire) that causes a person to act" and *reaction* as "a response, as to a stimulus." An MRU could also be called a stimulus/response unit. Placing the reaction before the motivation for it gives a muddled and awkward feel to a story; yet this is a common error of the novice writer and creates needless stumbling blocks for the reader. For a story to flow coherently, we must apply the principle of stimulus and response to every sentence and paragraph throughout the manuscript. With time and practice, the technique becomes second nature.

What's wrong with the following sentence?

She laughed at the scowl on her friend's face.

Quite simply, the reaction—laughter—is stated before the motivation for it.

A lazy fix might be:

Her friend's scowl made her laugh.

But that narrative is flat and telling rather than active and showing. Here's a better suggestion:

Her friend shot her a scowl, and she laughed.

Not only are the motivation and reaction in proper order now, but the sentence is also stronger with the insertion of an active verb.

Here's another example of an MRU problem:

Mary kissed her daughter's cheek as she turned to walk away. "Have a good day, dear."

The phrase beginning with *as* implies that Mary is kissing and turning away at the same time. Quite the physical contortion! Also,

ESSENTIALS OF FICTION: SPECIFY

Be specific, not general; concrete, not vague.

Don't say, "He held a gun," but "He slowly raised a .38 Smith and Wesson revolver, admiring his reflection in the stainless steel." The more specific, the more real. Don't say, "A man walked into the room and ordered a drink." Say, "The one-legged, redheaded dwarf marched up to the bar and ordered a Bloody Mary." Detail requires more time and thought and research. But a believable story is the payoff. —*Randy Alcorn* the reader may become confused and think that "she turned" refers to the daughter. The dialogue is out of order, as well.

Here's a possible fix:

> Mary bent and kissed her daughter's cheek. "Have a good day, dear." Then she hurried out to her car.

Now events are in proper chronological order with no ungainly physical contortions. In addition, the unnecessary mention of *turned* is eliminated in favor of a more specific and revealing action—hurrying out to the car. If Mary kissed her daughter and then walked away, of course she turned. It's doubtful she walked backward! Therefore, it's not necessary to insult the reader's intelligence by stating the obvious.

Another example:

> He stuffed the note into his pocket when he saw the teacher coming.

Obviously, this sentence just told the reader what the character did (the reaction) before giving him the motivation to do it. Not always, but often enough, words like *when*, *after*, and other time prepositions can be indicators of MRU problems. We need to take a second look at these sentences in our manuscripts to make sure we have our motivations and reactions in order.

Here's a possible fix:

> The teacher stalked toward him. His eyes widened, and he stuffed the note into his pocket.

The new sentences provide greater detail and create an active and emotionally charged situation—far more powerful writing than the initial version.

Like matter is made up of molecules, stories consist of MRUs. Mastery of the molecular structure of storytelling will build strength and health into the whole.

DEVELOPING YOUR CRAFT

PART TWO >

CHAPTER 8

PREPARATION

¶

How to Read Novels like a Writer
Linda Hall

A novelist friend recently commented that because she was currently writing a novel, she didn't have time to read any. She told me she was looking forward to the day when she finished her own book so she could get back to reading her favorite novels. When I questioned this, suggesting that surely she could find ten minutes a day, she added that she doesn't read novels while she's writing. She fears getting mixed up between her own work and the book she is reading.

I've since learned that my friend is not unique in this fear. I've even heard the damaging advice that novelists shouldn't immerse themselves too much in the work of others while they are writing, that to do so may hinder their own "writer's voice."

Nothing could be further from the truth. Not only will reading novels not detract from your own writing, it is an important step in developing your voice. No one is just like you, and no one writes just like you. Your writing voice is like your personality. Just as a personality cannot develop in isolation but is cultivated by socializing with others, so your writing voice only really develops as you read.

Read well and read widely. Read the classics. Read historical novels. Read the best sellers. Read the award winners. Read debut authors. Read international authors. And don't limit yourself to only Christian authors. Strive to develop your worldview. Novels can help you do this. The more scope and breadth your reading has, the more scope and breadth your writing will have.

HOW WILL READING NOVELS HELP YOU?

It is by reading novels that you learn to write them. Limiting yourself to reading books on how to write is as silly as trying to become a painter by reading books about how to mix paints and do brush strokes without ever studying the works of great artists.

Reading Increases Your Fount of Ideas

Ideas beget ideas. The more you read and write, the more ideas you will end up with. Years ago when I first decided I wanted to write a novel, I spent many months trying to come up with an idea. It was painful. I just didn't know where to start. I had no clue. Now, after penning fifteen novels, I have more ideas for future stories than I will ever hope to get down on paper. You will never use up all your ideas.

And just as your voice is unique, so the way you use your ideas is unique. A few years ago a group of Christian writers got together and decided to test this theory. We would all write short stories following a few rules. We had to begin with the same first line, the story had to include a few of the same things, and we needed to conclude with an identical sentence. As predicted, no two stories were remotely the same.

Reading Improves Your Ability to Write Descriptively

You may read a novel in which a tall, skinny, scraggly guy with a huge mane of yellow hair is described simply as a "sunflower." Now, to use that exact analogy would, of course, be plagiarizing or stealing. But reading that analogy can give you ideas. Maybe you could describe someone as a butterfly or a parrot, or maybe that little old lady with the church hat can be described as looking like a Victorian chair with a tatted antimacassar. This isn't stealing. This is merely looking at the way one author did it and trying it for yourself in a slightly different way.

Reading Deepens Your Well of Words

You need to immerse yourself in words. Be a student of words. When you come across a word you don't know, write it down, look it up or google it, and then try to use that word in a sentence. Now think, *How can I incorporate that word or thought into my own story?*

Reading Shows You How Novels Work

Reading fiction gives you a sense of movement and structure and pace and plot that no book on writing can offer. Reading novels can also give you a sense of sentence and paragraph flow. Why did that novelist use short sentences in that passage and longer, more languid ones in another? Did she use shorter sentences in paragraphs of heightened action? Maybe that's a technique you can try.

When you read wisely, when you read to learn, you read only those novels that are better than your own. This cutoff point is different for all writers but very easy to measure. If you are reading a novel and say to yourself, *I could write better than this,* well, you probably can, so put that book down and don't finish it. If, on the other hand, you are reading along and your reaction is *This is such beautiful writing. I wish I could write like this,* that's the novel you need to keep reading. That's the novel that will help you grow. That's the novel that will help develop your voice and teach you much that you need to know about writing novels. That's reading wisely.

READ NOVELS LIKE TEXTBOOKS

When you read for pleasure, you will absorb words and sentence structure and paragraphs. If, however, you want to be a bit more intentional, treat that novel like a textbook.

Gather together a handful of highlighter pens in various colors. When you come across words that describe how something looks, sounds, smells, feels, or tastes, highlight them in blue. Use pink for interesting analogies. When the writer describes a person looking like a sunflower, highlight that. When a ghost town is described as a dry breath or a sighing old man, highlight that.

Use a green pen for examples of showing and not telling. When the author could have written "She was sad when her dog died" but instead wrote "After her dog died, she lay down on the couch and covered herself with his pet blanket," that's an example of showing. That's an example of visual writing, writing that shows. Highlight that.

Use a yellow highlighter for ways the writer moves characters from scene to scene. Some writers struggle with this. Check well-written novels to see how the pros do it.

When you get to the end of a chapter and simply must move on to the next one, ask yourself why. What was the chapter hook that kept you from putting down the book? Read it over. Note it with an asterisk. Try to come up with something similar for your own story.

A purple highlighter can be used for dialogue that sounds natural and drives the plot along. If your story contains a lot of internal monologue and you are unsure of how to keep the story moving, find a captivating novel that includes a lot of internal monologue and see how the author does it.

How about humor? If your intent is to write a lighthearted novel, read them. If you write mysteries and thrillers, you might want to read a novel in this genre and highlight and make a list of the various clues that lead to the solving of the crime and the clues that are the red herrings. Study how they are ordered throughout the book.

Look at the novel as a whole. What made you want to keep reading it? Write that down on the front flap of the book. Then keep these "textbook" novels close to your writing desk and refer to them often.

If you are reading a library book, however, please don't mark it up! Instead, keep a notebook handy. Write out particularly descriptive paragraphs, make notes, pretend you are in school and must analyze this novel and critique everything about it. If you do this, I guarantee your writing will improve.

To succeed as a novelist, reading novels must be a priority. Don't be afraid. You won't lose your voice; you will only enhance it. And soon, students will be using *your* novels as their textbooks.

¶

The Work before the Work
Jane Kirkpatrick

It took some time in my own writing life to realize that the work before the work is what truly sets the tone in a novel. The more effort I put into clarifying the story before I sit down to write it, the more I know what I want to say and how I hope my readers might be changed by spending time with my characters and ideas, the better the actual writing process proceeds.

To begin, I've learned from some master writers in a book called *Structuring Your Novel: From Basic Idea to Finished Manuscript* by Robert C. Meredith and John D. Fitzgerald (Collins). When I first read that book, I'd already written four novels and one nonfiction title. My editor at the time, Rod Morris, recommended these writers, and I'm grateful. What those master storytellers suggested writers do before they begin writing changed each of my novels and nonfiction works and hopefully made them clearer and more accessible to readers.

These writers advised that aspiring novelists answer three questions: What is my intention in writing this story? What is my attitude about this story? What is my purpose in writing this book?

WHAT IS MY INTENTION IN WRITING THIS STORY?
A parallel question I ask myself is, "What is this story about?" It's really the elevator question that people talk about, where one has just a few floors to answer the question, "What's your book about?"

Too long an explanation and the person gets off the elevator before you've finished, or worse, their eyes glaze right over as you're speaking. You're looking for one simple sentence.

It may take several pages of writing to get down to that one sentence, but the effort can be well worth it. For a recent project, my sentence reads this way: "To tell the story of Jessie Gaebele's journey to become an independent photographer and the struggles with her mentor to find her own place."

It can also be a great exercise to imagine what other authors might have written about their works. How would they answer the question, "What is your book about?" See if they have answered that question by the time you've finished reading their work.

WHAT IS MY ATTITUDE ABOUT THIS STORY?

A corollary to help answer this question is to explore what I feel deeply about. Why have I decided to give up hours of sleep or time with family to write this story? Nothing could be worse for me than to have people read an entire book of mine and say to themselves as they finish, "Well, I didn't need to read that. There's no passion there. I've learned nothing new. I don't feel in the least connected to that story."

Passion drives our words. It's been said of writers that if we don't have to write, we ought not to. We should feel deeply about what we're working on and, in so doing, convey that passion to our readers. Writer Anne Lamott notes that "a moral position is not a message. A moral position is a passionate caring inside you." As writers, we want to convey that passionate caring inside of us.

A primary purpose of fiction, for example, is to move people. As writers, we need to know what and who is moving us. For that same work in progress mentioned earlier, here is my answer to the second question: "I feel deeply about the importance of integrity, wholeness, and the blend of soul and role in order to fulfill God's promise in our lives."

WHAT IS MY PURPOSE IN WRITING THIS BOOK?

This question often takes me the longest and the most pages to get to a single-sentence answer. How do I hope a reader will be changed by reading this story? Often I use words like "I want to prove that . . . ," which can bring clarity and passion to the central theme of the work. For my recent project, I wrote: "I want to prove that one cannot achieve wholeness (soul and role combined) or have the human spirit soar at the expense of another's dream."

After I've worked on those three questions and whittled them down to a single sentence each, I print out the three statements and post them near my computer. Then I begin to write. When I start to get lost halfway through my manuscript (this happens to most writers, even when they're certain of the path they're on), when I wonder why I ever thought I could write a book at all, I look back at the work I did before the work began to take shape, read those three sentences, and remind myself why it was I chose to tell this story.

What this process doesn't mean is that those three answers will remain the same throughout the writing. Before I begin my revision process, I ask myself the same three questions again. I'm often surprised by what the story had to tell me in the process of my writing it. For a recent project a major change came in what I felt deeply about. I discovered that I wanted to explore why it was that often talented, gifted people making their way to a successful career do foolish things that put them at risk of losing it all. The answer to my third question

AN INTERVIEW WITH FRANCINE RIVERS: PREPARATION

How do you start a novel? Do you start with a plotline or a theme?
Do you outline, or do you write more as a process of discovery?
I start with a question. I usually have something going on in my own life, something that is eating at me, nudging me. I use writing to try to figure out the answers. My goal is always to discover God's answer. What's his perspective?

For *A Voice in the Wind*, for instance, the question was "How do I share my faith with unsaved family and friends who don't want to hear the name of Jesus and who don't want to read a Bible?" Hadassah was the character who was dealing with that, and other characters come in showing their ways of thinking. For the book I'm currently writing, the theme is "Love one another." But when we say that, it sounds like a bumper sticker. So I'm exploring "How do you show that? How do you live that out?"

Sometimes the place I think I'm going is totally different from where I end up, from where God wants to take me. For instance, with *The Atonement Child*, I thought the answer was going to be about forgiveness. But it ended up being about sanctification, being set apart as God's holy people.

What is your writing environment like? Do you have to be in a quiet place?
I've had all kinds of environments. I've worked with a typewriter at the kitchen table, on a desk in the family room with the TV blaring behind me and three little kids running around, and in my husband's office with a laptop. It's just the past couple of years that I've had an office at home. I share it with my husband—we each have a workstation in there.

I need background noise when I'm writing, preferably music. I love all kinds of music. It sets the scene for me. I listened to a lot of Appalachian music while writing *The Last Sin Eater*. For a section of my work in progress that was set during World War II, I had music from that era playing—swing dancing, big band music. I also like movie sound tracks. Right now I'm listening to the music from the movie *Troy*.

changed too: I hoped to prove that "in art, one must always need to know the source of one's light."

One of the delights of writing fifteen novels over the past thirteen years has been the discovery that while I thought I knew what the story was about—its intention—when I finished the first draft, I was humbled by what the story had to tell me about myself. It's why, for me, much of writing is like praying, being and staying present in the moment of the story. C. S. Lewis once noted, "Where, except in the present, can the Eternal be met?" Staying present for the storytelling is much more important to me now than wondering how it reads or whether my agent might like it or whether it will ever sell. Doing that work before the work helps me stay present for the story.

THE IMPORTANCE OF PRAYER

One other practice I've begun through my writing life includes prayer. I often read poems, reread favorite prayers, find solace in the Psalms, and quiet my heart before I begin writing so that I can truly enter and live my story. I want desperately to put aside the "me" of the writing and allow God to speak through me those words he wishes others to receive. To quote the great poet Mary Oliver in her poem "Praying": "this isn't / a contest but the doorway / into thanks, and a silence in which / another voice may speak."

As writers, we're blessed with opportunities to let that other voice speak. Doing basic work before the work can help take us there and keep us listening and writing.

¶

Research: Immersing Yourself in History
Cara Putman

I may have been born in the seventies, but I've always held a love for and fascination with the life and times of the forties, particularly the World War II years. In many ways, it was completely natural to find my first novel set during that time. And I've enjoyed each adventure to uncover additional, little-known stories from that time period.

But how does someone who was born more than thirty years after the events she writes about weave them into a story in a believable way? My history minor alone isn't enough to give me a leg up. Instead, I believe there are several things a writer who wants to write about a historical time period needs: passion, commitment, and ability.

- You must have an absolute passion for the time period. If you don't, all the attention to detail that is required will drive you batty and you'll stop short of getting it right.

- You must have a commitment to accuracy. I'll drive hours out of my way to a tiny museum for the sole purpose of getting dates and time frames as right as possible for one of my books. I've done the research to understand the general setting and information, but that's not enough. I want the details to be as accurate as I can make them. For one of my projects that meant I used the actual language of the historical people I wrote about in the story when possible. And that meant sitting at the microfiche machines and spinning through dozens of newspapers to find a few golden articles.

- You must learn how to sprinkle in enough detail to convince readers they've traveled back to a time and place without boring them to tears. In the opening paragraphs of a novel taking place in 1940, I set the stage by referring to the Glen Miller record that skipped, the fabric and style of the heroine's dress, the kind of car the hero rode in. It's enough that people who lived it tell me it swept them back in time and that those who didn't live it can imagine it.

So if you know you have the passion, commitment, and ability to include only the key details, how do you find the right details? Here are a few tricks of the trade I've learned.

STUDY THE CULTURE

Find sources that can help establish the culture and media of the time. I have always loved the black-and-white movies from the thirties and early forties. By watching those movies I gain a sense for the styles of the era, how people talked, what they wore, and the stereotypes of the time.

Now you have to be careful. Much as I love Audrey Hepburn, I can't use her in a book from the early forties . . . she wasn't acting yet. So writers have to pay attention to copyrights on movies and who was popular when.

If your chosen time period is earlier, you'll need to rely on the books that were widely read, the radio (if it was invented), and newspapers to get a sense of the time. Magazines and store catalogs can also be helpful. Two of my favorite resources are excerpts from the Sears catalogs of the 1940s. The catalog was widely available, and it provides a good estimate of what the average American wore, plus it lets you know the prices of things.

INVEST IN RESOURCES

Search for resources that illustrate the styles and vehicles of the time. As I wrote one of my books, I realized I needed help describing the different styles in hats and clothing. I went online and found several great books, including one that gave me catalog illustrations and descriptions for the styles of my time period. It also gave me the details to back up things I knew, such as the fact that during the war women couldn't purchase nylon stockings, so they drew lines up the backs of their legs to mimic the seams in hose. But they also had makeup specifically designed to look like hose. Those are the details that make a book and a time period come alive.

Another resource I have lists the top cars of the 1940s. Again it contains details that I wouldn't otherwise know. Now I want to take a spin in a few of those vehicles.

INTERVIEW PEOPLE

Talk to people who lived during that time if you can. To learn more about the early 1940s, I interviewed my grandparents and others who lived then. One night I had a delightful conversation with a veteran who had traveled through the North Platte Canteen five times as a soldier. Each visit was different, and he gladly shared his impressions and memories with me. His stories reinforced those I had found through other resources.

When relying on people's memories, always double-check against factual sources like newspapers and magazines. As time passes, it is easy to soften the details, so you'll need to check them for accuracy. But the impressions and feelings can add richness to your characters.

FIND OTHER SOURCES

If you can't interview people, look for sources that did. I found several invaluable resources in published books, on public television broadcasts, and by spending a day with the Fort Robinson Museum curator, who had interviewed dozens of veterans when they returned to the fort. While I couldn't interview these people, others had.

Memoirs and journals are wonderful resources. Talk to the research librarian in the town your book is set in. If the town library doesn't have specific resources, the librarian will often know people to direct you to or be able to help you find the right people. Also, major universities often serve as the repository for government documents.

ESSENTIALS OF FICTION: DON'T SKIMP ON RESEARCH

Never compromise on research.

It's the reservoir from which you draw your story, so make sure the reservoir is full! And be sure you get the facts right—don't put a safety on a revolver or the wrong size engine in a 1972 Chevy Impala. Don't believe the myth "It's fiction, so you can just make up the details." Every factual error loses readers— why should they trust you? Always run it by experts. In writing my three murder mysteries, I consulted a homicide detective and other cops. When writing a novel set in China, I bounced it off of people who have lived in China, who know the language and the culture. Your book needs to ring true to have the weight of credibility. —Randy Alcorn

VISIT THE LOCATION

Even though I lived in North Platte, the setting for one of my books, for four years and still visit at least twice a year, there were details I had forgotten or simply didn't know. Also, I needed to dive into what the town looked like forty-five years before we moved there and sixty years before now. Actually walking the streets brought the town to life each time I sat down at my keyboard. I hate to write about a place I haven't visited and will schedule research trips so I can get a feel for the town. Each place has a unique feel that can only be captured by seeing it.

I love Google Maps because it allows you to see a street without visiting. The only caution is you'll miss many sensory details.

If you are writing or hope to write a historical novel, take the time to get the details right. With a little effort, your book will shine with the accuracy that makes readers feel like they've stepped back in time to join your characters. When you've accomplished that, your readers will thank you.

¶

Interviewing the Others
Anne de Graaf

What if we thought of the people group that is our greatest enemy—national, racial, family, or personal? What if we found some people from that group with the idea of interviewing them, of listening? Just listening. What would happen?

What if we went to places outside our comfort zones? What if we traveled to the far-off places, opened our hearts to the stories others could bless us with, brought those stories home, and wrote them in accessible ways for others?

These two things—seeking out an enemy and venturing beyond the borders of our comfort zones—make for conflict-ridden, suspenseful, high-energy writing with integrity. Expand your borders and your writing will excel as characters jump off the page and readers can sense between the lines that you care enough about your story to look for the details that make it come alive.

But we can't all afford to travel, you might say. Agreed. So seek out the people groups you're writing about another way.

- Post a card in the local market with the specifics of whom you hope to interview (e.g., "Looking for a Motswana from Botswana—preferably with knowledge of the diamond mines—to interview for a novel").
- Go to a local refugee center and ask to speak to people from that country; then ask them if they'd be willing to answer questions about home.
- Ring the doorbell in a wealthy neighborhood, explain that you're writing a novel, and find out if you could ask them a few questions because your character has a house like theirs.
- Volunteer in a prison.
- Teach English as a second language.

And what should you do when the moment comes and you're sitting beside your subject? Pray and never fear. Pray for Jesus' heart. Pray to see this person as Jesus does. Pray to want to love him or her. And pray that this interview might bless this person. Pray for healing; pray for words of wisdom and discernment, and listen to your heart for unexpected suggestions of what to ask next.

MORE INTERVIEWING TIPS

- Make a list of questions beforehand and write them into your notebook.
- If an interpreter is necessary, find one you can trust.
- Do your homework: Read everything you can on the subject so you can ask knowledgeable questions.
- Set the interview date and check back at least twice (once by phone) to make sure of the time and place.
- Double-check the spelling of all names and learn beforehand the proper pronunciation of the name of the person being interviewed.
- Learn at least five words in the interviewee's language: *hello*, *please*, *beautiful*, *delicious*, and *thank you*.
- Develop trust and make your subject feel at ease. Determine what he or she loves by looking around you—the canary, the pictures of grandchildren—and ask how many grandchildren there are, how old they are, their names.
- Don't try to get down every word; just write key words that will summon the sentence back for you, or use shorthand.
- Tape recorders can make elderly people and people with war traumas nervous, so you may not want to use them during your interviews. Afterward, though, document your impressions and ideas with a tape recorder. Of course, if the subject doesn't mind, recording is a good insurance policy, but transcribing an interview can make the process longer.

- Right after an interview, go back and fill in the blanks of the conversation in your notebook while it's still fresh.
- Don't try to filter during the interview or determine what is useful. Write down as much as possible. Later what you thought of as insignificant may prove crucial.

CHAPTER 9

THE DISCIPLINE OF WRITING

¶

Staying Organized in the Writing Process
Elizabeth White

It took me over a month to start writing this article. Every morning for the past six weeks I have looked at the neatly titled document on my computer desktop and thought, *Boy, I should totally do that.* Then I would think, *That looks like hard work. Whose idea was this anyway? Maybe I should be working on my revisions. Hey! Look at that spiderweb over there—RAID!*

Distraction, you think?

I comfort myself with the thought that I'm not the only one. Since bright, inquiring minds naturally flit in a million directions, struggles with focus are endemic to the creative personality. For writers, if the tendency isn't brought under control, one can become the Tasmanian devil of the literary world—a whole lot of motion and noise, with little accomplished. Unfortunately, I know this from frustrating experience.

Little by little, however, I have discovered some simple strategies to conquer my TDS (Tasmanian devil syndrome), and I would like to share them with you. Right after I wipe the dust off the TV and balance my checkbook and . . .

Ahem. My personal type of TDS is a very quiet, subversive one. The kind where you are sitting in a room full of people and zone out into your own interior world—and forget you're at your future daughter-in-law's bridal shower. The kind where you get on the Internet to look something up and you keep clicking on links until three hours have gone by and you can't remember the original question. The kind where you suddenly remember your Eighteenth Century Novels final was yesterday. Sneaky.

Since I choose not to pursue medication, I've learned the fine arts of calendaring, filing, and sticky notes. And today I declare myself not cured, but under relative control and capable of completing large, complicated projects like writing a novel.

USE A CALENDAR

I'll have to confess that I did not come to this in a blinding flash of revelation or even learn it in a seminar. It started with my husband literally begging me to try a Day-Timer system: "The odds of you actually remembering something are astronomically higher if you write it down." Grumble, grumble.

So I bought one of those black leather notebooks with monthly and daily calendars. Surprise, surprise, I started remembering most, if not all, of my appointments and deadlines (once I got in a habit of looking at the thing every day). Now it's almost an obsession, keeping to-do lists and checking them off. And now that we're in the twenty-first century, I keep all that on my iCalendar on my Mac—but I still carry that black notebook around everywhere I go. Maybe one day I'll get a BlackBerry or something.

CREATE A FILING SYSTEM

The second thing that revolutionized my writing life was a computer filing system. For every project I start, I set up an electronic folder—titled by the name of the book—with nine subfolders: *business, chapters, characters, cover, drafts, fan mail, outlines, research*, and *reviews*. (Don't forget to save everything and back it up on a flash drive. You'll be glad you did.)

1. The *business* folder contains correspondence with editors and my agent. I try to save all proposals, rejections, acceptances, and anything in between—as well as my e-mail responses. Then I have a record of everything related to that project, in case questions come up later.

2. The *chapters* folder is simply where I save individual chapters as I set up a master document in Word. I also have a "Leftovers" document there, in which I can save pieces of the manuscript that I cut but don't want to lose (in case I change my mind, which frequently happens).

3. The *characters* folder is one of my favorite files. Each of my main characters undergoes a development process including a "Hero's Journey" (see Christopher Vogler's excellent *The Writer's Journey*); a biographical "diary entry," which is a first-person account of some significant scene or scenes of backstory that feeds and informs the present story; and a goal, motivation, and conflict outline (see Deb Dixon's *Goal, Motivation and*

Conflict). I also track secondary characters in a separate document as they appear in the story, making note of any physical or emotional traits. That way I don't have to search through an entire three-hundred-page document to find out if the next-door neighbor's dog was a Labrador or a golden retriever. Also, if possible, I find photos that resemble the characters and stick the JPEGs in this file. Most publishers like to see the author's physical vision of the characters because it helps the artists who develop the cover. Plus, it's a nice creative inspiration for me, the writer.

4. The *cover* folder, obviously, contains JPEGs of the cover artwork, as well as taglines, back cover blurb drafts, and anything else related to the cover.

5. Because every manuscript undergoes several revisions, the *drafts* folder keeps all the versions organized. I number each one, leaving the current, working draft outside in the main folder. Many times I've gone digging through old drafts for one reason or another. I never throw these out until the book is in print.

6. The *fan mail* folder is set up from the beginning, just for fun. Come on, we writers are exhibitionists at heart. We all want an audience!

7. The *outlines* folder is perhaps the most critical of all. When I'm planning a book, I take the protagonist's and villain's hero's journeys and compare them to make sure there are enough places where they intersect. If not, I adjust and make notes in a document stored in the outlines folder. Then I take GMC charts and do the same thing. Last, I develop a "snowflake" design document (see Randy Ingermanson's excellent article on

his Web site www.advancedfictionwriting.com) for the story. Ideally all of those should match. They help me come at the story in several different ways to write a coherent and complete synopsis. Then, as I write the first draft of the manuscript, I fill in a spreadsheet with each chapter vertically subdivided into scenes and analyzed horizontally for POV character, date and time, location, event, and approximate word count.

8. Anytime I look up something related to the book, I put it in a Word document and stick it in the *research* folder. Any correspondence with experts or sources is saved as well. Photos are helpful here. One other thing to note: I keep names and addresses of people who have helped me with research and offer them a free copy of the book. I always *ask* if they would mind if I acknowledge them as an information source, however. Not everyone wants his or her name in the front of a book.

9. Reviews obviously come later, but it's important to have them all in one place as they come in—they're invaluable for blogs, interviews, Web sites, and other marketing tools. If it's a print review, I type it into a Word document or scan it as a JPEG. I try to copy and paste online reviews into a document, as well as noting the URL for link purposes.

JOT DOWN NOTES

The third tool that keeps me from a padded cell is the sticky note feature on my computer desktop. (You can find free sticky note programs to download from the Internet if you don't already have one installed.) Let's say I'm writing along and I need to know what year the stethoscope was invented (true story). Instead of getting on the Internet (at the risk of losing three hours to the history of gallbladder surgery), I fill a sticky note with all the things I need to look up while I'm watching TV later that night.

Stickies are also useful for making notes during revisions. That way I don't forget, for example, to change the heroine's hoodie from University of South Alabama to Ole Miss.

These three strategies have made my personal TDS manageable. I still inevitably feel the pull of sorting socks, making my grandmother's oatmeal cookie recipe, or calling my little sister. But at least when I wander off, I've got a plan to bring myself back where I should be. And there's something reassuring about consistency, even for us Tasmanian devils.

¶

Doing a Fast First Draft
Linda Ford

How often do you spend an hour in front of your computer trying to get into the story? How often do you go back and forth on the same two pages until your writing time is done? Do you end up with nothing to show for the hours you spend at the computer? Is it frustrating? Would you like to get up from the desk with ten new pages written? Maybe even twenty?

Well, I have news for you. It's possible to make your time more productive. It's called doing a rapid write—getting the story down in the shortest time possible. I am talking about getting a sloppy first draft down.

A fast first draft is exactly that—writing a draft as fast as you can, perhaps in as little as seven days. The idea is to get the story down because you can't fix a blank page. But in practical terms, it means writing fast and furious without regard for editing. It's a very effective way of shutting off the internal editor and allowing creativity to flow.

Okay, stop protesting that you can't write that way. You *can* if you decide to, and I suggest you give it a try. I resisted the idea for a long time, but the promise of productivity enticed me. The first time I tried this method I was pleasantly surprised. I finished a first draft in ten days, and when I went back to revise, it was surprisingly strong. Of course, you might have to change your attitude about a few things like perfection. But you might also find that making a few changes in how you tackle the blank page enables you to be much more productive.

BENEFITS OF WRITING A FAST FIRST DRAFT

Writing fast and intense means I don't waste so much time going back over old ground trying to reconnect with the story. But the biggest reason for me is that it forces me to be intensely *in* the story. I live the story. The longer I write, the more convinced I am that my brain knows more than I do. Maybe yours does too. This is one way of giving your brain the chance to tell what it knows without you getting in the road. I suppose this is just another way of saying we have right brain–left brain tendencies and writing fast is a way of getting the internal/infernal editor off our backs and letting the right brain work.

Something almost magical happens when I fall into the story— I become part of it. Threads remain fixed in my mind and don't get dropped. I remember details about the characters that I can weave in. If nothing more, I have a finished draft. And revising or rewriting is easier than writing.

STARTING A FAST DRAFT

First, prepare.

Preparing involves two different areas of my life. I have to get my bills paid, finish the laundry, tidy the house, and prepare some food or at least have some in the house. I need to have pressing things like government forms off my to-do list. It also helps to warn the family what I am doing and what they can and cannot expect from me for the next few days. For instance, I will deal with *really* important matters, but I don't want to mediate arguments about whose turn it is to wash dishes.

That said, I confess that I don't put life on hold to do my rapid writes. I set a goal that pushes me, but I still stop to make dinner in the evening. I still take care of my paraplegic client, of course. In other words, I don't wait for life to be perfect, or I'd never do it. You may have the luxury of putting your life on hold and writing eight, ten, twelve hours a day. If so, take advantage of it. Otherwise, make it work as best you can. But don't let the excuse of having a busy life keep you from this experience. Even an hour can produce results.

Then there is the prewriting preparation. How much of this a writer needs to do depends on his or her writing process. Some need only an idea and two characters to start. Some need plot cards neatly arranged on a whiteboard. Some have fifty or sixty scene cards. I need a solid story outline—not a lot of details but a clear idea of each major turning point. I need solid goals and motivation for my characters and a clearly definable conflict. I generally have a working synopsis done before I start the fast draft. I usually don't start a fast write until I have the first three chapters figured out. (I hate those initial chapters when everything has to be set up.) However, you might find this isn't necessary for you.

Consider joining a Book-in-a-Week (BIW) group if that appeals. You may be able to find a group online or through your local writing group chapter. They can be a lot of fun and provide a challenge and accountability. But don't let a group be the only reason and only time you do this. Don't let it become another form of procrastination.

TIPS FOR FAST WRITING

How do you write fast? How do you get around the mental blocks? I have a few suggestions.

- Set a timer. Fifteen or twenty minutes is good. Don't lift your fingers from the keyboard until the timer goes off. Write. Even if it's garbage. With a computer, deleting is simple. Writing is hard. So write and forget trying to get it right.
- If seeing mistakes on the screen bothers you, turn off or cover the monitor. Remember, this is not a polished draft. It's the story you are interested in, and writing this way makes the story alive in your head. Remember the motto of rapid writing: You can fix a page. Just get the first draft out.
- Disconnect your modem or unplug your computer from the network until you are done writing. Don't let the Internet and e-mail distract you.
- Don't look back. Don't go back. Keep a pad of paper at your elbow, and when you think of something that you want to change in previous chapters, make a note and keep going. Remember—only forward motion.

- If you can't find a word or have forgotten a name, use *XXX* or some such thing to mark the spot and move on. (I use *X* because I like the thought that *X* marks the spot.) You can look up the information later. This isn't the time to find the best noun and verb. This is storytelling time. If you don't know what happens in a scene, give yourself a few minutes to think it through, and if you can't figure it out, leave yourself a note to indicate what needs to happen at that point and move on.

- If necessary, do some scene work each day prior to writing so you know the elements of the scene and what you want to do with it. You might consider identifying goal, motivation, conflict, and disaster or change. You might want to jot down sensory details—sights, sounds, tastes, etc.

- For some, setting the mood with music, candles, and scents works. Experiment and discover what helps you find the zone of your story. One thing that works for me is listening to music with headphones. The headphones signal to me as much as to others that I am not to be interrupted.

- Write. Write. Write. Push yourself. You might be pleasantly surprised to discover how many pages you can write in a day when you really try.

EVALUATE AT THE END

When you reach the end of your draft, look back at the process. Did you find it easier than you expected? harder? Did you feel more connected with the story? more connected with your characters? more connected emotionally? Did you find it difficult to leave the mistakes? Were they as bad as you feared?

What would you do differently next time? Would you do a more detailed synopsis? a less detailed one? If you used scene cards, did they help or hinder? If you didn't use them, is this something you might like to try? What time of day worked best for you? Did you learn any little tricks that helped you along the way?

It's important to evaluate, assess, and adjust until you find a way that works beautifully for you. Because, of course, you are going to try this again. And again. I can tell you that it has become so much easier for me as I do it over and over. In fact, I confess, I look forward to getting a fast first draft down. Surprisingly, as I go along, I find I need less and less polishing because I learn little lessons with each draft. However, whether that is the same for you or not is immaterial. Getting a fast first draft down is its own reward.

I challenge you to try this. You too might surprise yourself. Warning: It can become addictive. The joy of falling into a story and writing fast and furious is so wonderful I always write a fast first draft now.

❡

Tunnel Vision—a Writer's Friend
Carolyne Aarsen

Panic is not an emotion I embrace or seek out—that fluttering in my heart, that feeling like I'm running out of air, that overwhelming sense that events are crowding in on me and pushing me into a corner. But when I became published and multiple deadlines from multiple projects became a reality, so did panic.

The first two books I wrote were done at leisure. More hobby than vocation. When I sold them they were complete and had been lovingly edited over a course of five years. Then I signed my first contract for a book I hadn't started. I gladly immersed myself in my imaginary world, writing, rewriting, editing, rewriting, so thankful to be paid for doing this utterly enjoyable work. However, in reality land, the clock kept ticking. And as the deadline closed in on me and I realized I wasn't going to finish at my current pace, I canceled appointments, shut myself in my writing room, and morphed into this crazy person.

When the book was finished and I surfaced to a house in chaos and a grumpy family, I realized I couldn't live like this. I needed structure, but I was an artist and my muse was flighty. Structure? Surely that would kill my creativity. Over a period of a few years, a few panic attacks, a few stress rashes, and a lot of headaches, I realized that the only way to avoid this was to make a schedule and stick to it.

Four days of the week I write. And I work hard on those days. The fifth day is set aside as a buffer day because I've also learned, over eleven years of writing, that things come up. I keep weekends open

ESSENTIALS OF FICTION: WORK HARD

Don't buy the myth that writing is easy.

It's not. I heard one author say, "Writing is like giving birth to barbed wire." Others say writing is 5 percent inspiration and 95 percent perspiration. Many books that are hard to write are easy to read. Books that were easy to write are invariably hard to read. Some writers seem so natural, so effortless. Don't be fooled. It takes a lot of effort to appear effortless. With everything else competing for your reader's attention, you must work to earn it. Many people say they want to write a book, but what they really want is to *have written* a book. Big difference! —*Randy Alcorn* for sanity's sake and give myself an extra week at the end of the allotted time as a buffer week. Again, things come up. Then I give myself a week off before editing, which I've also plugged into my schedule.

Life has a way of happening to you while you're busy plotting out your schedule. I've taken care of a foster child with multiple handicaps, I've spent hours traveling to visit an ailing father and stand by him as he lay dying, I've driven two hours to visit my mother, and I've put aside my work to help my husband or my kids. My schedule hasn't completely alleviated panic from my life. But it has given me a better space. Maybe for you, one buffer day might not be enough. So change it. Give yourself two buffer days. Two buffer weeks. By laying out your schedule and only focusing on what lies directly in front of you, you decide how hard or fast you want to work.

Which brings me to my most valuable habit.

Tunnel vision.

Keep the focus narrow, tight, and manageable. Focus on the work for today and only today.

The devotions I do each morning give me a time to pray the Lord's Prayer. Each time I come to "Give us this day our daily bread," I am reminded that I only need to worry about today. So when I pray for my daily bread, I'm not just talking about food. I'm talking about what I need . . . for today. I'm reminded that I only need to focus on . . . today.

Each morning, I sit down in front of my computer and open up my calendar program and see what needs to be done today. Ten pages. For today, that's my focus and my goal. Today. If I am faithful with the time that has been granted me on this day, I will get the book finished.

Trouble is, many, many times I know exactly why I didn't meet my goals for the day. I wasted the time given to me. I frittered it away checking out my items on eBay and reading e-mail; then I look at the clock as it inexorably marks the seconds and the minutes toward the end of the day and I feel that all-too-familiar panic hitting.

That's when I haul out another tool to further tighten my focus.

CONQUERING THE BLOCK

Writer's block . . . every aspiring writer has heard of it. Many have experienced it. Some writers say it doesn't exist. Others decree it is overcome only by sheer willpower. Can it be overcome, and if so, how?

If it's creative anxiety, like stage fright before a performance, there is only one cure for it—just start writing. As we force words onto the page, we begin to tap into the creative side of the brain. It's the critical side of the brain that shuts us down, makes us fear that what we have to say isn't worth the time or that our words are a pathetic expression of the story in our imagination. This kind of writer's block can only be answered with the willingness to put words on the page, knowing that when the right time comes, we will revise, rewrite, and polish. But we can't revise what we haven't written yet. So we just write.

Is your resistance something repairable? Are you tired? hungry? Perhaps physical illness is robbing your creative energy. If a nap or a snack is required, then I do what needs to be done and come back to the page. Other writers say going for a walk or taking a shower breaks up the resistance. Basically, the cure is any non-accomplishment-oriented activity that helps you get out of your own way. If the cause is physical, then deal with that problem first. Be assured that the writing will be there when your physical being is strong enough for it.

Brainstorm with another writer, whether online or in person. When you're helping another writer come up with ideas, the pressure is off of *you*. Your internal critic has no vested interest in the ideas you toss out and therefore backs off to let you create.

If the problem is boredom, there's a good chance the story will bore your

I set a timer for forty-five minutes and shut everything else off. I push away the urge to check e-mail, play solitaire, or surf the Internet, and I narrow my vision. Just forty-five minutes of uninterrupted and undivided attention to the writing. It's only forty-five minutes, I remind myself.

editor, which means your readers won't ever see it. The boredom is your opportunity to change direction before it's too late.

Perhaps you suffer "writer exhaustion" from going without a restorative break between projects, or perhaps general life stress has overwhelmed creativity. Then refill the creative well. Forget about the words and do whatever makes your soul feel restored—reading; walking; observing creativity in art, sculpture, or craft; even sleeping. Nourishment of the soul is as important as nourishment of the body.

In some cases, negative influences leave a writer feeling incapable of formulating a thank-you note, much less a riveting story or an insightful article. If the negativity comes from a toxic critique group, then it may be time to rethink that association. If it comes from family, choose the most effective course of action—continue to toil away in secret or lovingly confront the negative speaker. In any case, you must find positive reinforcement. Whatever the source, find at least one person who will affirm your worth as a person and your skill as a writer.

Herein lies the most important truth of all: what you accomplish as a writer is between you and God. If we don't care for the tools he's given us, we can't expect to follow his calling. If we are faithful in all aspects of the calling, then he will take care of what follows—the bills that need to be paid, the sales figures, the subsequent contracts, etc. Fulfilling your contract promises to your editor is part of your faithfulness to God. He will provide the words, the stamina, and the creativity you need to do what he has called you to do.

—*Janelle Clare Schneider*

And when the timer finally goes off, I am surprised at how much I get done, how far I can get on my quota for the day.

Then, if I need to, I do it all over again.

Of course, as writers, we complain that we can't work under these strictures. We must be free. Where's the room for creativity? for inspiration?

Moment of truth? I don't write because I'm inspired. Mostly I show up at the computer at my appointed time and I start writing. One page at a time. I don't write only when I feel like it, because if I did, I wouldn't write.

I write because it's my job. I write because if I didn't, I would be missing a huge part of me. I write because my schedule says "Today Carolyne Aarsen has to make up two pages from yesterday, and she's not allowed to get up and cut her fingernails until she has done at least half of today's quota. But once the manicure is done, she'd better come right back and finish up for the day."

And yes, the schedule is restrictive. However, an interesting sideline has been the freedom it has given me. Freedom to let go of the work when I'm not working. Freedom to go and take care of my grandbaby for a few days because I plugged that time in. Freedom to go shopping and dawdle away a day because I completed my work for the week.

I don't have to think about the pages I need to get done next week. They are written down. When I get to that day, I will take care of them. I don't need to think about my worship committee meeting. It's written down. It doesn't need to enter my consciousness unless there's something I need to do . . . today . . . for that particular committee.

Now that I've narrowed my focus and stayed faithful to the work of today, I've become more relaxed and more confident when I set out a publication schedule and more relaxed in other areas of my life.

When I am doing my devotions I can truly focus on asking God for what I need . . . for today. Then I can be faithful with the time given to me . . . today.

Tomorrow is written down in my calendar. Tomorrow will take care of itself.

¶

Finding a Twenty-Fifth Hour in Your Day
Rick Acker

So you don't have time to write? Join the club. Very few writers—and virtually no beginning writers—have time to write. Our days are already full. All our time is taken up by jobs, housework, school, small group activities, etc. Not many people have two or three free hours per day that they can devote to writing. Yet every day millions of people somehow find time to write, and thousands of them manage to crank out a book per year or more. How do they do it?

START WITH A TIME AUDIT

For a full week, write down everything you do, breaking it down into half-hour increments. Be specific and detailed. For example, a general description of my morning from 6:45 to 8:15 would be "commuting." That's not an obvious time slot for writing, is it? But a more specific breakdown shows something different: 6:45 to 7:15, drop daughter off at high school and drive to train station; 7:15 to 8:10, sit on train; 8:10 to 8:15, walk to office. I can't write while I'm driving or walking, of course, but I can while I'm on the train. So it turns out that I actually have fifty-five minutes of writing time during my morning commute and another fifty-five in the evening. In fact, right now I'm using that time to write this article.

Be honest in your time audit. For instance, I might be tempted to describe my Sunday afternoon as "spend time with family." That doesn't sound like wasted time, does it? I'm not supposed to abandon my family so I can go write, am I? Well, it depends. Specifically, it depends on whether a completely candid description of my Sunday afternoon would be "watch back-to-back football games while another family member is in the room doing something else."

Once you reach the end of your audit, go through each time slot

ESSENTIALS OF FICTION: REWRITE IT

Rewrite again and again.

A first draft is the lump of clay; repeated revisions shape it into art. Someone asked Hemingway why he rewrote an ending nearly forty times. His answer: to get the words right. Beginnings and endings are critical—and middles are extremely important too! Don't lower the bar. Don't think editors or readers won't notice whether you've done six rewrites or only one. It will show up. Consciously or unconsciously, they'll sense how much work you put into this. Search for the perfect word, maybe a surprising one—it makes the setting, the character, the action *real*. Don't say, "The sky was dark gray," but "The sky looked like it had been rubbed hard with a dirty eraser." Some pages will be better than others, but every page will be good, because a good writer won't tolerate anything less.   —*Randy Alcorn* and ask yourself, "Does God really want me to be doing this instead of writing?" If your answer is no to seven or eight hours of time per week, then you've identified your writing time. If you answered yes all or virtually all of the time, congratulations! You are a better and more efficient person than 99.9 percent of the human race. However, you might want to consider whether you could free up some writing time by multitasking. For instance, instead of going out for lunch, consider brown bagging and writing while you eat. Or carry a note-pad around with you and write whenever you're waiting for a doctor, a load of laundry, a bus, or anything else that leaves your brain and hands idle for a few minutes.

MAKE WRITING PART OF YOUR ROUTINE

For most authors, writing is like exercise: it gets a lot easier once it becomes a habit. We're more productive if our brains are expecting to write at a particular time and place. For romance writer Tamara Leigh, that time is 8:00 a.m. (right after she drops her boys off at school) and the place is her local Starbucks, a caramel macchiato in hand. Lyn Cote's mental trigger is having breakfast and watching the first part of *Live with Regis and Kelly* because "they always give away prizes, and that gets me in a good mood." Gayle Roper avoids both caffeine and mornings, finding that she writes best between 3:00 and 7:00 p.m. Their routines are all different, but the key is that they're all routines.

Take another look at your time audit with the goal of creating a routine. Is it possible to write at the same time of day three or four times a week? Can you do it in the same place? If so, you have the beginnings of a writing habit.

One note: Having a daily writing routine doesn't necessarily mean writing every day. For example, one author I know generally writes every other day and spends his "off" days doing research and thinking through what he'll write the next day. Find a schedule that works for you, but make it a regular schedule if possible.

MAKE YOURSELF ACCOUNTABLE

Okay, you've identified your writing time. Now you need to make sure you use that time efficiently. For some authors, that's easy. Charlene Ann Baumbich, for example, says, "My brain kicks into fiction writing mode any time I sit down at my computer, close my eyes, and say to myself, 'Get out of the way, Charlene, so your characters can let the story lead all of us where it needs to go.'"

Most of us aren't that lucky. It's very easy to wind up staring out the window, listening to your iPod, and vaguely pondering what you're going to write. We need to put pressure on ourselves to be productive. There are lots of ways to do that. Here are some that have worked for me or other published novelists:

Have someone waiting for your pages. Most authors have a writing partner, critique group, or other "writing cop" who monitors their progress. For me, it's my wife, Anette. Every day when I get home from work, she's ready to critique what I've written. So if I've spent my commute watching the scenery roll by or reading the paper, I have to tell her. She's generally pretty easy on me, but I'd still rather not have to stand in front of her and say some variation of "I didn't write today because I was lazy/got distracted/wasn't focused." On the positive side, if I've written something good that day, she'll get excited and I'll be motivated to start writing again the next morning.

Set goals and reward yourself for meeting them. Figure out how many words you can realistically produce during a writing session. That should be your target whenever you sit down to write. You probably won't hit it every day (I meet my quota about half the time), but it will give you a useful yardstick to measure your daily writing against. And hitting it will be easier if you have a little something to look forward to. For Janelle Schneider, for example, "sometimes it's quick and simple like reading a magazine. Other times it's an hour or two with my quilting projects, or scrapbooking. . . . Sometimes it's even a nap. Depends on the day and on my mood."

Make writing a job. Most of us are more efficient at work than we are at home, so treat writing like a job—a job you like, but a job nonetheless. As Sharon Dunn explains, "I thought when I got my laptop I could live every writer's fantasy, writing in bed with my pajamas on . . . not. I kept drifting off and falling asleep, and when I wasn't doing that I was thinking about how nice it would be to take a nap. What I found was that I have to treat my writing like a job. I get dressed, wash my face, comb my hair, and take the long commute up the stairs to work at my laptop, which is now on a desk."

Arrange penalties for not writing. This trick comes from Christy Award winner John B. Olson. If he's having trouble motivating himself, he has a friend fine him fifty or one hundred dollars if he misses his daily or weekly writing target. This encourages him to write, of course, but it also turns his family (who might otherwise be tempted to distract him) into a team of cheerleaders pushing him to meet his goals on time. This technique may sound a little extreme, but it works. I know: I was the designated fine collector for his last book—which had over sixty separate writing goals—and I never got a penny out of him.

HAVE FUN

It's a lot easier to find time for something you enjoy than something you don't, right? So write what you enjoy. Don't try to force yourself to churn out an Amish romance or a vampire story just because that's what's hot right now. Chances are, you'll get sick of it after forty or fifty pages and never finish. And even if you do make it to the end, you'll probably find that the market for Amish books and vampire books—and even Amish vampire books—is glutted.

The same thing can also apply when you find yourself stuck in the middle of a story you're otherwise enjoying. By stuck, I mean really, really stuck, of course: You've made writing part of your routine, you've tried every accountability trick mentioned in this article and a couple that aren't, and none of it's working. You're frustrated, mad at your book, and your writing partner collected two hundred dollars in fines from you last week. To put it mildly, writing is not fun.

Try having some fun. Skip ahead to a part of the book you've been dying to write—the climactic confrontation between the heroine and the man who murdered her family, the scene where the star-crossed lovers can finally fall into each other's arms, or the clever trap the detective uses to catch the jewel thief. Once you're enjoying writing again, go back to the part that frustrated you before. Nine times out of ten, you'll find a way around whatever problem seemed so insurmountable. And before you know it, you'll be holding a finished manuscript in your hands—even though you never had time to write it.

CHAPTER 10

FINDING YOUR VOICE

¶

The Rules, Voice, and When to Deviate
Mary DeMuth

When I sent my short stories to a writing professor who'd invited them, I fretted, waiting a month before Sandra Glahn gave me feedback. I'd written in obscurity for ten years, self-publishing a newsletter for stay-at-home moms and developing church newsletters. I'd penned a few stories, created artificial deadlines, read writing books, all while my children grew from babyhood to childhood. Sending my work to Sandra was my first toe splash into the publication-seeking ocean.

Her advice to me:

- Kill your adverbs and adjectives.
- Use stronger nouns and verbs.
- Follow the correct format.

In addition to her rules, I studied and unearthed more rules:
- Don't write in fragments.
- Avoid run-on sentences.
- Keep clichés to a minimum.
- Try to eliminate negatives.
- Keep POVs consistent; avoid head-hopping.
- Be sure you have the correct antecedent for pronouns.
- Vary your sentences (don't use simply a noun-verb construction).
- Don't use too many gerunds.
- Avoid passive voice.
- Show, don't tell.
- No exclamation points!
- Keep punctuation within quotes.
- Learn proper capitalization rules.

I worked hard the next two years slaying adverbs and adjectives and beefing up my nouns and verbs. I followed the correct format, using the Tab key to indent, with only one space after a period. And through all that exponential growth, I became a columnist, wrote a novel, and secured an agent.

So the rules saved me, right?

Yes, in many ways. My prose morphed from flabby to muscular. I became less enamored with flowery phraseology and more interested in clarity. Following the professor's guidelines changed my writing for the better.

But I've learned something counterintuitive as I've linked myself to rules: There does come a point at which my writing begins to suffer if I shackle myself there. I'm reminded of a class I took at a nationally prominent writers' conference. The teacher, a veteran agent, pointed to a man in the back row. "Your piece," he said, "must've been brilliant. But you've edited and edited and edited the life out of it. It's dead now—clinically correct, but dead." You'd think the writer would react with sadness or defensiveness, but he actually looked relieved. He'd been given the permission to be himself, to write comfortably in his own skin, to break the rules as his voice necessitated.

My advice to new writers? Be humble and listen to every critique that comes your way. Folks will let you know about your fragments, your addiction to *was*, your penchant for double adjectives. In that initial state of your career, the only thing you should do is nod, listen, and acquiesce. But as you grow in your craft and the rules become second nature, over time you'll begin to venture out, experimenting with your voice. One day you'll know you've found it, and in that discovery you'll have the gumption and maturity to venture away from all the rules that kept you so safe before.

When you find your voice, you don't have to take into account every scrap of feedback. Of course you'll still need to maintain your humility and keep a teachable heart, but you'll have the discernment that seemed so elusive at first to know what to discard and what to keep.

Picasso lived this journey on the backdrop of portraits. Before he became known as an abstract portrait painter, Picasso perfected the classic forms of portraiture. He'd mastered every element of the craft, only to later deviate. I doubt his later pieces would've had the depth of character and beauty had he painted them at the onset. Nor would anyone have taken him seriously. By mastering the craft first, Picasso not only earned the right to deviate, but he found himself.

It's the same for us. If we charge out of the writerly gates bent on breaking every rule, we will not have gained the valuable perspective that comes from gritty work, dogged determination, and the unglamorous pursuit of craft. If we truly want to deviate brilliantly, we must first be brilliant in traditional forms. That early mastery will only enhance, broaden, and deepen our later prose.

There are no shortcuts to mastery, no magic potions that project us from mediocrity to beauty. Only humility under the tutelage of the craft and the rules. As we are trained by those rules and learn to humbly accept critique, our voice and word personality will develop.

I love how the author of Hebrews confirms this process: "No discipline is enjoyable while it is happening—it's painful! But afterward there will be a peaceful harvest of right living for those who are trained in this way" (Hebrews 12:11, NLT). I firmly believe that after we've been trained by other writers in the craft (either through critique or by reading great writers), we will yield the fruit of a unique voice.

Permit me to show a bit of my own voice revolution and how some of the writing rules faded in the transition. When I initially wrote the opening scene for my first novel (yet unpublished), I placed the reader on the porch, in a physical place, eventually venturing into the protagonist's head. I added details like Augusta's age, that she was an aspiring writer, that she harbored fears of death—all clinically good things. The intro reads:

> Why Augusta sat on the porch swing that foggy Monday morning, she did not know. *Maybe I'm hoping for a miracle.*
>
> "Porches are for miracles," Mother had told her when Augusta lived as a skinned-knee tomboy perched in the climbing trees that lined the streets of her childhood.

"You just never know *what* miracle the day will bring, and a porch is as good as anything in helping you watch it unfold."

Forty-three-year-old Augusta Brinkworth longed to embody her mother's oft-repeated advice—that today she would be one who captured the moment, whether the moment held some sort of private delight scribbled on her mind or if it would be announced to others through the nib of her pen. She hoped this same pen would liberate her from a childhood fear—that if she wrote and wrote and wrote, she'd no longer think that yes, today, someone will die.

A few years later, I dusted off the manuscript and retinkered with the beginning. Note the evolution—how I shied away from the porch and placed Augusta smack-dab in the midst of the action. How I used her poetic view of life to hint at her desire to write. How I eliminated some details in light of others. And how I embraced sentence fragments.

Augusta always knew Thomas would die young. Always knew God would thrust his angry finger through the muggy Ohio air and point right at him. "Your time's up," the Almighty would say. And Thomas, being obedient to the depths, would nod quietly, then slip into glory without so much as saying good-bye.

The word *accident* repeated itself with each slap of Augusta's shoes against shale. *Accident. Accident.* The word screamed in her head, longing to release, but clenched teeth kept her terror to herself. Olya followed at her heels as they passed stilled shovels, empty water pumps, and halted railcars standing sentrylike in reverential silence. The quarry's Dinky engines saluted the two wives as they raced toward the rock quarry's belly.

Thomas, you promised me there'd be no accidents.

When I penned that second draft, I gave myself permission to tell the story without worrying as much about the rules. What ruled me then was my voice—that pesky quality that took me years of writing in obscurity to master.

I remember the e-mail confirming my voice suspicions. It was the summer of 2003. I'd written over a hundred columns for my local newspaper. I'd been in the habit of sending each column to a group of folks who enjoyed reading them, my writing professor friend one of them. Sandra Glahn e-mailed me back immediately with these words: "Methinks you've found your voice." The professor who'd laid down the law was now giving me wings.

ESSENTIALS OF FICTION: STAY INVISIBLE

Stay invisible; avoid all author intrusion—it pulls readers out of the story.

Imagine watching a play in which the director stops the action and comes out on stage, points to the characters, and says, "See, she loves him, but he doesn't realize it; he's still thinking about his old girlfriend. Get it?" Writing is like *The Wizard of Oz*—the guy behind the curtain doesn't want to be seen! Don't try to impress the readers with your vocabulary—they'll know you're there. When you keep using the same phrase (e.g., "a thin smile"), readers start thinking about you, not your story. Now the magic is broken—the story's not real. *—Randy Alcorn*

Yes, we need rules just like we need playground boundaries when we're younger. We learn to play behind the fence, not venturing beyond. But someday, we grow up. We see that there's more to explore beyond the fence. We are mature enough to know not to dash in front of cars. Once we've aged, we earn the right to be free because of the process of growth.

As writers, it's the same. We start small. We learn the craft. We master the rules. We grow up. And then we venture. Mastery comes before the adventure, and voice is the vehicle to writing beyond the rules.

Finding and Honing Your Writer's Voice
Camy Tang

These days, the one thing that captures an editor's or agent's attention the fastest is a writer's voice.

Voice sets the stage for the story. It establishes ambiance and immerses the reader in the fictional world. Voice can prepare the reader for the type of story—for example, a dark vampire novel versus a thriller—purely by the words used, the cadence, the rhythm of the sentences in the first paragraph.

Voice serves to distinguish one writer from another. Someone could read passages from different authors with good writer's voices and be able to tell the difference in flavor from one to the other, and sometimes even recognize a certain author purely by the voice.

A strong, unique voice will hook a reader's attention within the first paragraph. It will make the reader go on to the next paragraph, and the next. It will engulf readers in the "fictitious dream" of the story, which they won't easily snap themselves out of.

But how does a writer recognize his or her own writer's voice? Is it innate? Can it be learned or acquired? Can it be honed?

FINDING YOUR OWN VOICE

Many writers—beginning and intermediate—use a rather bland voice. They might be too timid or strive to emulate a favorite author. The result is a neutral writer's voice that acts like a wet blanket thrown over a story and characters that would otherwise zing with possibilities.

Each writer has a unique voice. It's usually similar to his or her speaking voice and is as identifiable as speaking patterns are from person to person.

The key is drawing it out.

Voice usually comes out the more a writer writes. Writers dedicated to finding and honing their voices write thousands upon thousands of words. They won't always be words used for publication, but they won't be wasted words.

Utilize writing prompts (Writer's Digest has daily writing prompts online at www.writersdigest.com/WritingPrompts) or write short stories. Write every day for two to three weeks, longer if you can.

Do not edit yourself—just write. Voice usually comes out in raw writing. Therefore, don't analyze your writing or criticize yourself. Don't censor yourself. Don't think, *That's good* or *That's bad*. Don't think about what can be said in public or in private. Don't worry if what you write even makes sense. Don't think about if it could ever be used for publication. Don't worry about staying on topic—tangents are fine. And don't be afraid of uncharted ground.

This might be the hardest part for you, and these weeks might also work to teach you to write without trying to correct or revise yourself. Don't be discouraged, because polish can always come later—just not now.

After those two or three weeks, when you've acquired a large collection, put that writing away for two weeks. Feel free to write other things during that time, but don't look at the things you wrote during the earlier period.

After your "cooling off" period, go back and analyze your writing from the first weeks. Highlight passages or phrases that particularly impact you or please you—anything that strikes your fancy. Is there a way of writing you fall back on again and again? Is there a certain atmosphere to the stories or scenes? Is there a rhythm or cadence to the prose that seems to come out every so often? Is there a particular timing you utilize often when forming sentences or delivering hooks? Are there types of words you use that are tied by a certain emotional bond or theme?

Those are glimmers of your voice.

MIX IT UP

If your writing still seems rather bland or diluted, repeat the experiment: Write more, for longer than three weeks. Utilize more writing prompts or freewrite about anything that interests you. Try different genres, even those you're not familiar with. Try both past tense and present tense. Try omniscient point of view, limited third person, and first person.

Interact with external stimuli—different scents, sounds, objects, tastes. Try different aromatherapy oils or candles. Experiment with various sounds—some that soothe, some that excite, some that frighten or build tension. Movie sound tracks can be great for this. Surround yourself with objects or pictures that evoke emotions in you, and try to prompt the gamut of emotions—fear, joy, sadness, contentment, loss, anger. Try different tastes in your mouth as you write—sweet, salty, hot, creamy, crunchy, savory, unctuous, biting. Touching different textures can also wake emotional memory and stimulate creativity—soft, furry, sharp, smooth, sandy, hot, cold.

Mix up your writing and venture outside your comfort zones. This will help you bring out your writer's voice.

EXPERIMENT WITH RHYTHM

While many writers find it difficult to write to music, music can sometimes help a person find his or her natural rhythm. Each writer's voice has a rhythm and cadence, but sometimes preconceived notions or distractions can confuse or mask that internal urge.

Freewrite or use a writing prompt to write to a certain song or style of music. Experiment with various musical rhythms and beats to find something—or a set of things—that resonate with you as you write. You may need to try various styles of music, some with words, some without. Try both fast and slow, syncopated or on beat.

Pay attention to your body and tastes, and to how the music impacts you as you write. Are there genres that seem to have more emotional impact in your writing? Certain music will stimulate your internal rhythm and bring out greater creativity and vibrancy in your writing. Try to figure out what style, beat, instrument, or cadence affects you the most.

EMOTION IS EVERYTHING

As you discover your writer's voice, you can enhance it and polish it with the same types of exercises described above—external stimuli work best.

While you are working to bring your voice out more, focus on emotion. Use stimuli that evoke stronger emotion. Visualize situations or choose writing prompts with high emotional impact; then write.

Voice is often enhanced in highly charged scenes, and for an emotional high in your story or novel, you want your voice to be at its strongest and best.

Emotion is what keeps a reader riveted to the page. The clearer and sharper the emotion in your writer's voice, the more engaged that reader will be.

REFINE YOUR VOICE

Once you have discovered your voice, also pay attention to how it connects with readers. While you may be happy with your writer's voice as it is, ultimately you're writing for other people—your readers—not yourself, and you'll need to hone your voice so that it will positively impact those readers. For this stage, you will need critique partners to provide feedback on how your voice comes across to someone besides yourself.

A good writer's voice is wonderful to read, like chocolate mousse to the senses—rich, decadent, but light and not overpowering. Your voice should draw readers into the story, not be abrasive or shove them away. Your voice might need some softening to make it more inviting to readers rather than full of hard edges that make reading difficult.

Your voice might need polishing to create a smoother flow, so readers aren't hung up on odd phrases or a jerky cadence. Sometimes word choices need to be tweaked a bit to make the writing more accessible to readers. If a reader is grabbing a dictionary every page, it disrupts enjoyment of the story. Ask your critique partners to highlight any words, phrases, or sentences that jolt them out of the story world or make the reading difficult or slow.

Polish your voice, but remain true to yourself. Don't rub all the gilding off your work. Pay attention if more than one person mentions the same thing, but be thoughtful in how you take any feedback you get about your voice. Also make sure your critique partners know to focus on the voice, rhythm, and atmosphere—don't get bogged down by feedback that pertains to the characters and plot rather than the voice.

DISTINGUISH CHARACTER VOICES FROM YOUR OWN

Take your writer's voice a step further and distinguish your characters' voices from each other and from your own. Don't make the mistake of having all your characters sound alike—or worse, all like your own voice. Each character should have his or her own distinct style, but formed with the clay of your unique writer's voice.

When writing a novel or short story, do several exercises, which you won't use for the story but which will help you refine each character's voice. Take a certain situation or scene and write it from one character's point of view, paying attention to how that character would speak and act. Then write that same situation from a different character's point of view, paying close attention to how that character would speak and act differently. Repeat this with each main character in your story.

Keep in mind the people around the character, whom the character is speaking to. Keep in mind relationships—is the hero talking to his mother or his coworker? Slip yourself into the character's skin, become the character in entirety. How does the character view the world?

Try to experiment with personalities very different from your own. If you are an introvert, try writing several different extroverted characters. Also experiment with different occupations and the emotions and skills required for those occupations. Think up a situation

AN INTERVIEW WITH FRANCINE RIVERS: VOICE

How does your reading influence the way you write?
I read voraciously. I tend to read analytically. There are dozens of writers who can write circles around me with their use of language and similes. That's been a struggle for me, to remember that I have my own voice and not to try to be another voice. Each of us has a unique way of expressing ourselves. I think it damages us when we do too much comparing, too much admiring of others' work. Reading one young novelist recently, I realized she's light-years ahead of where I was at her age. But I had to remind myself, "This is her voice. I have a different voice and a different call." It's a challenge to remember that. So my advice would be, study, but don't imitate.

Some of your punctuation is very deliberate. How much thought do you place on those types of things as you're writing a first draft? Or is that something you layer in, in subsequent drafts?
Oh yes. I'm very aware of punctuation, commas in particular. My husband helps me with that too. Nowadays the trend is to omit them. But leaving out a comma can change the whole cadence of the sentence, as well as the meaning. I think it's really too bad that they're doing away with them. We're losing the richness of the language.

that would put a character in danger emotionally or physically, and write that situation with several different characters in various occupations.

This experimental writing will not only help you refine the characters' voices, it will help you understand your characters better, and it will refine your own writer's voice at the same time. You will be expanding your skills and learning to exert more control over your voice without losing its richness.

PRACTICE CONSISTENTLY

Write daily, preferably. Don't let weeks go by without writing something.

Also don't feel that everything you write has to be used for a story or publication. Much of what you write as you discover and refine your writer's voice will be things no one else will ever see. This is not wasted time or words—it is like the training athletes go through to prepare for a race. In your case, for your next novel or short story.

Even while you're working on your novel, write a little each day outside of your project. Do a hundred-word response to a writing prompt or some freewriting. Keep up the exercise so you'll be in shape as you work.

And above all, persevere. Just as athletes are not Olympics-ready in a few weeks, writers take time to develop their voices.

Are you up to the challenge? Do you want a writer's voice that will wow an editor? Then write!

CHAPTER 11

WRITING WITH EXPRESSION

❡

Writing to Change Lives
Karen Kingsbury

People ask me what it's like spending so much time with people who are not technically real, in the sense of not having actual flesh and blood. I tell them to ask my husband, Don. He's the one who sees the craziness firsthand.

One day I was working on a book in the Baxter series and a favorite character—Irvel—was about to pass away. Irvel was an older woman with Alzheimer's, so no question it was her time to go. Her dying would be completely the result of natural causes. But the sorrow remained. The closer I came to her death, the slower I typed until finally, she passed. At that point I had to set my laptop computer down—out of sight next to my chair—and have a good cry about losing Irvel.

About that time, Don bounded into the room, his typical happy, energetic self. But as soon as he saw me, tears streaming down my face, he stopped short. "Honey!" He looked alarmed. "What happened?"

I took a moment to find my voice, still choking back the sorrow of the situation. Finally I was able to eke out a tearful "Irvel died!"

He stood without moving, and the color drained from his face. He swallowed hard. "Irvel? Oh no." He blinked twice. "Do we know her from church . . . or school?"

My tears came harder. "Honey!" I shook my head. "She's one of my characters!"

Don relaxed his stance. "Well . . . I don't have any sympathy for you." He rolled his eyes all the way to the ceiling. "I mean . . . you killed her!"

Yes, Don often says I'll make a very interesting old woman one day, unable to tell my kids from my characters. "I can just hear you," he tells me. "'That Ashley! She never calls, never writes!'" And it won't even occur to me that (a) We don't have a child named Ashley; and (b) Ashley was a character in the Baxter series.

So yes, I spend my time with imaginary people. But I also spend a great deal of time with my husband and kids. Not long ago, our youngest son, Austin, climbed into our bed late one evening. I was sitting up, working on the last chapter in a novel, and he snuggled next to me. "Hey, Mom." He pointed at the screen. "You writing a book?"

"Yes, honey. Almost finished."

"Good. Cause I've been meaning to ask you a few questions about book-writing."

I stopped typing and looked at him. "Okay. What do you want to know?"

His eyes lit up. "Well, first . . . those covers on your books are so cool. I love the colors and the way the people look." His expression grew curious. "Do you make those?"

"The covers?" I smiled. "No, lots of talented people at the publisher work to make the covers. I might have a little input, but for the most part I see it when it's finished and I'm always amazed—just like you."

His face fell a little. "Oh." He thought for a few seconds, and his eyes danced to life once more. "I know, what about the inside of the book. The way the letters line up nice and neat and the little curlicue things at the top of each chapter." He squinted. "Do you do that part?"

I could see where this was headed. "No, buddy. That's not my part either. Interior designers at the publisher take care of making sure the inside of the book looks nice."

"Really?" His little shoulders fell a notch and the sparkle left his eyes. Again he thought for a minute, and finally he raised his brows. "How about the bookshelves at the mall? We go in a bookstore and your books are always lined up in a row. That takes a lot of work, unloading the boxes and stuff." He narrowed his eyes at me. "Do you do that?"

I frowned. "No . . . no, that's the work of the sales staff at the publisher who send the books out and the bookstore staff who open the boxes and put them on the shelves." I found a weak smile for him. "I have nothing to do with that."

He looked at me for a long time, and finally he shrugged. "Wow." He gave me a quick kiss on the cheek and bounced down off the bed. "You really don't do that much, do you?"

And the thing of it is, I don't.

The process of putting a novel in the hands of a reader involves hundreds of people, all with jobs as important as mine. The part I'm responsible for is the writing, because I'm a writer.

You too are a writer.

I'm often asked, "How do you become a writer?" I give the only answer I know—if you want to be a writer, you must write. But if our writing is to last, if it is to change lives, there are three things we must remember along the way.

BE HONEST

We must tell the truth when we make up our stories for the world to read. This means finding a way to be honest in our storytelling. Once, a while back, I was working on a novel called *A Time to Dance*. It's a deeply emotional story about the struggling marriage of two longtime believers. The story needed humor if it was going to make it, because the teary parts already filled the pages. So I asked God for humor, for something I could infuse into the story that would give readers the comic relief they would need to continue.

About that time our family took a trip to SeaWorld for spring break. For some reason, of vital importance that day was a stop at the 11:30 a.m. sea lion show. We literally dragged our kids off the swings and slides and raced around the park so we could make this show on time. At that point, we were a family of five because we had not yet adopted our boys from Haiti. Austin was only eighteen months old, so he spent the day in a front-carrier strapped to Donald's chest. I wore an enormous backpack carrying all our worldly belongings except maybe our beds and the refrigerator. In all, we were not a light-traveling outfit. We looked like nomads from a foreign land, making our way around the park desperate for a seat at the sea lion show.

Once we finally made it to the top of the stairs, just one row remained open—about three-fourths of the way down. Now, the stairs turned out to be very steep, because in Southern California that's how they get the most people into a small geographical location. You almost need a lead rope to make it down the stairs. I figured out later that the way they make the stairs so steep is like this: regular step, half step, regular step, half step. Only I didn't know that at the time.

"That's us!" I announced as I spotted the empty row of seats. I planted one foot on the regular step, but the next foot missed the half step entirely. With nothing but air supporting me, I began to tumble and fall down the stairs. People thought I was part of the act. I realized somewhere along the way down that my backpack was unzipped, because personal things were preceding me along the steep incline.

When I finally stopped rolling and falling, I was right exactly at our row. I stood up, dusted myself off, waved at the worried crowd, and motioned back to Don and the kids that yes, they could join me now. At the end of the show, I turned to my husband—who hadn't cracked a smile yet. I winced a little. "So . . . how did that look?"

I tell you the truth when I say the man has never quite recovered from the laughter that overtook him in that moment. I was bruised and battered, but we had more than a good laugh that day. I had a funny story for *A Time to Dance*. The reason I could use it? The story was honest.

Here is how you make your fictional stories honest: If it makes you laugh, it can be reworked for a scene in your story. If it makes you cry, ask yourself what triggered the tears and rework it for your next chapter. If you are left awestruck by a scene or a moment, bring it into your writing. In this way, you will keep your work honest. The letters I receive most of all from readers say this: "Thank you for writing such real characters." The reason they're real? The reason your work will be real?

Because we must write in a way that is honest.

BE HARDWORKING AND HOPEFUL

My dad always told me, "Whether you think you can or you think you can't, you are right." This is especially true for us writers. We must work hard and we must pray, believing that God is taking our writing to the place where he alone can showcase it. Wherever that place is, and however many people eventually read what we've written—we must always be hardworking and hopeful.

There is a YouTube video clip that's made its way around the Internet. It shows a very old woman in the crosswalk of a residential area. She is wearing a fuzzy gray hat and a fuzzy gray coat, and in her hands she holds the straps of a fuzzy oversize purse. But the fact of the matter is, she's not making much progress getting across the street. The reason? She is sound asleep. Yes, there she stands, clutching her purse, her head slightly bowed, napping away.

Just then a business guy in a convertible BMW screeches up to the intersection and nearly runs her over. He is *so* mad at her for sleeping in the crosswalk. How dare she get in his way, when he has important things to do, places to go, people to see. He revs his engine angrily a few times, and when that doesn't wake the woman, he lays on his horn. Startled from her dreams, she jerks her head up and begins making her way across the intersection again. This woman is slow, and my guess is she's earned the right to take her time. Watching her in the video, I couldn't help but think she might need another nap before she actually reached the other side. Either way, she is trying.

But it isn't enough for Joe Business Guy. He is ready to pull his hair out. How dare she be too old to walk fast? He revs his engine at her in a threatening manner and honks several more times as she moves toward the middle of the crosswalk. Now—and here's where I love her spunk—the woman never once looks at the guy. Not once. But as she passes inches from the front of his car, she simply swings her big bag at his bumper. What happens next remains one of the most wonderful moments ever recorded. Though she couldn't have planned it, her purse exactly hits the guy's air bag sensor, and before the guy can honk one more time, his air bag explodes in his face. We see the little old lady continue on her way, undaunted, never looking back, and in the background we watch Joe Business Guy picking pieces of his steering wheel off his cheeks and forehead.

I watch that video and I think that's how it is for those of us who write. The world will rev its engines and honk at us. We will at times be distracted, discouraged, defeated, and depressed. But like that woman, we must stay on the crosswalk. We must keep our eyes focused on our destination and continue our journey. Never mind the world's distractions. We are writers, and we must stay the course. We must be hardworking and hopeful. We must write.

BE HIS

Finally, if we are to write fiction that will touch hearts and change lives, we must be God's. Philippians 2:14-16 tells us, "Do everything without complaining or arguing, so that you may become blameless and pure, children of God without fault in a crooked and depraved generation, in which you shine like stars in the universe as you hold out the word of life—in order that I may boast on the day of Christ that I did not run or labor for nothing."

This is our calling, that we might hold out the word of life to the world, and that we do this through our writing. For me, Christ is the story. He is not a patch to add into my plot, or a marketing ploy. The world can write about the physical, intellectual, and emotional aspects of people. So can we. Ah, but we also can tell about the spiritual—and the story is nothing without that piece. We are the most blessed of all writers because we are called to tell the *whole* story. All people are spiritual because we are created in Christ's image. We are either running toward God or running away from him. Tell that part of the story, because that is what he is calling us to do.

Last fall we were making chocolate chip cookies when it came time to add the vanilla. Three of my kids were nearby, and Tyler, our oldest son, said, "Mom, I love vanilla. It's great how you need just a little bit but it flavors the whole batch of dough."

We all agreed as Kelsey, our only daughter, stirred the vanilla through the cookie mix. But the mention of vanilla brought another son, Sean, running into the kitchen. "Wait! I hate vanilla!" He stared at the batter. "Is it already in?"

"Yes." I frowned. "I guess I forgot about you and vanilla."

He looked at me, hopeful. "Can you take it out?"

A few of the kids giggled. I put my hand on Sean's shoulder. "Honey, the vanilla is already mixed into the dough. There's no way to take it out now."

Kelsey gave me a knowing look. "It's like that with God, isn't it? A little bit goes a long way, and once he's in the mix, it's impossible to remove him."

Such wisdom from my nineteen-year-old. But her lesson stands for us today. As writers, our work should be so infiltrated with the Christian worldview, so true to the message of the gospel, that we could no more take Christ from our stories than we could take vanilla from a batch of chocolate chip cookie dough.

You must be his writer. Let him tell the story. Keep it honest, be hardworking and hopeful, but most of all, be his. Be the pen in his hand. In that way, though you surround yourself with imaginary people, and though you will be responsible for only a small part of the final project, you will write stories that bring glory to God. And since the gift of writing comes from him, there really is no other way.

¶

Writing Novels from the Inside Out
Mary DeMuth

As a book mentor, the biggest flaw I see is lack of character emotion. When writers ask me how to up the emotional ante in their stories, I tell them to write the novel from the inside out.

What does that mean, exactly?

Writing from the inside out means taking risks internally. It means facing your demons, even if they threaten to strangle you. It means going places in your past you've locked the door to. If you dare, this will change your novel utterly, grabbing your readers by the throat, throttling their emotions, and keeping them turning pages until The End.

But writing a novel from the inside out will not only change your prose and your reader's experience, it will change you.

When I turned in my first novel, I worried I'd receive one of those long, single-spaced documents that told me my book was just fine, if only I altered the entire thing, rewriting 97 percent of it. When I received the twenty-six-page, single-spaced letter, I fretted. I didn't have to rewrite the whole thing, thankfully, but I did have much work to do. Most of the letter dealt with lapses of logic, plotting problems, and character issues. But the lion's share of the critique centered around one thing: my main character's lack of emotional response.

I reasoned the notes away, remembering my own situation that somewhat mirrored my character's. I'd been sexually abused at five by neighborhood boys. My character, Mara, experienced the same horror at nine at the hand of General, a bully. I came from a family that didn't tolerate negative emotions, so to please my family I didn't outwardly react to the abuse leveled at me. Although I did exhibit some telltale behaviors, I kept my mouth shut, and I told myself not to cry.

Enter Mara. And General. How did Mara respond to her attacks? With stoic resignation, as I had. And although it is clinically true that childhood victims of sexual abuse lack an emotive response or spend a lifetime keeping their secrets, that kind of stoicism did not endear my reader to Mara. Wrestle as I might with my editor's suggestion, in the end, I knew she was right. Mara needed emotions.

So I cried through my revisions. In one of the most cathartic writing experiences of my life, I assigned Mara the emotions I was not allowed to have. In that grieving, God chose to heal me afresh. As

I made it through to the other side of edits, I reaped a better book, with a character readers wept for.

How can a novelist probe his or her own depths in a story? Through skillful questioning and layering. Because I believe we write stories that have some emotional connection to us as authors, this is not as complex as you might think. Start with these questions:

- Why did I write this book?
- What about this book had to be written?
- What character most represents me?
- What character represents my opposite?
- Which scene evokes the most emotion in me? Why?
- If my readers could come away from my book with one prevailing emotion, what would that be?
- Why is it so important to me that the readers experience my book this way?

Once you've answered those questions, take some time to ask the Lord what it is he wants to accomplish through your story. Seek his face in terms of your own healing. Perhaps there is something he would like you to explore as you write, some type of healing he's been kindly pestering you about. When these questions are answered (his intent for the book, his intent for your healing or growth), take a scene that most clearly represents both intents and paste it in a separate document.

For the sake of example, let's say you have a protagonist, Ellie, who pursues men who are just like her absent father. In that pursuit, she chooses the wrong sort of men, often sabotaging her life.

Your original scene looks like this:

Ellie stopped short. She should have yelled at Drake, should've told him to leave, but something held her there. She stood in the bathroom, a mascara wand in her hand, bathed in Drake's affable gaze. Yes, it was his eyes that kept her there. His blue-like-the-sky eyes, bewitching her into a mediocre life.

Now let's consider that you have experienced an abandoning relationship with your mother. It is not the same as the situation Ellie finds herself in, but you both share feelings of abandonment. Recall a moment when you felt abandoned. Journal about that time beneath your scene. Identify what you felt, why you felt it, what your actions were. Consider what consequences the abandonment reaped in your life. How did the injury affect your decisions, good or bad?

Here is my journal entry:

I remember waiting in the corner of our home as a little girl, shaking, worrying, fretting. I would count to one hundred, hoping that by the time I reached that

ESSENTIALS OF FICTION: CREATE AN "AHA" MOMENT

Write to bring the reader to an "aha" experience, where some new and important perspective or value emerges. People are reading for escape and entertainment, sure, but also for enlightenment, to fill some inner voids, to come back better prepared to face the real world. A test of depth and substance is whether a book lends itself to rereading. C. S. Lewis said that the best book is the one you want to read again and again. Try to write a story that doesn't yield up all its treasures in the first reading. —*Randy Alcorn* nice, round number, my mom would magically come through the door of our little locked house, rescuing me from my fear. I worried incessantly with a monster-shaped fright that being alone necessitated that bad guys would break in and kill me. But my mother was bigger than the bad guys then, and I knew if she'd just make it home in time, I'd be safe. I spent a lot of time worrying about her return, and I learned one thing: I would instantly forgive her for her tardiness once I saw her face. All the fear and rage waged in her absence turned into my insatiable need for her in her presence. I forgave, forgave, forgave, even apologizing when I didn't need to. This followed me into my adult life, making me an over-apologizer, making me long for acceptance and presence more than a gutsy desire to be treated right.

Now return to the scene. Rewrite it using those pesky emotions. Make Ellie dig deeper; make your reader feel her anguish.

Here's a possible rewrite:

Ellie fingered the mascara, wishing it were the magic wand she believed in so fiercely as a child when she dressed up like a princess waiting for Daddy to come home to her tea party—a party she'd set for three years. The wand didn't work then, and it wouldn't work now. Drake edged closer, holding her captive with blue eyes, the eyes the same color as the Pacific Ocean at dusk, but put more plainly: the exact shade of Daddy's. She sucked in a breath, wondering if Drake sensed her panic. Sure, he called her "my pet" and told her which opinions she was allowed to have, but he loved her. He needed her. And he was as real to her as the daddy that never rescued the abandoned princess. "I'm sorry," she heard herself say, the litany of words she'd perfected for Drake over and over again. "Of course you're right." She glanced away from his eyes, but he propped her chin heavenward and drowned her with his gaze, holding her there. She could stay there the rest of her life. Lord knows, she would.

See how repainting the scene with an emotional tie to the past strengthens a reader's empathy? And deepens the story?

Once you've re-crafted a scene by looking to your own emotional landscape in the past or capturing one ripped from the headlines of today, take your before and after copies to a friend, critique partner, or critique group. And see which one has more emotional impact.

To become an inside-out novelist, you'll soon learn that fully living life in all its messiness will enliven your stories. You must live life, then use life. And through all that, write in a position of humility, asking God to reveal parts of you that need direction or healing. He is faithful to use your words not only to deeply impact your reader, but also to change your heart from the inside out.

CHAPTER 12

HANDLING REJECTION

¶

The Power of Humility
Hannah Alexander

For a novelist, the path to success can be littered with potholes and rocks, sharp curves and sudden drops. Humility can help smooth the way.

When we pour our hearts onto a page, we can become vulnerable to criticism. The opposite can be true as well, and even the humblest of us can fall prey to pride. After all, how many people can create worlds that readers will want to visit? That's quite an accomplishment. But don't get caught up in the dream.

Do you have your complete masterpiece whittled and honed, rewritten and polished? Then put the manuscript away for a week or two, even longer if possible. Focus on something else—preferably a book or two about the process of writing. Several authors of articles in this book have written excellent how-to books about the craft.

I completed my first novel-length manuscript two and a half decades ago. I glowed with happiness, amazed that I was actually able to focus long enough to complete such a difficult task. My friends read my novel and loved it. My mother was so proud. Life was good. I didn't have a clue what I was supposed to do with the finished manuscript, and so I put it away for a while, purchased some books about novel writing, and started work on a new story.

Though I didn't realize it all those years ago, I did the right thing when I began work on another story immediately. Had I known how difficult my own road to publication would be, I might never have started that next novel, or the next.

Studying my craft was fun, and it was also a good thing for me. With a little humility, even the most seasoned, educated, and well-published writer can learn something new to improve his or her skills. As you read how-to books about your craft, it's likely you will experience several "aha!" moments—things you hadn't considered and steps you did not take with your completed masterpiece. Take notes; underline passages. This waiting period will give you some necessary distance from your work.

When you return to your manuscript, try to do so with the mind-set of an editor, not a creator. Chances are the pages you slaved over still need more work. Read the words as if you were reading someone else's story, and apply what you studied during your waiting period. If you don't find places that need to be repaired, you're not looking hard enough.

Every author has strengths, but we also struggle with weaknesses. Find yours, admit them, and then work on them.

Once you've reworked and reread until you're sick of the whole thing, turn it over to someone who will be unbiased, able to tell you the truth about your work. This could be a critique partner, a teacher, or a freelance editor who will charge you a fee for services rendered. Your mother probably can't help you here. The opinion of a close family member won't usually count, because unless this person knows what constitutes good writing, you'll simply have your ego stroked as you are fed words of praise.

It's difficult for most writers to accept criticism about their work. If your chosen critic returns your prized masterpiece to you with abundant red ink, you may feel as if you've been personally attacked. Don't plot revenge, and don't argue. I have a friend who does freelance editing. She's good. She hits her clients hard. When they rewrite to her specifications instead of taking offense, she knows they may have a chance of reaching publication someday, because they have been humble enough to listen, learn, and improve.

Please understand that I'm not saying you should make every change suggested to you. After all, this is your story, and unless the editor is a professional connected to a credible publisher, you must balance your humility with knowledge of what will and will not work for your story.

Your next lesson in humility will come when you begin marketing your work, which will best be done at a professional writers' conference. If you're fortunate enough to pitch a brief synopsis to an interested publishing house, send the editor your proposal as soon as you arrive home from the conference. And then wait—preferably while continuing to study the craft or working on a new writing project. If you then receive a request for the complete manuscript, celebrate! You're one of the few.

If you receive a form rejection slip, file it in a special place. Don't throw it away, and don't feel as if the world has ended. You've just begun your marketing campaign. The more rejection slips you collect, the closer you are to your goal. You can't sell your work if you don't send it out, and those rejection slips are evidence that you've been doing your job.

Your first rejection may come at any time during the marketing process. That's only the beginning. I have friends whose stories were purchased the first time they tried, but that's a rare occurrence. When first marketing my work, I heard speakers talk about being able to paper a wall with the rejection slips they received. I was horrified, but I decided I wouldn't let that stop me. I saved my rejection slips until I had enough to paper my whole office. I could have earned a degree in humility.

Thirteen unpublished manuscripts and fourteen years later, I finally sold my first novel.

After the sale, I kept writing new stories, but I was also able to use my backlog when I signed with a second and third publisher. Some of those first manuscripts—rewritten and well edited, of course— won international awards.

Once I sold that first novel, I discovered that professional editors usually have finesse. They give liberal praise before taking the knife to your words, but if they think your work is good, they will take the time to help you hone it. Bless them for it. You don't always have to agree, and editors are open to discussion, but you can learn so much about writing from a good editor. The more you learn, the better your next work will be. Very few authors on the best-seller lists are overnight successes. They have worked hard to improve their craft, and they have been open to critique and editing. Being humble enough to accept help has served them well.

Humility is one of those ingredients that can help you transform what is merely a well-crafted piece of writing into a work of art. Learn your lesson well, and someday you may see your title on that coveted space of a best-seller list.

¶

When God Says Wait
Janelle Clare Schneider

Writing comes from our souls. Because we want to please God with all we do, we're particularly vulnerable with our writing. More than anything, we offer it as our gift to him, our effort to share the miracle of grace. In fact, we have a sense of calling about this task. Rejection strikes not only at our sense of professional ability, but even deeper, at our sense of what God wants us to do.

These words don't come lightly. My own writing career started so quickly and easily that I was afraid to tell any other writers about it. It didn't seem to me that I'd paid my dues, and I didn't want unpublished writers thinking my path was typical. However, it's now been over five years since I've been under contract. For a while, my writing had to take a backseat to my personal needs and the needs of my family. Since I've resumed writing, I've been unable to acquire anything more than rejection letters, everything from the form "no thank you" to "I really enjoyed reading this story, but it's not right for us."

So what are some ways to use this "waiting time" effectively?

First and foremost, we must keep writing. If this is something we're called to do, not just a little hobby, we can't give up on it no matter how discouraged we feel. Continuing to work at our craft is

RETHINKING REJECTION

Like it or not (and usually we don't), rejection is part of the writing life. No matter how we sugarcoat it, *rejection* is synonymous with *ouch*. Keep rejection from becoming a disaster by viewing it as a stepping-stone rather than a barricade.

The first step in doing that is to change your goal from "getting published" to "glorifying God." Publishing can bring satisfaction, but it is not the key to lifelong joy and fulfillment. That comes only from obeying God's call on your life. So write for God first and publishers second, and I guarantee that you will grow . . . as a writer, and also as a Christian.

Also, don't take a rejection too personally. *You* aren't being rejected; your *story* just doesn't "fit." Did you research the publisher's current needs? Good stories are sometimes rejected for lack of a place to put them. Or maybe you've chosen the right publisher, but they've just contracted something similar. If you receive positive feedback along with the rejection, celebrate those strokes and send the story out again.

Maybe now just isn't your time. Many writers wait years to see their first manuscript accepted; and most will tell you, in retrospect, the timing was perfect. So remember God is able to see the big picture. Trust your heavenly Father with the timing, and keep trying.

Now, here's a tough thought to swallow: maybe *you* aren't ready personally. Being published is wonderful in many ways, but it brings its own challenges. You may face unfavorable reviews, low sales, or contest losses. It can be overwhelming to face deadlines, editors, marketing, and readers while at the same time trying to meet the needs of your family. Spend time in prayer *now* asking God to prepare you for the challenges and demands ahead. Those will be hours well spent.

Yes, rejection is painful, but there are no wasted steps in a God-directed journey. If God has called you to write, there is a purpose for that call, and the Lord has his reasons for moving at the pace he does. If you will remember that God has it all under control, then he can take that disappointment and use it to mold you into a stronger, more usable vessel.   *—Kim Vogel Sawyer* an expression of our love for Jesus. Write because you love him. Write because you love the words. Write because you can't *not* write.

Find a genre, a cause, an inspirational thought, anything that makes the words start pushing to get out. Write for the pure joy of it. When the initial push of enthusiasm is expended, go back and edit. Make the piece as good as you possibly can. Whether that piece ever attracts an editor or not, the process of writing it will hone your skills.

Volunteer writing assignments can assist in this. They come with deadlines—perhaps more flexible than a contract might demand, but deadlines just the same. Meeting your commitments keeps your "writing muscles" in shape.

Spend some time reading, too. Read as many how-to books on writing as you can. Read novels in your chosen genre and figure out what makes them work. No effort expended on developing your writing potential is ever wasted.

Do something that feeds your creativity in other ways. I know very few writers who express themselves exclusively through their words. Some paint. Others do carpentry. I like to quilt and to scrapbook. Since neither of these activities generates an income, they have become my "play." There's nothing like some carefree play to lift the mists of discouragement.

Stay in touch with other writers. Whether this is one other writer friend, a critique group, or an online group, the contact with others who share our passion is important. Their daily struggles with deadlines, editors, and "just don't feel like writing today" keep us in touch with our own writer souls.

But a word of caution here: when in the company of other writers, it's all too easy to play the comparison game. We must remember that our success ultimately lies in God's hands. When I compare myself to another, I begin to doubt God's wisdom and sovereignty.

Find ways to give back to the writing community. Offer to judge a contest. Mentor a writer with less experience than yourself. Perhaps offer to assist in organizing a workshop for your writers' group, or work as a volunteer for a local writing conference. Find a way of investing in the writing world beyond your own computer.

Finally, remember whom we're writing for. God is the one who gave the calling, and he's the one who will determine how that calling best expresses itself. It's all about his purpose, not our own. Whether we're ever published or not, may we each someday hear him say, "Well done, good and faithful servant."

WRITING CHRISTIAN FICTION

PART THREE >

CHAPTER 13

DISCERNING YOUR CALLING

¶

How I Felt God Calling Me to Write for Him
Robin Lee Hatcher

In my early career as a novelist, I was a believer but I wasn't walking in obedience to the Lord. However, in the early nineties, my heart went through a restoration process as Jesus drew me back into close fellowship with him. As I grew closer to God, I became less and less comfortable with the books I'd written for the general market. There was little difference between what I wrote and what someone who didn't know Christ might write.

However, I was nervous about making a major career change. Was it necessary for me to leave my publisher and change my career focus? "God, can't I reach more lost people with a Christian worldview in my secular books than I can writing for those who are already Christians? Isn't writing for the Christian market preaching to the choir?"

To which he answered, "Yes. And the choir is sick."

How could I argue with that, since it was a perfect description of me?

As God was changing my passion for what I wanted to write, he was also bringing me into contact with more Christian writers and editors. I began to ask him to make it clear to me what I was supposed to do, what stories he wanted me to tell. For months I prayed the same thing: "Show me, Lord, what I'm to do. Make it clear to me." I needed to know without question what path I was to take.

One Sunday at church, two missionaries from Sri Lanka were

AN INTERVIEW WITH FRANCINE RIVERS: CALLING

You are one of the pioneers of Christian fiction. What challenges did you face writing for a fairly new market?

I would not call myself a pioneer. Lloyd C. Douglas was there before me; Lew Wallace, who wrote *Ben-Hur*. Then later Bodie Thoene, Frank Peretti—they were in the market before I was, and it was a great inspiration to me to see that they were great writers. They brought "reality" back into Christian fiction and opened the door for all the rest of us. I was just in the door early on. Other doors were closed to me, and this one opened.

I think I was plucked out of the general market and put into Christian fiction at just the right time. I think we see God beginning to work in all of the arts—not just books, but also music, movies, painting, artwork.

What has been the biggest challenge in your career?

Finding the answers. When I start a book, I have the question, but I have no clue where I'm going to go with it. In my pre-Christian life, I could lay out a plan, a formula, a story. But with the kind of writing I'm doing now, I don't know where that question's going to take me. I need to get out of my own way and go where God's taking me. I'm learning that now through a personal speaking to us, and when one of them quoted Ephesians 2:10 (NASB)—"For we are His workmanship, created in Christ Jesus for good works, which God prepared beforehand so that we would walk in them"—I heard God say into my heart, as distinctly as any audible voice, that not only had he already prepared the good works for me to do, but that those good works were beyond anything I had imagined or hoped for or dreamed of. I knew then that he was opening that final door to a ministry of writing stories that would glorify him, and all I had to do was step through it.

At that moment, I lost my fear of changing the direction of my

situation in my family too. "Letting go and letting God" is probably the hardest lesson I'll ever learn in this life. And I'll be learning it one day at a time as long as I live.

What has been the most satisfying moment of your writing career?
Every book has one. Every book has an epiphany moment, where I realize, "Oh, that's why! That's the answer! That's the lesson God has for me." It may take an entire year to get to that point. One scene from *An Echo in the Darkness* stands out in my mind—the scene with Hadassah at Julia's deathbed. When Julia said, "How can I not believe in Jesus after seeing what he did for you?" my character spoke words that didn't come from me: "He didn't keep me alive for me, he kept me alive for you." God's heart was fixed upon Julia. I got goose bumps; I knew that was the lesson God had for me. Why are we Christians here in this world, where we so obviously don't fit in? We're here to be salt and light, to point the way to Christ. We know that in our head, but that day I knew it in my heart and my spirit. That's why I write—to get to that epiphany moment to receive God's answer for why I'm working on this particular project.

career. That was because I would no longer be writing books to please myself. I would be writing books to please God and trusting him to use them as he willed.

I cannot claim that leaving behind a career in the general market to enter a writing ministry has been smooth and easy. There have been successes and failures, highs and lows, joys and disappointments. Occasionally fears and doubts have raised their ugly heads. But knowing I am where God placed me, that I'm doing the work he called me to do, keeps me moving forward and looking upward with trust.

I have heard unpublished novelists say that God wouldn't have given them the desire to write if he didn't mean for them to be published. I don't know how to respond to that kind of statement, I suppose because I know too many unpublished writers who have worked hard at their craft, who have talent, and yet have not been able to make that first sale. But what I can say is this: If God has called you to write, you need to write and then leave it up to the Lord what he does with it. He may have a reason for your writing that you cannot even conceive at this point.

I have learned something in my thirty-plus years as a Christian (and have had it driven home by my wonderful pastor). The three most important things in life are these: (1) Come to know the God who created you; (2) discover why he created you; and (3) then do it for all you're worth for the rest of your life.

As believers who feel called to write, our first desire shouldn't be publication but to be in the center of God's will. Seek that first and the rest will take care of itself.

¶

Writing: Ministry or Profession?
Rene Gutteridge

I've come to find, after nearly a decade of working as a Christian novelist, that balance is often key to happiness, but definition is key to sanity.

What I mean is that it took me a very long time to come to peace about what exactly it was that I was doing. Early on, I had grand expectations: I would write my books; they would be lightly edited, then published, sent out to hundreds (of thousands . . . like I said, I dream big) of stores, and gobbled up by adoring fans eager to be entertained while also getting the side benefit of being spiritually enriched. That, ladies and gentlemen, was going to be my ministry.

I soon came to learn that you don't actually always get to write what you want. Turns out, *I* was not the only factor to be considered when publishing a book.

Huh.

The more I became immersed in the business of professional writing, the more I wondered where, exactly, the ministry was going. Suddenly, it wasn't as simple as writing with purpose.

It turns out writing is a small part of the whole deal, which can be very hard for a writer to take, because generally we're not very good at other things, like talking with nonimaginary people about nonimaginary problems.

Writers can get pretty comfortable hiding in our little and dark caves, wrestling with the challenges of the craft, hurtling to new simile-usage heights, expanding our vocabulary by playing online Scrabble.

But we quickly learn we can't hide in a cave. There are decisions to be made, beyond whether or not we should kill Frank on Tuesday, and if his wife or a stalker should off him.

You're going to be expected to make contact with the outside world and make decisions about money and rights and foreign trade. You're going to end up disagreeing about the color of the title on the cover. And when you suggest that perhaps purple might be appealing, you could very well find yourself on a conference call with the editor, publicist, art director, and your agent. And if you do indeed find yourself on a conference call, you're expected to add to the conversation and not just sit there and breathe heavily while trying to type quietly because you just came up with some witty dialogue for the scene you really wish you could be working on.

Or, perhaps, you find yourself with two really good offers from two really good publishing houses. Your agent assures you that you cannot offer chapters 1 through 14 to one house and 15 through 28 to the other so nobody's feelings are hurt.

I don't want to have to make these decisions! I'm in this for the ministry!

I'm a writer, of the godly sort! I pray and I read the Word and I write what the Holy Spirit puts on my heart. I'm often divinely inspired on a daily basis, and climbing down the mountain to discuss such trivial matters as contracts and copyrights sort of takes the shine out of the shekinah glory, you know? It seems irreverent to a writer. We worship God and we hold the craft in high esteem. The craft, we are quite sure, does not include sales projections on mass-market books. And where does a bidding war fit into ministry?

Ministry is from the spirit and the soul, uninterested in production costs and market trends. We are about matters of the heart. We like to pull all that information out of your head, needle it straight into your main artery, and cause you to feel things you never thought possible.

Our expectation is that we will change your life by the words we write, the stories we create, the characters we mold out of blood, sweat, and tears.

Once upon a time, the business of being a professional writer caused me great conflict. I found myself constantly worried about the ministry value of addendums and escalating pay scales and corporation taxes. While my mind wandered toward the unbelievable list of write-offs writers are afforded, my conscience worked overtime reminding me that it's not about money.

No, it is absolutely not about money. Except my insurance premium just topped a thousand dollars. But money doesn't matter. I'd do this for free.

No, I wouldn't. I really wouldn't.

I would've, back in 1994. Truly.

But now, I can't.

Or won't?

I'm depraved and wretched. What business do I have in ministry?

See? I'm just giving you a little taste of the agony.

That is, before lightning struck me at Target.

Lightning strikes get such a bad rap, but it turns out they're not always deadly and you can get a jolt more effective than an energy drink. I was driving to Target to spend the money I shouldn't be making from the craft that can't be busied with business when I realized that what I needed was a definition for what I do.

Is it ministry?

Or is it a profession?

And can it be both?

Oddly I came to a pretty quick conclusion for myself. It cannot be both.

Yes, business can certainly have ministry value, but I could never make the two work together. Because every time I made a decision that benefited me in some way, I felt guilty that it was not benefiting someone else. It was like trying to push two opposing magnets together.

Perhaps someone with a healthier sense of perspective could navigate through the maze of ministry and profession, but I have a sensitive conscience, and I found that I could not do this without overeating at some point during the day.

So I created a definition for what I do. And once I had that in place, I began using that definition to help me make the decisions that I needed to make. I immediately stopped calling my writing "ministry."

Relief swept over me, and I decided I could actually go look at my royalty statements with a more critical eye.

But wasn't it more than just a profession?

Yes, it was. And that's where I carefully formed these words: *my writing is a profession I've given to God.*

That was it. Almost immediately I found ministry again. It came from the strangest places, like critiquing a manuscript for free because someone didn't have enough money to pay for a critique otherwise. I started pen palling with female prisoners, finding great joy in corresponding with a delightful woman who has an amazing ability to tell stories. I offer to answer questions from struggling writers and volunteer my time writing drama for church. I give books away!

All this felt so freeing because nothing was involved except the pure joy of helping another soul.

And with that set aside and in its proper place, I could grab ahold of this business called writing and delicately maneuver through the craft and the contracts, all the while remembering that I have given this profession to God. He guides me; he sustains me; he gives me wisdom. He allows me to have a good financial year or provides when I have not made enough to pay the smallest of bills. I can be charitable and savvy and live with myself all at the same time. I can make good business practices glorify God. And I can take my craft to the level that is good for business.

My expectations weren't wrong! They just needed a little reshaping, some definition. Sanity is tacked down and in place.

Now, back to my cave.

CHAPTER 14

DISTINCTIVES OF CHRISTIAN FICTION

¶

What Makes Christian Fiction Christian?
Ron Benrey

The seemingly simple question, What makes a Christian novel Christian? is surprisingly difficult to answer. I discovered this paradoxical truism several years ago, when no one in my fiction critique group could define the essential requirements for a successful Christian novel.

Oh, most of us could recognize an authentic Christian novel when we read one, but "I know it when I see it" doesn't offer much guidance for first-time novelists who want to write Christian fiction that publishers and readers will buy.

As I searched for a more useful answer, I found that my local public library—not my local Christian bookstore—provided the most comprehensive definition of Christian fiction:

- Stories about people, places, and times of the Bible told from the perspective of the Christian religion
- Romance novels written from a similarly religious point of view
- Contemporary stories in which the characters' Christian faith is tested by the challenges of real-world issues
- Stories that emphasize a Christian way of thinking in the plot

At the time, this collection of statements struck me as true, but I eventually concluded that most are too vague to be helpful—chiefly because they can apply to mainstream fiction as well. Many secular novels have Christian themes; many have religious perspectives; many retell stories from the Bible; many star Christian protagonists—including more than a few that feature Jesus Christ in a leading role.

More research—and lots of pondering—eventually led me to conclude that Christian fiction has two characteristics that are so universal we can treat them as requirements when we begin to write a Christian novel: an explicit Christian message and an ultimately Christian worldview.

SENDING A CHRISTIAN MESSAGE

The message your novel sends is the Christian teaching that you want readers to take away when they read your novel. If you prefer, it's the "Christian moral" of the tale you've told.

For example, countless Christian novels teach readers to "let go and let God." They depict protagonists who stubbornly—and foolishly—insist on doing things their way until a crisis finally forces them to turn over their lives to God.

Other popular Christian messages include the following:

- A sinful person gains salvation by trusting Jesus Christ as his Lord and Savior.
- Every human being—even a contemptible villain—is redeemable by God.
- Faith in God will help a person get out from under the guilt or shame that has been holding her back.
- There's reason to have hope in the future, because though evil does exist, good will eventually triumph.
- It's beneficial to forgive wrongs and grievances—and to show love for neighbors and enemies.
- God answers sincere prayers—although the answers may be surprising.
- The "foolishness" of the gospel makes sense.

You can spend a lifetime writing novels that tell wholly different stories yet deliver the same Christian message book after book. When my wife, Janet, and I planned a three- or four-book series, we often zeroed in on a single message for all of the novels. This set the stage for us to examine the teaching from a different perspective in each story. On the other hand, many successful novelists switch messages along with story lines.

WORLDVIEW IN ACTION

Everyone has a worldview—you, me, and the various characters in our novels. Worldview is the collection of beliefs and assumptions that we apply—usually without thinking about them—when we interpret the world around us and interact with other people.

Christian fiction should demonstrate the Christian worldview in action—through the thoughts and deeds of key characters and via the ultimate direction of the story. A Christian worldview will reflect the following beliefs:

- There is a Creator God who created the universe and is ultimately in control.
- Humans were created in the image of God and have innate value; each of us was put on earth for a purpose.
- God has revealed absolute truths and established moral absolutes.
- God loves humankind, seeks a personal relationship with each of us, and redeemed the world by entering his creation in the person of Jesus Christ.

On the flip side of the coin, a truly Christian worldview will preclude some of the popular plot twists used in secular novels, which often affirm the non-Christian idea that a noble end justifies an ugly means:

- A hero who happily lies, cheats, or steals to accomplish his purpose
- A heroine who cheerfully revenges a past wrong done to her
- A hero who has flexible definitions of right and wrong—and is willing to act as cruelly as the villain if that's what it takes to win

Avoid Unrealistic Christianity and Christians

It's possible, alas, to go too far in the other direction and present an unrealistic picture of an ostensibly Christian worldview. In those situations, the novel's message becomes wildly improbable and, at times, theologically doubtful.

- Some novels depict God as a cosmic vending machine: The hero says a quick prayer and *zap*, God provides an instant and complete solution to his problems.
- Other novels are populated with Christian characters who are all-knowing, even-tempered, consistently forgiving, and sympathetic to all—veritable fonts of *agape*.
- Still others show us impossibly wise Christians who change the hearts and minds of intransigent characters merely by quoting a handy verse of Scripture.

Real life and good fiction don't work this way. Prayers may not be answered, and Christians are not necessarily wise, nice, or loving. Moreover, we're following in Jesus' footsteps when we invent stories that communicate Christian teachings. He used stories to teach, advocate, and inspire—and he never candy-coated his parables to make them more convincing.

Fast-Changing Worldviews

There are many competing worldviews in circulation today—including several that encourage selfishness, greed, and cruelty to others. It's not unusual to see a key character in a Christian novel begin with a decidedly non-Christian outlook and move toward a strong Christian worldview at the end of the story. This is perfectly acceptable Christian storytelling.

A real person's worldview can take decades to shift, but fictional characters are often required to do rapid worldview pirouettes during the relatively short-term crises they experience. Readers will accept fast-breaking change—if writers make the accelerated turnabouts seem plausible happenings rather than merely convenient plot devices.

How do you do this? The best way to study the techniques is to read successful Christian novels and see how their authors achieved credible worldview shifts. One common trick is to show that the protagonist has previously considered a different frame of mind but hasn't acted on it yet.

An interesting related question is how a Christian worldview finds its way into a novel. Some writers argue that a Christian novelist automatically writes with a Christian worldview. I'm part of the

AVOIDING PREACHY FICTION

Fiction can capture a reader's mind and emotions with vivid illustrations of spiritual truth. As Christian writers we want our stories to honor God, but the line between storytelling and sermonizing is a fine one. When we cross that line, we risk alienating our readers and diluting the message we care so deeply about. By employing a few simple techniques, we can successfully blend our fiction and our faith without becoming didactic.

- Keep a proper focus in mind. A novel becomes preachy when the author's desire to make a point becomes more important than telling an entertaining story. Fiction can teach profound lessons, but only when it also satisfies the reader's desire to be entertained.
- A person's actions speak louder than words, and that is true in fiction as well as in real life. A character's actions will make a lasting impact on a reader long after his or her words have been forgotten.
- Dialogue *can* be used effectively to explore a story's message. But when one character launches into a diatribe directed at another character, readers assume (and rightly so) that the lecture is really directed at them. To avoid this, writers should make every piece of dialogue consistent with the character's behavior and relevant to the plot.
- Be especially careful with characters who are clergy. Fiction readers tend to skip lengthy sermons and prayers. As a general rule, keep sermons, prayers, and Scripture references brief. To ensure that the

group that disagrees; I need to keep worldview firmly in mind when I design a story line, or else my characters—who tend to reflect human values—may veer to the "dark side" without my permission.

Don't Preach to Readers

It was legendary movie mogul Samuel Goldwyn who reportedly said, "If you want to send a message, call Western Union." Goldwyn recognized that moviemakers—and by extension, novelists—often

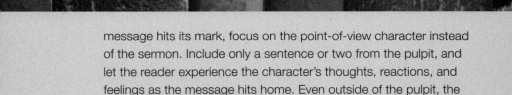

message hits its mark, focus on the point-of-view character instead of the sermon. Include only a sentence or two from the pulpit, and let the reader experience the character's thoughts, reactions, and feelings as the message hits home. Even outside of the pulpit, the tone of the fictional preacher will be interpreted by readers as directed toward them.

- Profound spiritual truths are often communicated through the use of symbolism and metaphor—in large and small ways. An allegory of our Christian walk or a retelling of a biblical story can be very effective in communicating a spiritual message. Symbolism can also be used on a smaller scale to illustrate a point.
- Readers love subtlety. Explanations destroy subtlety. In elaborating a point, the author diminishes the impact of the message and may even cheat the reader out of the chance to have a profoundly personal experience.
- Incorporate a spiritual element. A good Christian novel is not merely an entertaining story in which the characters stop every so often to whisper a prayer. The best and most effective Christian novels have a spiritual element woven so intricately into the story that if the element were removed, there would be no story left. —*Virginia Smith*

become destructively preachy when they try to say something "deep" in their creative works. Moviegoers (and readers) are likely to tune out or get annoyed when a disconnected sermon pops up in the middle of a story. The critics of early Christian novels complained that they were often more tract than action, more propaganda than entertainment.

The Christian fiction you write must avoid the trap of overt preaching but still communicate a distinctly Christian teaching to your readers. You perform this seeming magic trick by integrating the Christian message within each story rather than tacking it on top as some sort of religious afterthought.

I find the best way to accomplish this is to design a Christian subplot, using the same plotting model I use to architect the main plot. I focus on effective storytelling and trust that evangelizing will follow.

A GROWING RELATIONSHIP WITH GOD

Regardless of your story line, regardless of the Christian message you deliver, it's probable that one or more key characters in your novel will experience an improving relationship with God. This is a staple of Christian fiction. In fact, not long ago, every Christian novel included at least one conversion scene that showed a focus character accepting Christ. These days, few Christian publishers require conversion scenes in the novels they publish—most will accept stories that show progress in a lead character's Christian walk.

A familiar variation on the theme is the hero or heroine who enters the novel as a weakly committed Christian and—challenged by the story line forces, encouraged by companions who are solid believers—becomes a stronger Christian over the course of the story.

Despite changed editorial requirements, many Christian authors

I know still insist on incorporating full-blown conversion scenes in their novels. They argue that readers want and expect this climactic moment in a story that's genuinely Christian, and that anything less leaves the story incomplete.

The good news is that you get to choose the depth of growth in your character's relationship with God when you write Christian fiction. If a conversion scene doesn't suit your story, you don't have to include one. If it does, honor a fine old literary tradition and develop a powerful example for your novel.

¶

Writing the Nuances
of Christian Content in Fiction
Randy Singer

A powerful story without a biblical worldview is a great escape to nowhere. But a spiritual message without an entertaining story is a sermon, not a novel. A strong story should leave readers asking important questions, and one of the primary goals of my writing is to show biblical truth in a way that will resonate with both believers and those who are not yet Christians.

Does that mean my characters have to be Christians or have to become Christians during the course of the story? Not necessarily. But on a spectrum of spirituality, my stories should move readers incrementally closer to God. This can be done by raising spiritual questions, by painting spiritual allegories, by illustrating spiritual concepts, and yes, by writing dramatic conversion scenes (though one must be careful to avoid unrealistic, oversimplified, or clichéd conversions).

Spiritual journeys in real life are messy, episodic, nuanced, and unpredictable—more of a roller coaster than a rocket ship. Our fiction should reflect this—a call to write with all the shades of gray that we see in real life. But the trick is to do this in a way that doesn't compromise the black-and-white message of the gospel.

In one of my recent books, *By Reason of Insanity*, for example, I tried to address an issue that is becoming increasingly important in our culture. Many unbelievers don't believe in the supernatural at all. If something can't be explained through logic or the scientific method, it doesn't exist. The main point of this book was to show that a spiritual dimension exists and cannot be explained away. I was trying to nudge readers off the far end of the spiritual spectrum, to at least raise questions about the existence of a spiritual dimension. But I didn't stop there. I also wanted to show what it's like when someone is willing to sacrifice their own future for somebody they love and take the punishment for that person. This, of course, is what Christ did for each of us.

My two main characters in this book are both unbelievers. Quinn is a most unlikely person to show what grace means. He's a Vegas lawyer who gambles and drinks. But he struggles with the same skepticism that many unbelievers do, and I thought readers who haven't yet come to know Christ might identify with him. By the end of the story, Quinn can't deny there is a supernatural and spiritual realm, though he has no dramatic conversion experience.

Yet Quinn is the one who sacrifices his future for somebody he loves. A gambling Vegas lawyer as a Christ figure? Yes! Why did I choose him? Because I hoped that my unbelieving readers would identify with Quinn's struggles and personalize his triumph. And maybe in this process they would understand a most important biblical truth: "Greater love has no one than this, that he lay down his life for his friends" (John 15:13).

We also see God begin a real work in the life of my other main character. Granted, Catherine doesn't become a believer by the story's end. I have written many conversion scenes in previous books and don't hesitate to do so if it feels natural to the story. But in this case, it would have felt forced if I had brought Catherine's spiritual journey to a conclusion. By the end of the book, she knows she needs to start trusting God. She knows that The Revealer of Mysteries (a phrase used to describe God in the book of Daniel) is at work in her life. She has learned that God loves her and has been pursuing her. This seemed like a natural, realistic place to end the story.

Some readers might be bothered by this. *What happened to Catherine? Did she become a Christian? How can you leave us hanging?* But did you ever notice that the Master Storyteller sometimes left us hanging as well? What about the older brother in the story of the Prodigal Son? Did he reconcile with his younger brother? Did he heed his father's advice or continue pouting? Apparently Jesus thought it was more important to raise the right questions than to provide all the answers.

Another lesson we learn from the Master Storyteller is that important spiritual truths can often be conveyed through secondary characters. In the story I've been discussing, the two main characters are balanced by several secondary characters, both good and bad. Rosemarie is an expert witness and friend of Quinn's and, in my mind, the moral center of the story. She has a strong knowledge of Scripture and helps the reader understand some difficult

Old Testament passages. She tries hard to keep Quinn from doing immoral or unethical things (often without success), and in a critical scene, she helps Catherine make a personal connection to Christ's ultimate sacrifice on the cross.

At the other end of the character spectrum, Harold is a fundamentalist preacher who sheds an unfortunate but realistic negative light on Christians. He protests at newsworthy events, spewing judgmental diatribes at attendees. Similar incidents in real life have made national news, such as when Dr. Fred Phelps and his church members have picketed military funerals and said hateful things.

This is an image Christians must overcome in order to share the

AN INTERVIEW WITH FRANCINE RIVERS: DISTINCTIVES

You handle some tough subjects in your novels. Redeeming Love *and the* Mark of the Lion *series covered some gritty issues, and you've also dealt with the abortion issue in* The Atonement Child. *Did you experience resistance from publishers?*

With *Redeeming Love*, there was lots of resistance. The editor I'd been working with for years said no way, it had too much to do with God. I don't know how many times that book was submitted before it was finally accepted by a Christian editor at Bantam. She got resistance too, and it was still a while before it was published. They didn't know where to put it. Then when I got the rights back a few years ago, there was resistance from the Christian publishers due to the subject matter.

A Voice in the Wind was turned down a number of times by publishers who didn't believe I was a Christian. There were some rather hurtful letters, and understandably so. They would say, "We've looked at her work, and none of her work is Christian, so we don't want to have anything to do with her." Finally one publisher at least flew me in to talk face-to-face. They initially asked if I'd be willing to use a pen name and dissociate myself from my previous gospel with credibility. Why shouldn't we acknowledge that this image is out there—unfortunately caused by those who don't really reflect the true love and grace of Christ? Did Jesus call out the hypocrisy in some of the religious leaders of his day, or did he pretend it didn't exist?

By acknowledging this problem and showing it, we can contrast Harold's judgmental actions with the sincere and credible witness of someone like Rosemarie. The point is not to ridicule Christianity, but to help unbelievers understand that persons like Dr. Phelps do not reflect the true spirit of Christ.

At heart, the themes addressed in the world's greatest literature—justice, forgiveness, self-sacrifice, hope, and love, among others—are

work. I said no, but I was willing to talk about where I came from and why. I was concerned that if I changed my name and people did some research and found out what I'd written before, they would feel like I was lying about who I was. When I explained that, the publisher agreed, and the executive who had brought up the idea eventually became one of my strongest supporters.

I ended up getting a lot of spiritual and emotional support from my publisher while I was writing *The Atonement Child*. That involved a lot of difficult writing, dealing with my own abortion back in college.

Can you give prospective authors any suggestions on how to write honestly about tough subjects for a Christian market?
Don't be afraid to walk through the darkness. God is with you there, too. Some of the hardest writing I've had to do has taken me back to things I didn't want to relive. But God can take the worst in your life and use it to his good purposes. As King David says in 1 Chronicles 28:20 (NLT), "Be strong and courageous, and do the work. Don't be afraid or discouraged, for the Lord God, my God, is with you." God won't forsake you.

all spiritual themes. Our job is to help readers look at them from a biblical perspective. To do so, it's not necessary that we pound readers over the head with Bible verses. Sometimes a flawed character in a compelling story can personify God's truth in a way that will penetrate the mind and speak to the heart.

God is pursuing the real-life Catherines and Quinns, helping them to see beyond the shallow caricatures of Christianity to a real God who loves them and will use any means possible to break through their intellectual defenses and help them understand the love of Christ. Often he uses friends or sermons or circumstances. But sometimes he uses stories.

¶

Closing the Bedroom Door
Terri Blackstock

When you write a Christian novel, you make an implied covenant with your readers to give them a clean story, one that doesn't put a stumbling block before them. They can read the book without guilt and pass it on to their teenage children without worrying about the content. But if we're writing about real-life marriages and authentic relationships, should the sexual element be left out entirely? How can we write true to life without crossing the line?

For the first thirteen years of my writing career, I wrote secular romance novels. Because I wasn't walking closely with Christ, I pushed the boundaries of my Christian conscience and wrote books that were filled with graphic sex. Eventually I realized I wasn't using my gift the way God intended, and in fact, I was writing stories that graphically depicted sin in such a way that it caused my readers to sin. In 1993 I repented and gave my career to the Lord. From that point on, I vowed to write only things that glorified him.

When I started my first Christian novel, I leaned too far the other way. In my zeal to glorify God with my work, I avoided sexual chemistry like the plague, as though it didn't exist for Christians. Fortunately I had a great editor who showed me that my books should depict real people with real relationships that have real challenges in the real world.

I came to understand the difference between authenticity and titillation. Secular romance novels are designed to titillate the reader. But a Christian novel, whatever the genre, shouldn't make the reader feel defiled in any way. As a writer who's inviting my readers to enter a world I've created, I have a responsibility not to lead them into scenes with graphic images that put lust in their hearts.

But by the same token, I don't want to imply that Christian husbands and wives have chaste relationships, or that people who are in love and *not* married never have temptations. To keep scenes from being flat and characters from being cardboard, I have to portray human feelings. If a plot calls for a love scene between a married man and woman, then I do what they did in the movies before 1960—I simply close the bedroom door when I get to the threshold between kissing and intercourse. It's easy to suggest the intimacy of a healthy marriage without planting images in the reader's mind.

But what about characters who aren't married? It's not realistic to pretend that they don't have hormones or that they never feel sexual chemistry. In that case, I don't close the bedroom door. I just make sure they avoid the bedroom entirely. I acknowledge that they feel that chemistry taking over, then pull them apart, either through a ringing phone or a knock on the door or through their own Christian consciences kicking in.

In *River's Edge*, my characters Blair and Cade are desperately in love. Their chemistry has built over three books in the series, and they're very much drawn to each other. It would be foolish and unrealistic to pretend they don't have sexual feelings. But Cade is a man of deep integrity, and he's a strong Christian. He stops them before they go too far.

> After a moment, he got up and followed her into the kitchen. Leaning against the counter, he watched her fuss over putting ice in the glass. He met her eyes and saw her swallow. Then she looked away and let her hair fall back along her face.
>
> If only she understood how beautiful she was.
>
> "Come here." He took her hand and pulled her toward him. She came, looking up at him with those wide eyes that seemed so uncertain—even a little afraid—as if she might be misreading his interest and making a fool of herself.
>
> Slowly, he bent down and slid his fingers through her hair, against her soft neck. Her pulse raced against his fingertips as she melted in that kiss. She caused a longing deep inside him, a sweet homesick pull for some home he'd never had. It made him ache.
>
> When the kiss broke, he kept his forehead against hers and let that ache linger.

It wasn't safe, the two of them here . . . alone like this, with these feelings that seemed bigger than the strength he had.

"I'd better go."

"Why?" Her question was a breath against his lips.

"Because I really want to stay."*

His decision to let his Christianity triumph over his hormones makes him more heroic in the reader's eyes, and their longing makes the romantic part of this plot more compelling. When a relationship is not consummated and the chemistry is allowed to build, the readers want to keep turning the pages, and their emotions are impacted instead of their hormones.

But there are times when your story will call for you to delve a little deeper in your depiction of intimacy. In 2 Samuel 11, we're told of David's relations with Bathsheba. In Genesis 38, we're told of Judah's relations with his daughter-in-law, who disguises herself as a prostitute. But in neither case is the reader given cause to lust or fantasize about what happened. The Scriptures include these situations to teach an important lesson about sin and its consequences. If you have some greater purpose, you may find it necessary to be a little more descriptive.

Elizabeth White chose to do this in her novel *Off the Record*. Her hero, Cole, is remembering the night he eloped with his wife, due mainly to hormones after a night of drinking. The author gives a very clear sense of what happened without dragging the reader through the sinful details, and Cole recalls it with a sense of shame.

---

* Terri Blackstock, *River's Edge* (Grand Rapids, MI: Zondervan, 2004), 116.

Now he knew for sure why she'd eloped with him. . . . The simple truth was she'd been a twentysomething daddy's girl blind with grief and some obscure form of survivor's guilt. So blind she'd turned to the first presentable male to pour a couple of Hurricanes down her at Pat O'Brien's and offer a comforting shoulder.

Not that he'd had any intention of moving past the stage of rumpled sheets in a cheap hotel. His intentions, however, rammed full-tilt into the reality. Even with her considerable brainpower overcome by alcohol, there were some things Laurel wouldn't do without a ring on her finger and her name on a license.

And Cole had found himself so consumed by lust and selfishness—not to mention copious quantities of rum and fruit juice—that he'd figured it would all work out in the end. . . .

He should have known. If he'd learned anything growing up in the shadow of Yoknapatawpha County it was that . . . at the end of it all you might not see the truth until you woke up stone-cold sober in a New Orleans hotel with a long-legged, angry redhead in your bed and a paper cigar band on your finger.*

The readers come away from this scene knowing the marriage was the result of drunken lust, but they get the picture without seeing the sinful details, and their mind isn't drawn into their own lustful fantasy.

Robin Lee Hatcher, in her book *The Forgiving Hour*, tells the

---

* Elizabeth White, *Off the Record* (Grand Rapids, MI: Zondervan, 2007), 245-246.

story of a woman forced to forgive the woman who had an affair with her husband. In a love scene between Dave (a married man) and Sara (who doesn't know he's married), Robin's intention was to show the consequences of following passion without thought.

> It had to be fate, their meeting. They were meant for each other. So why wait?
>
> "I've never known anyone like you," he whispered in her ear. "No woman's ever made me feel this way before."
>
> He thought she was a woman. Wouldn't he see her as a mere girl if she denied him what he so obviously wanted? They belonged together. Waiting wouldn't change that.
>
> "Sara?"
>
> "Yes."
>
> It was more than a response to her name. It was a decision. It was inevitable that they become lovers, and now was surely the time.*

Robin breaks the scene here, closing the bedroom door to the reader. Then, in a later scene, she opens it again to show the aftermath.

> Sara felt Dave sliding away from her and stirred in her sleep. "Mmm," she mumbled. "Where are you going?"
>
> "It's time I left for home."

---

* Robin Lee Hatcher, *The Forgiving Hour* (Colorado Springs, CO: Waterbrook Press, 1999), 60-61.

Opening her eyes, she made out his form, sitting up on the side of the bed. She reached out, touched his back with her fingertips.

"You should have told me this was your first time, Sara." There was a hint of accusation in his voice.

"I didn't think it would matter. Did it?"

Without answering, he rose from the bed and started to dress.

Even though she couldn't see him clearly in the dark bedroom, Sara blushed and glanced away, embarrassed. Now that the sweeping passion was over, now that she was fully awake, she experienced her first wave of guilt and shame. She pulled the sheet up to cover her nakedness.*

Instead of a graphic description of an intimate and sinful act, Robin gives us a graphic description of the guilt and shame that follow. This plays into Sara's character and ultimately into the Christian message of the book. Yes, the scene is one of sin and deception, but Robin was careful not to plant graphic images in the readers' minds.

In Tosca Lee's novel *Havah: The Story of Eve*, she describes the unabashed intimacy between Adam and Eve before and after the Fall with more sensual imagery than most Christian novels because of the subject matter and the overall message of the book. In this scene, she avoids a play-by-play of their intercourse and instead focuses on their frenzy in devouring the forbidden fruit, their emotions as they freefall from grace, and the eternal consequences to come.

---

* *The Forgiving Hour*, 62.

Perhaps my hand trembled as I held it out. Perhaps I already knew. Either way, I ate and then gave it to him.

He ate.

That is it.

We fell upon the tree like hungry locusts, never knowing when the serpent left.

We shared them between us, throwing one away before we finished it, plucking another, if only to take a single bite, licking lips and fingers—our own and each other's. I had wanted him earlier—I claimed him now. We fell together, the night renewed between us by day, twining in the sunlight the way we had in the darkness.

Having done, we lay in the shade of that tree, beneath the climbing sun, and slept the sleep of the dead.*

That scene leaves me with a chill, and my mind lingers not on the sensual act of Adam and Eve as they fall, but on the eternal consequence of their disobedience and the "sleep of the dead."

Ultimately each publisher has its own restrictions, and each story its own requirements. The downfall of a Christian writer could be in pushing the envelope just for the sake of it, to break what he or she perceives to be the rules of faith-based fiction just for the sake of edginess. Readers choose Christian fiction because it upholds their values and doesn't compromise their consciences. Keep that covenant with them, and they'll trust you enough to keep buying your books.

---

* Tosca Lee, *Havah: The Story of Eve* (Colorado Springs, CO: NavPress, 2008), 67.

Break it, and they'll stop buying your books and warn others away from them too.

⁋

Evil in Fiction
Athol Dickson

It is widely said, "Art imitates life." This is an insult to art. From a grocer or a doctor's lips it may be harmless enough, but when an author takes it to heart, we can be certain of bad books to follow.

Good novels do not imitate life; they enrich life. In this respect a good novel is like a good friend. No one would say, "Friendship imitates life," for everybody knows friendship is no mere imitation. On the contrary, because true friends are rare indeed, friendship often makes a mundane life worth living.

If friendship is the stuff of life, so it is with art. Therefore, the novelist who merely imitates life does not understand his task. To the extent an author succeeds with imitation, his work will be irrelevant, for every reader lives a real life. What use have readers for imitations?

To change analogies, such an author is like a cook who serves up photographs of soup. The resemblance might be excellent, but the appetite is unappeased. Readers want a cook who tastes the stock and says, "It could be better," then adds a pinch of thyme to bring the flavor out. Readers want a novelist who shows them something richer than the basic facts of life. Readers want the truth, which is quite a different thing.

AVOID IMITATION EVIL

The Scriptures tell us life is not as it should be. This world is cursed, which explains why novelists who merely seek to imitate life mostly give readers stories filled with evil. This mistake is especially unfortunate in the author who hopes to explore Christian themes for the benefit of unbelieving readers. Knowing it is necessary to understand the disease before one can fully appreciate the cure, he sets out to express the full dimensions of the evil that Christ has conquered.

Thus far his strategy makes sense. Most great novels do portray horrific evils, which are then overcome. But because the Christian author mistakenly believes art imitates life, in order to portray fictional evil, he thinks it necessary to flirt with the real thing. Imagining an audience of hardened skeptics ready to pounce upon the slightest variation from real life, he thinks his fiction must be "edgy" to be relevant. He serves readers real profanity to convey a foul-mouthed character; his words approach the pornographic to portray a prostitute's profession; he drags readers' minds through scenes of gore to show the truth about a murderer. Such a slavish devotion to the facts is regrettable for several reasons.

Imitation Evil Precludes Imagination

First, it fails to take advantage of the novelist's most powerful tool, the reader's imagination. "Show, don't tell," the sages say, but as with almost every rule, it is an oversimplification. It leaves out the importance of deciding what to show and how much should be shown.

Imagine a longshoreman who uses a profanity in every sentence. Now imagine a nun who uses that profanity just once. Which will have more impact? Which will most inspire imagination? Of course readers expect a longshoreman to curse fluently and often. That is exactly why we should not imitate his language. It is factual, but also superficial. The reader already knows it. He or she wants something new, something original. Why should readers engage our imaginations if the author only imitates the well-known facts? Show something unexpected. Show a longshoreman who knits to relax, for example. Readers can dream great dreams about such a man.

Imitation Evil Is Everywhere

Second, the Christian author's strategy of imitating evil dulls the very impact he desires. Remember, he wants readers to appreciate the cure, so he first presents them with the disease. He also wants to imitate the evil of this life as accurately as possible in order to establish his credentials as a "relevant" author and get the reader's full attention. But this is a losing game because he has merely joined the crowd.

Imitation evil screams for attention everywhere these days, from books and magazines to billboards and video games and motion pictures. The more we are exposed to evil, the more callous we become. From this it follows that the way to keep readers cognizant of evil is to show it only slightly or obliquely, lest they tune it out. A writer shows the deeper truth of evil best by shining light most brightly on what is good, while never letting readers forget what waits within the shadows.

Adolf Hitler loved dogs, so they say. Only a fact like that can hope to make evil on the scale of the Holocaust relevant. Hitler's love of dogs brings the gas chambers to life because I also love dogs, and if a man could do such vastly evil things while loving dogs, might I? To merely give escapism to your readers, to shut down deeper thinking, by all means show them bodies piled like cords of wood in gruesome detail. But to create some sense of the true evil in those camps, to explore the real underlying horror, it is best to mention the evil in passing while focusing on Hitler's love of animals.

Imitation Evil Costs Credibility

Third, we find an irony at work within the Christian author's strategy, for by imitating evil in order to be relevant, he achieves the exact opposite. What could be less useful than a Christian author trying to establish his credentials among unbelieving readers by imitating the very evil that oppresses them? Would a shepherd go among the lambs disguised as a wolf?

Some may point to Paul, who "became like one not having the law . . . so as to win those not having the law." But let us not omit the words Paul also said: "though I am not free from God's law but am under Christ's law" (1 Corinthians 9:21). To be sure, Jesus ate with tax collectors, sinners, and prostitutes, but he did not imitate the evil that earned such people those descriptions, not even a little, just to make a point. On the contrary, it was the difference in Jesus that attracted them. Nothing is more relevant to an unbelieving reader's heart than that same difference in a story.

BUILD HATRED FOR EVIL

Having discussed three reasons to avoid mere imitation of life's evil, it should be quickly said that the author must not make the opposite mistake and avoid evil altogether. On the contrary, he must dig deeply into evil in its truest forms, for as was mentioned previously, to understand the cure, one must first know the disease. But as was also said, it takes more than the mere facts to get at the truth.

The Christian novelist's task is to build hatred in the reader for the evil in his stories—a hatred of the evil and a deep desire to see it vanquished. It is not enough to cause offense. What we want is outrage. Therefore, to the extent that evil titillates or revolts his readers, the author has failed. Titillation makes his readers a friend of the very thing the author wants them to oppose alongside Christ. Revulsion shuts down readers' imaginations, because when they look away, the novelist has lost them.

While dealing with evil in his or her work, how can a Christian author tread this narrow path between proper hatred and outrage on the one side and useless titillation and revulsion on the other?

Write Evil Strategically

First, we must always remember that evil is a potent instrument to be used strategically. This means we must never portray evil simply because it seems realistic under the circumstances.

Readers place themselves in an author's hands, perfectly content to let the story tell them what it will—so long as it is a good story—with no compulsive loyalty to real-life details. This is a grave responsibility. Every novel is a fantasy of sorts, and every novelist a wizard weaving spells within his or her readers' minds. Thus an author has an obligation to present only those facts about his or her world worth knowing. We ought to ask, "What is the purpose for including evil in this scene? What does it contribute to the story?" It is not enough to say, "This character would do such-and-such an evil thing under these circumstances, so I have to show it." After all, we as authors have created the circumstances, therefore we are responsible for any evil that our characters might do. Heaven help us if that evil is unnecessary!

If the story can possess equal truth and power without showing evil in a certain scene, let the Christian author leave it out; otherwise we become part of the problem we set out to solve.

Use Evil Sparingly

Second, evil is always best examined sparingly. One example of this was already mentioned: the difference between a longshoreman who curses constantly and a nun who curses only once. If the actual profanity must be printed on the page (and sometimes it must), then let it be done in an isolated way that shocks readers into outrage or contemplation, rather than merely dulling their senses with thoughtless repetition.

Focus on Evil's Effects

Third, we as Christian authors would be wise to focus more on the effects of evil actions and less upon descriptions of the evil acts themselves. In an adulterous sex scene for example, the truest evil is not found in the act of sex, but in the death of trust and love. Where then would attention best be placed: on a graphic physical description of the bodies in the bed or on dialogue and action that convey the truer nature of the evil?

For another example, consider our longshoreman once more. Put him in a subway speaking to a stranger about knitting—an old woman, let us say, whose handiwork he admires, but who is not accustomed to his language. Again, where is the true evil of the man's profanity? Is it in the sound of his words themselves, or is it in the way such thoughtless language isolates him? Rather than depicting this man's dialogue as spoken, would it not be much more powerful to focus on the effect, the barrier to potential friendship and the hurt and confusion in the longshoreman when the old woman does not seem to want to speak of their mutual interest?

Contrast Evil with Good

Finally, evil is most truly seen in stark contrast to good, for all evil is a mutation of something good. In other words, the truth about evil is best understood in terms of the good it ought to be, not in terms of the evil itself. We already saw one example of this in Adolf Hitler's love of dogs. Consider another in the Gospel of John, where it says, "They crucified him" (John 19:18). That basic statement of fact is the only reference to the evil act, but after all the beautiful things Jesus has just finished saying in the upper room and in the garden, "they crucified him" is exactly enough. We all know what it means, and after focusing on Christ's beautiful words, our sense of the evil done on the cross would be less true if John had realistically described the spikes going in. We would then be thinking of pitiless iron and gory flesh instead of the deeper evil happening there: the fact that Jesus was the personification of all the love that ever was or ever will be, yet he was still crucified.

The Christian novelist has an obligation to enrich his or her readers' lives. Unlike those who do not know the Lord, we can point toward peace amid the evil that surrounds us. We can lead readers toward the path to paradise. We know how to "have life, and have it abundantly" (John 10:10, NASB). Let the slavish imitation of this life never cross our minds. Rather, with deep devotion to our craft and art, let us write with all our hearts as if writing for the Lord and thereby plant a new reality within our readers' minds, a reality that transcends this life altogether.

NETWORKING
& MARKETING

PART FOUR >

CHAPTER 15

SOLICITING FEEDBACK

¶

Confessions of a Critique Groupie
Virginia Smith

I thrive on the red ink of my critique partners' pens. My manuscript doesn't feel polished until they've given it the once-over. At one point in my career, I belonged to four different groups at once. I freely admit it—I'm a critique groupie.

My critique partners taught me how to write. When I joined my first group, I'd never heard the term *point of view*. No college professor taught me about plot movement or character motivation or how to avoid head-hopping. Instead, I learned fiction basics from a group of fellow writers who set aside time every two weeks to pick apart my amateurish stories, point out potential improvements, and help me polish them until they shined. No doubt my peers privately lamented my lack of skill at first, but they stuck with me, and I with them. I learned to produce a piece of publishable fiction from my critique group.

GROUP MEMBERSHIP BENEFITS

Joining a critique group is a little like joining a Bible study group. We must be willing to commit our time and skills to helping others grow in their writing ministries. In return, we reap the benefits of shared knowledge and support in this crazy profession of writing. And those benefits are many. There's a biblical principle involved here: As we give to others, we are blessed.

That's true in a very literal sense in a critique situation. In helping others spot the flaws in their work, our editorial eyes become adept at identifying similar problems in our own writing. One dear lady in my group submitted a chapter of her novel, and as I read, I noticed an overuse of the noun–verb–prepositional phrase sentence construction: "Sally sat in the car. She glanced at her watch. Larry coughed from the backseat." The writing felt stilted and awkward, and I spent some time coming up with a few alternatives to suggest. When I returned to my manuscript, I was surprised to find instances of the same repetitive sentence construction. I'd become sensitized to spotting it in her work, and my work benefited.

Because we are all marvelously unique, group brainstorming sessions can take delightful twists that a single writer might not conceive on their own. As that wisest of Israel's kings, Solomon, wrote, "Two are better than one, because they have a good return for their work: if one falls down, his friend can help him up" (Ecclesiastes 4:9-10). When I've written my character into a corner and can't figure out how to get her out, my critique partners have come to the

230

rescue with some tremendous solutions that have made it into my published books.

Another benefit of group membership that must not be minimized is the support we receive from like-minded people. Writing can be a lonely occupation, rife with rejection, where encouragement from professionals within the publishing industry can be hard to come by. No one can quite commiserate with a painful rejection like someone who's experienced it. Critique partners help each other develop the thick skin that's so important to this profession. It's harder to give up when you have a group of people holding you accountable to continuing on the road, no matter how bumpy the ride may be.

FINDING THE RIGHT GROUP

Every group has its own dynamics, so selecting the right one is critical. Each member should define his or her expectations and be willing to articulate them to the rest of the group. It isn't necessary that every member have the same goal; of necessity, face-to-face groups are usually comprised of writers at various skill levels who may have widely differing writing goals. A writer whose goal is to record her memoirs for her grandchildren can still provide valuable feedback to someone who hopes to write the next Great American Novel, especially if that person is also a reader of the genre. The type of feedback for each of these members will be different; as long as the writer's expectations are being met, that's okay.

But the professionally minded writer might require more knowledgeable feedback than others in the group can provide. That person may decide a group isn't meeting his needs, and when that occurs, he should feel free to move on. The commitment of membership in a critique group is real, but it should not be considered permanent.

The most effective groups are those comprised of like-minded writers at a similar skill level who are learning the craft together. When one member develops a skill, he or she passes that knowledge along to the others in their critiques. In one group I belonged to, four of the five members all made their first professional sales within a year. Obviously the group served an important purpose in the developing careers of its members.

When selecting a group, consider the format for meetings. One face-to-face group I belonged to required that writers submit their work at least a week in advance of a meeting, and everyone came prepared to provide feedback. The critiques I received there were usually more detailed and pinpointed finer skill issues. Another group allowed writers to read their submissions aloud, and critiquers discussed the piece afterward. Those critiques tended to spot broader issues related to consistency and structure.

The Internet makes it easy to form groups with people who share a common goal and skill level. The submission schedule can be flexible, and group members can respond at their own speed depending on their availability. It is still advisable to have a specified timeline for submissions and responses, though. Otherwise members lose the benefit of learning to work within a schedule, a discipline for any writer who will someday be required to meet editorial deadlines.

LEAVING A GROUP

Even an effective group can outlive its usefulness for a number of reasons. If the members are not committed to increasing their skills, their critiques will eventually become predictable and unhelpful. Writers' voices can begin to sound too similar to their critique partners'. Novelists may find that as their productivity increases, the limitations of the group submission schedule (typically a chapter or two every month, depending on the size and composition of the group) no longer fit their needs. For these reasons and others, every group should establish a time, perhaps annually, for each member to reevaluate his or her continued participation.

When a writer decides it's time to move on, he or she takes the benefits of group membership along. The lessons learned have left an impact on each writer's style and skill level. Plus, the relationships formed in critique groups often continue. I've gained some incredibly talented critique partners from the groups I've belonged to over the years, individuals with whom I trade manuscripts privately. And I've developed friendships with people I wouldn't have had the opportunity to meet had it not been for my critique groups.

¶

Developing a Critique Partner Relationship
Tamera Alexander and Deborah Raney

As iron sharpens iron, so a friend sharpens a friend.
PROVERBS 27:17, NLT

Writing can be a lonely pursuit, and it's easy to become so close to your own work that you can no longer be objective. A writing critique partner can provide encouragement, a new perspective, growth in the craft of writing, and a kick in the pants when necessary.

We have been critique partners for more than five years—ever since we met at a writers' conference and Tammy volunteered to critique one of Deb's manuscripts. While not all critique partners become friends, friendship has been a natural outgrowth of our working relationship. Over the course of critiquing almost a dozen manuscripts, we have learned much about what to look for in a critique partner—what works, what doesn't, how to handle conflict and competition, and how to "agree to disagree" with grace.

Here are a few of the things we've gleaned through our working partnership.

FINDING A CRITIQUE PARTNER

- First and foremost, *pray* about the person God might pair you with.
- Ask God to keep your heart teachable.
- Seek someone whose strengths make up for your weaknesses and vice versa.
- Join a critique group. One-on-one partnerships often develop naturally out of larger groups.
- Ask a nonwriting friend or relative who is well-read to critique your manuscript. Perhaps barter babysitting or cooking or housecleaning in exchange for those services.
- Attend local or national writers' conferences and connect with another writer you meet there.
- If feasible, sign up for a paid critique at a local or national writers' conference you're attending.
- Consider paying a professional editor for a critique. An organization that both of us are members of is American Christian Fiction Writers (www.acfw.com), and there are numerous

well-qualified editors within the ACFW membership, as well as critique group opportunities.

- Become your own critique partner. Keep your skills sharp by reading books on self-editing, such as *Revision & Self-Editing* by James Scott Bell (Writer's Digest Books) or *Self-Editing for Fiction Writers* by Renni Browne and Dave King (Collins).

- Take advantage of online opportunities to post your work for critique. If someone likes your work or sees potential in it, he or she may be interested in partnering with you.

- Offer to critique for a published author. It's a long shot, and we're certainly not suggesting you start contacting novelists at random, asking to critique their work. But if you've established a relationship with a published author at a conference or online, it might be a possibility, and it's a great way to learn.

BENEFITS OF A CRITIQUE PARTNER

- At the point when you most need to be objective, you are too close to your own story to read it as an unbiased reader, let alone evaluate it critically. Your critique partner is able to offer perspective that you may have lost.

- You bring only one opinion or viewpoint to the reading of your own work. A critique partner brings a different point of view since he or she has likely had a different upbringing and different life experiences and therefore has a much different "filter" through which to read your work.

- Someone who's not so close to your story might come up with ideas or plot directions that you never would have dreamed of.

- Almost any two people working together bring two sets of strengths to the table and offset each other's weaknesses.
- Brainstorming! With today's technology, critique partners don't have to be next-door neighbors or even live in the same state. With applications such as Skype (skype.com) and iChat (for Macs), you can "video brainstorm" anytime, day or night. And it's free! Plus, if you use something like Google Talk, you'll have a "text copy" of all those ideas for future reference.

PARTNERSHIP VERSUS A CRITIQUE GROUP

- It takes much more time to critique three or four manuscripts from group members than one from a partner.
- Too many cooks can sometimes spoil the soup. Writing by committee can really mess with a writer's voice. It's a fine balance to stay true to your voice while also striving to remain open and teachable.
- You really develop a safety net within a one-on-one relationship, which fosters trust and the ability to speak the truth in love. We have grown to the point that we can be very blunt in our assessment of each other's work, but that doesn't mean we point out only the negative. We're careful to make note of what we admire about each other's writing too and generously sprinkle plenty of encouragements throughout our critiques. A good critique is one in which the writer clearly sees what needs to be changed and feels equipped and empowered to address those issues—not beaten down into the dust, ready to give up.
- By concentrating on the one-on-one relationship, you're able to focus more on that person's unique strengths and

weaknesses as a writer. And likewise, your partner can do the same for you.

BENEFITS OF A CRITIQUE GROUP

- When you're first starting out, it's good to have input from multiple writers because, chances are, you have a lot of writing basics you still need to learn.

- Having multiple critique partners can help you find your voice as a writer. When Tammy was in a critique group early on, she would watch for similarities in critiques from her writing partners. Would three of the four writers make the same comment about a certain character or plot point? Or would it be only one writer making that particular comment? That helped her to develop confidence in her own voice while still weighing the counsel of others.

- When you desire a quick response or input from more than one person about a particular aspect of your work, a critique group is helpful. Life sometimes gets in the way of responding to tasks as quickly as we'd like. This is true of writing partners, especially if you're both on deadlines. The chances of having someone available to read your work in a timely manner are much greater if you're part of a group.

- There are many styles of critiquing, and being in a group can help you learn *how* to critique. Again, it's not just about pointing out what's wrong but about equipping another writer to be the best writer possible. Writers often have their specific areas of expertise as well—be it a strength in characterization, dialogue, plot, creating believable story worlds—

so being part of a group can expose you to a wider variety of writer strengths.

Whether you're already in a writing critique group or a writing critique one-on-one partnership, or you're still looking for that right group or person, the goal is to keep improving your writing skills and honing your craft. None of us ever ceases needing to learn, needing to grow. We want to give God our best, and as King David said in 2 Samuel 24:24, "I will not sacrifice to the LORD my God burnt offerings [or in our case, our writing] that cost me nothing."

So be willing to pay the price, hone your craft, and give God your best. And keep your eyes open to the possibility of a critique partner to share the "cost" along the way.

§

Beware of CGD:
Critique Group Dependency
Angela Hunt

Years ago, I read an anecdote in *Reader's Digest* that went something like this: A young husband watched his wife cook a ham and was mystified when she cut off the end of the ham before placing it in the pan. When he asked why she did it, she said, "Because my mother did."

So they called Mom, asked her the same question, and got the same answer: "Because *my* mother did."

So the newlyweds called Grandma and asked why she always cut off the end of the ham before baking it. "Simple," she said. "Because my baking dish was too small for the whole ham!"

Ah, gotta love that. Sometimes logic should overrule the practices we adopt.

I'd like to address a problem I've seen arising out of critique groups. Before you start tossing rotten tomatoes, let me say this: I know that critique groups can be helpful, beneficial, and fun. But lately I've recognized an epidemic raging among would-be novelists—I call it *CGD* or *critique group dependency*.

I've seen firsthand how CGD can stifle a writer's voice and fill his or her head with nonsense. I know critique groups have been around forever, but almost every aspiring novelist I meet at a conference has joined one and picked up a set of "rules" that are too much like Grandma's undersized baking pan. These groups are adamant about what should and should not be done, and often they're the blind leading the blind.

For those who suffer from it, CGD tends to stifle creativity. At a recent writers' conference where I taught, I went through a stack of manuscripts and kept reading comments like "My critique group feels this is too [insert adjective]. But I think [insert comment]."

Why would you let a critique group wield that kind of influence? If they offer a suggestion and you are persuaded by their logic, great, they've been helpful. But if they offer a suggestion and it goes against everything in your gut, forget it! The people across the table are not editors. They have no purchasing power. They may not even have any publishing experience behind their opinions—and trust me, things look different once you've been at this awhile.

I've seen some really odd things in manuscripts as a result of critique groups. At one conference, I evaluated a stack of novel proposals. Several of them contained mini book reports on other novelists' works and read something like this: "My book is a little like Karen Kingsbury's [insert title here] except that my book features a [insert noun] and she works in [place] instead of [Kingsbury place]."

What in the world? I asked my class where this came from (since I'd only seen it in that particular region), and they said they'd been told to do it like that. By whom? Well, someone heard it at a conference and came back and told their critique group . . . and there's Grandma's too-small pan again.

No, no, a thousand times no. Think logically—why make your novel sound derivative instead of fresh and original?

I know where that particular idea springs from, but the concept has been twisted like an ugly rumor. Publishers would like to know of novels similar in tone for marketing purposes or of similar books on the market when you're writing *nonfiction*. But that information should be presented at the end of the proposal, more like an afterthought than a selling point.

I've also seen manuscripts where the author second-guessed every other line based on feedback from her critique group. Let me assure you of this—a writer's voice needs to be confident. At some point you have to trust yourself. Writing is both an art *and* a science, and at certain times the art overrules the science. Yes, there are rules and you must know them, but sometimes the rules should be broken. If you break them, you have to break them with aplomb. And if questioned, you'd better have a reason more valid than your critique group's opinion.

Finally, CGD can result in overexposing the book that's dear to your heart. You can talk the magic and enthusiasm right out of your work if you're not careful. Others can pick it to death and leave your darling looking like a pampered Persian left out in the rain. You don't want a critique group to drain your enthusiasm.

Though I've never belonged to a critique group, I know they can be helpful. If you've found a good one, count your blessings. For the record, I'm not adverse to feedback, but I usually use a single test reader because there are already too many voices inside my head. I am forever grateful to my test readers!

So whether you use one test reader or avail yourself of a critique group, be aware of CGD and its symptoms. You don't want to throw out good material just because it doesn't fit Grandma's pan.

CHAPTER 16

BREAKING INTO PUBLISHING

¶

How to Write a Proposal
Mindy Starns Clark

You've written the Great American Novel—now what? Now it's time to create a book proposal, the tool you will use to introduce yourself and your novel to agents and/or publishers and convince them to take a look at the entire manuscript.

In theory, once you've pumped out tens of thousands of words for your story, a simple little proposal should be a piece of cake, right? Not necessarily. In reality, some authors find the process of proposal writing excruciating and more difficult, even, than writing the novel itself. Creating a proposal needn't be intimidating or painful, however. It simply requires some careful thought, attention to detail, and an understanding of what it is that publishers are hoping to find when they open your packet and start reading.

PROPOSAL ELEMENTS

Because different agencies and publishers have different submission guidelines, there is no single "approved" format for fiction proposals. Despite minor variations, however, most fiction proposals consist of the same four common elements: a cover letter, a synopsis, a one sheet, and sample chapters.

Cover Letter

The cover letter for a book proposal should be professional, engaging, and brief. Never longer than a single page, the cover letter's purpose is to set up the accompanying synopsis, one sheet, and sample chapters in a way that piques an editor's interest and keeps him or her reading. The tone of the cover letter should be enthusiastic but not overly "salesy." Most of all, it should reflect the author's voice.

There are no hard-and-fast rules for what goes where in a cover letter, though most authors begin with their novel's hook, a one-line irresistible teaser that hints at the book's unique premise and tone. A great hook is like an enticing movie preview in that it gets the viewer in the mood for the story by implying all that lies ahead without taking the time to provide extensive information.

Author Kristin Billerbeck opened her proposal for the Spa Girls series with the following words:

> Three friends. One spa. And an infinite amount of oversharing.

Not only is her hook engaging, it also communicates the author's voice and the book's tone.

So how do you come up with the best hook for your novel? If you're having trouble condensing an entire book into a few choice words, try the following exercise, a variation on what's known in the industry as an elevator speech.

Imagine that you're on the third floor of an office building waiting for the elevator, manuscript in hand, when a Big Name Editor just happens to come along. You've heard rumors that his publishing house is acquiring new projects, and you already know that your book would be a great fit—if only you could get someone there to take a look at the full manuscript. As the elevator doors open and the two of you step inside, he asks if that's a manuscript you're clutching and, if so, what it's about. (Come on, an author can dream, can't she?) You're both heading for the first floor, so you know you have about fifteen seconds to answer his question. Given that you're suddenly filled with poise, confidence, and clarity, what would you say? Your best answer to that question is your hook, the sentence(s) you should use in your proposal's cover letter.

Along with your hook, be sure to indicate the novel's title, genre, target audience, and length. If you are simultaneously submitting this proposal to other publishers, say so. Somewhere in the letter, you should also indicate that the novel is complete and ready to send out, exclusively, upon request. With few exceptions, editors and agents will not look at proposals for unfinished first novels. You have to write the whole book before you try to sell it.

Besides presenting information about your novel, the cover letter also introduces you as the author, usually in a single paragraph. In this paragraph, be sure to point out your previously published works, if any, and state your unique qualifications for writing this novel. If you have no published works and no obviously unique qualifications, don't be too concerned. With fiction, editors pay much more attention to the quality of the writing than the résumé of the writer.

Conclude your letter with a polite call to action. In his proposal for *The Notebook*, author Nicholas Sparks ended his cover letter with this simple question: "May I send you a copy of the completed manuscript?"

His approach is straightforward and professional, and it encourages the reader to move on to the other elements of the proposal so that they can answer his question.

Synopsis

Let's face it: Writing a synopsis is tough. You've just finished telling your story in three to four hundred pages; how can you possibly describe it in one or two?

"You'd be surprised at how many of your peers, published and unpublished, can't write a decent synopsis of their own novels," says Jeff Gerke, founder and publisher of Marcher Lord Press. "When I first read the proposal for a fantasy I ended up publishing, the synopsis was so terrible I almost rejected the book without even looking at the sample chapters."

Often synopses fail because authors misunderstand what's required. The main goal of a synopsis is not to wow an editor with fun, breezy advertising copy peppered with coy questions and vague promises. According to Gerke, a synopsis can include some snappy copy, but it should never be too much of a tease and it should always include a description of how the tale ends.

Use your synopsis to relate the high points of the story as a whole, and be sure to include not just plot elements but also character development, inner conflict, and even spiritual principles.

I learned this by sitting on the other side of the desk; on several occasions I have had the privilege of representing my publishing house at writers' conferences, evaluating proposals as an acquisitions editor would. This experience always deepens my appreciation of the job editors do, and it helps me learn firsthand how *not* to pitch a novel. Over and over, I will ask authors to tell me about their book, and they will immediately launch into a play-by-play recounting of the plot. After about the fifth ". . . and then this happens and then that happens," my brain has checked out.

It is the rare author who understands that what happens next is only one part of the whole. A great synopsis will give a basic recounting of the plot, yes, but it will also highlight other elements of the story, such as theme, character growth, or spiritual development.

Author Marlo Schalesky included the following paragraph in her proposal for *Beyond the Night*:

> The world shows us how to love with an eye to self. But self deceives. It teaches us love filled with passion. But passion fades. It gives us love marked by desire. But desire betrays. God calls us to a higher love, one like his own, a love that lights even the deepest darkness of pain, fear, and adversity. That's the love that changes lives and reflects the purpose of our God. That's the love that does not fall or fail. And that's the kind of love that forms the heart of Paul and Maddie's story in *Beyond the Night*.

As you can see, by including the spiritual basis for the story, she communicates the novel's impact within a much richer context than a simple recounting of the plot would reveal.

Remember the elevator speech exercise for creating a hook? To write a synopsis, use the same trick—only start with the two of you on a higher floor. Imagine that you now have a full ninety seconds before the elevator reaches the lobby. In that amount of time, how will you describe your book in a way that will convince the publisher to ask for a full proposal? Once you figure that out, you'll have the basis for your synopsis, which should be at least one page long (but never more than two) and so polished that it shines.

One Sheet

One sheets actually originated with the film industry as handy marketing tools for screenwriters. A one sheet is—you guessed it—one page long, and it features all of the salient points that an editor would appreciate having at his or her fingertips when reviewing your proposal or sharing it with other departments at the publishing house.

A one sheet features your name, contact information, book title, genre, word count, audience, hook, and blurb (a paragraph-long description of your book's premise, similar to the summary that would go on the back of the book).

Other elements that can be on a one sheet include the following:

- More detailed biographical information
- Personal experience that is relevant to the story
- Historical notes
- Selling points
- Series information

- Previous publishing credits
- Marketing analysis
- A list of comparative titles

When researching potential publishers for your proposal, be sure to find out which of these optional elements are expected and then tailor your submission accordingly. A good one sheet will feature your proposal's salient points in a handy reference format, and it is geared toward presenting your manuscript's potential in the best possible light.

Sample Chapters

Despite all of your hard work on the cover letter, synopsis, and one sheet, most editors will jump to the sample chapters first anyway, reading a page or two to see what your writing style is like.

Unlike nonfiction, the sample chapters that you submit with a fiction proposal should be the first two or three chapters of the manuscript—a minimum of thirty pages and a maximum of eighty—not sections culled from different points in the book. You already know that those first few chapters should sing; if they don't, you need to give more attention to the book itself before spending time on a proposal.

When representing my publisher at conferences, I'm frequently astounded at the premature nature of most sample chapters I'm given. It's not that the writers are untalented or don't have good ideas for their novels. It's that they simply have a ways to go before their writing reaches the level of competence that publication requires. I've seen stilted language, amateurish dialogue, mistakes in grammar and punctuation, and much more. Before you send a proposal to anyone, make sure that your writing is well edited and publisher ready.

PROPOSAL MECHANICS

When fully assembled, your proposal should include the following:

- A one-page cover letter
- A one- or two-page synopsis
- A one-page one sheet
- Sample chapters, thirty to eighty pages total, with a title page for the book that includes your contact information

You also have the leeway to include at least one more page of pertinent information if it will truly help an editor or agent better understand your fiction project. For example, when I sent in the proposal for my first mystery novel, I included each of the items listed above plus a one-page synopsis of the entire series. In that synopsis, I began by explaining that the series premise was flexible enough to span three books minimum or twelve books maximum. (Given that the popularity of series frequently waxes and wanes, I knew that publishers would appreciate the flexibility that my story line offered.) Next, I described each of the subsequent books in individual paragraphs. Finally, I concluded with a small section that outlined the overriding romantic story arc and character growth that began in the first novel and would conclude in the final one. That proposal helped to sell the entire series, which ultimately spanned five novels.

As for formatting your proposal, there are no specific rules beyond making it as professional and editor friendly as possible. According to Ron Benrey, author of *The Complete Idiot's Guide to Writing Christian Fiction*, that means using a standard font and size, normal margins, and plain white paper. Benrey says that "gizmos and doodads" such as fancy clip art or colored paper will not impress an editor; in fact, things like that tend to make editors skeptical about your writing.* Keep it simple and professional and allow your words to speak for themselves.

WHAT PUBLISHERS WANT

Kimberly Shumate, acquisitions editor for Harvest House Publishers, says that when editors read fiction proposals, they are usually looking for the following:

- Fresh ideas that are well conceived and have a broad appeal
- Professionalism of the author, especially in meeting deadlines
- The ability to sustain characters and plot for an entire novel
- Believable characters in refreshing stories that move quickly and provide tension through action, not narration
- Crisp dialogue that flows well and is free of clichés

Of course, the very first criterion that any proposal must meet is that the book is appropriate for the publisher. Make sure you do your homework when choosing where to submit and that you query the publisher first before sending the full proposal. By sending a proposal for a mystery, for example, to a house that accepts only romance novels, you will waste time and postage and very likely irritate an editor—which is never a good thing.

HOW *NOT* TO IMPRESS A PUBLISHER

As shown in the following real-life examples provided by agents and editors, you must avoid at all costs a proposal that comes across as impolite:

---

* Ron Benrey, *The Complete Idiot's Guide to Writing Christian Fiction* (New York: Alpha Books, 2007), 255.

Please advise on the preferred manner of submitting for acceptance—*not* refusal—acceptance.

illiterate:

> I know your website said you don't take unsolicated manual strips. Can you please tell me how to solicate my manual strip?

or even downright wacky:

> You must send me a large advance, or I will tell God to hit your part of the country with severe weather patterns.

My favorite proposal faux pas was an editing error sent to agent Chip MacGregor. From the first line of the cover letter it was obvious that the author forgot to turn off his translation software (which provides alternative words in brackets) before sending. The salutation read:

> Dear Chip [potato, chocolate, buffalo, fish and]

Be sure that you avoid similar missteps and instead demonstrate professionalism from the first page of your proposal to the last.

DO YOUR BEST AND LEAVE THE REST TO GOD

A great fiction proposal is professional, succinct, and utterly engaging. Creating one is hard work, but if you have written an excellent book and have chosen carefully the agents and/or editors to whom you will submit it, that proposal can be the first step in a long and satisfying career as a novelist. Be sure that you cover every step in the process with prayer and that, as a Christian author, your work is pleasing to God both in content and effort.

For what it's worth, that first book proposal is almost always the hardest. Once you are an established author, your proposals will likely become easier and much less structured. After writing eleven books with the same publisher, I am now able to pitch new projects with nothing more than a synopsis and a conversation. Not all of my ideas are accepted, of course, but between the projects I pitch and the ones they accept, I have been able to produce a steady stream of fiction since that first book, with more contracted for the future.

So even if you find the proposal-writing process excruciating, remember that it's a necessary part of the road to publication and that it does get easier with time. Remember, too, that a great proposal can make all the difference between a manuscript that languishes in your computer and one that finds its way to a receptive publisher, bookstore shelves, and ultimately the hands of eager readers.

¶

How to Write a Compelling Synopsis
Nancy Mehl

Although it's important to make your synopsis sound interesting, your agent or publisher needs information—not just hype. Think about combining the basic facts of a newspaper article with the excitement and drama of a movie trailer. You will need to merge the *who*, *what*, *where*, *when*, *why*, and *how* elements taught to journalism students with a touch of the kind of enthusiasm found in cinematic previews. How is this done?

WHO?

You must introduce your protagonist. Your target will want to know your main character's gender and approximate age. Why? Because he or she needs to decide what kind of readers would be drawn to your book. If a publisher is concentrating on middle-aged female readers, presenting a proposal or manuscript that would appeal more to young men will cause your work to be rejected.

A warning: although you must clearly define your protagonist, don't unload all the information at once. Doing this creates an information dump that can weigh down your synopsis. So how can this be handled effectively? Here's an example:

> Sylvia Renfro is a young woman with a problem. She wakes up one morning to find her husband and two-year-old daughter missing.

Without actually stating her age, I've made it clear that she is young, yet old enough to be married and have a small child. You can scatter more information about Sylvia throughout your synopsis if you need to, but gender, age, and marital status are the most important.

WHAT?

Explain the situation your protagonist finds herself in. *What* is it about this situation that will make it a story worth reading?

Let's go back to Sylvia. Obviously Sylvia's husband and child are missing. So? Maybe they're playing outside.

> A quick search of her house only adds to her confusion. Where are her daughter's toys and clothes? And what happened to her husband's things? Sylvia runs to a neighbor's house only to be told that she has been living alone . . . for the past several years. Yet the memories of her family are as real as the terror that seizes her mind and makes her heart race.

Now we know *what* the story is about.

WHERE? (AND WHEN?)

It is important to present the location of your story. This can be a critical element. Does your story take place in a large, contemporary city? in a small town? in America? in another country?

Is your setting in an Amish town? Although currently a popular setting for stories, if the marketplace is overrun with Amish novels, your publisher may pass. Is it a cozy mystery? If so, don't set it in New York City.

I'm also adding *when* to your *where*. When does your story take place? Is it a historical novel? a contemporary story? Your target needs this information to define your genre and decide if your manuscript will fit the publisher's needs.

WHY?

Why does your protagonist allow herself to be pulled into the plot? For Sylvia, it's personal. Her family is missing. Personal relationships can be a compelling excuse for a character to walk into a dangerous or difficult situation. Motivation is key.

Every author must ask these questions when writing a novel: *What is it that keeps my main character from walking away? What is it that compels her?* Many manuscripts have been rejected because this element wasn't addressed.

Unfortunately some writers never ask themselves this question. Their protagonists simply make unbelievable choices that involve them in dangerous situations. In your plot and your synopsis, this won't work. There must be a solid *why* for your story to proceed. Be certain you share this reason in your synopsis. Agents and publishers will be looking for it.

HOW?

A synopsis needs a conclusion. Although book reviews and movie trailers should never reveal the ending of a story, in a synopsis, it must be included. And it must make sense. How do you, as the author, bring about a satisfying conclusion to the story? Does Sylvia find her missing family? Did she have a family? How does she discover the truth?

Remember, the agent or publisher has to be in on the plot. Don't tease them. Like a finished puzzle, you must show your target a complete picture.

This sounds like a lot of information, but it can be done within the recommended one or two pages of a synopsis. How? Write it out—including all the information that must be there—then start cutting. You'll be surprised how much you can trim by simply deleting unnecessary information and sticking to the important facts. So cut, cut, cut until you have a concise synopsis that will tell your target everything he or she needs to know.

Next? Spruce it up and make it sound exciting. Read it out loud

FORMATTING YOUR MANUSCRIPT

Publishers may have specific requests for manuscript formatting. It's worthwhile to double-check this in a writer's market guide or on a publisher's Web site before submitting your manuscript. In general, the following formatting guidelines are acceptable.

- Include a cover page with the title of your project; your name, mailing address, e-mail address, and phone number; and the word count. You may also wish to list your agent's contact information under yours.
- Use 12-point Times New Roman font and set standard margins (one inch or 2.5 cm) on all four sides.
- Specify left alignment and double spacing. Do not add any extra spacing before or after paragraphs.
- Create headers that include the title, your last name, and the page number.
- Indicate a line or scene break by typing [###] or [***] and centering it on the page.
- At the end of each chapter, insert a page break after your last sentence.
- Do not use two spaces after a period at the end of a sentence; if you're in the habit of using two spaces, retrain yourself or use the "find and replace" function in your word processing program to replace two spaces with one space wherever they occur.

—*Siri Mitchell*

to yourself and to others for feedback. How do the hearers respond? Is it compelling? Does it make them want to read your work?

Once you know what should be included in your synopsis, it's your job to make it interesting. If you follow these guidelines, you'll be on your way to crafting a synopsis that will be a quick, clearly stated, and attention-grabbing read.

¶

What to Expect from a Writers' Conference
Deborah Raney

A writers' conference offers writers at all levels of expertise and publishing experience a chance to jump-start a career, improve the writer's craft, network with like-minded wordsmiths, and make connections with leaders in the publishing industry. Attending a conference with realistic expectations and a teachable spirit is the secret to a successful conference experience.

Here are some tips to ensure the best return on your conference investment:

GO WELL PREPARED
- Do your homework ahead of time and learn all you can about the faculty who will be at the conference.
- Study the conference schedule and choose the workshops and continuing sessions that best fit where you are in your

writing journey. But don't be afraid to change your schedule, if allowed, once you arrive and hear the faculty introductions.

- Read conference blogs and participate in available forums about the conference beforehand.
- Rewrite and self-edit the manuscript you hope to propose at the conference. Then practice a short pitch—preferably in front of a mirror, into a tape recorder, or with an honest and trusted friend—so you are ready for those meetings with editors and agents.
- Pack with learning in mind; include a notebook, your favorite pens and highlighters, your laptop computer, and whatever else you'd take into a regular classroom.
- Pack light so you'll have room to bring home souvenirs, handouts, and the wealth of books and resources the conference bookstore—and new writer friends—will likely have available. Don't forget your Bible. Most Christian conferences provide a wonderful opportunity for spiritual retreat.

If you do these things, you've done everything in your power to go prepared to get the most out of the conference experience.

GO WITH REALISTIC EXPECTATIONS

Most conferees will not sell a manuscript the first time they attend a conference. If you go with the idea that you simply *must* sell something or your money and time will be wasted, then you can't help but feel defeated before you ever set foot in the auditorium. If instead you view the conference as a next step in the journey to becoming a competent, working writer, you will free your thoughts and emotions to simply soak in the wealth of information you'll encounter at the conference.

If this is your first conference and you are especially nervous about talking to editors and agents, don't stress about making a pitch during your appointments. View your meetings with publishing people as a practice run or an opportunity to ask questions of an editor, agent, or author whose brain you'd like to pick. Then make your priority simply to soak up information in the workshops and continuing sessions.

As the conference progresses and you feel more comfortable, perhaps you can gather the courage to pitch your project. Many conferences have faculty-hosted tables at meals. Get your feet wet there, and save the more daunting one-on-one meetings for later in the conference, or even for next year when you've had twelve months to apply everything you learned and you can come back as a veteran, knowing what to expect.

DRESS APPROPRIATELY

Wear something that makes you feel attractive and confident, yet comfortable. This might sound like petty advice, but if you are comfortable with the way you look and feel, you'll be less anxious and more self-confident. Wear something you can put on and forget. I always advise attendees to dress up just a little, especially if you have an appointment with an editor or agent. Err on the side of being overdressed rather than underdressed, but don't feel you need to go out and buy a new wardrobe for the conference.

If you don't have anything appropriate, borrow something or check out the local Goodwill or Salvation Army for a couple of new outfits. Mixing and matching is another option. You could probably wear the same black pants–black shirt outfit throughout the entire conference. If you jazz it up with different jewelry, scarves, jackets, etc., each day, no one will be the wiser.

SERVE OTHERS

Finally and most important, get your mind off of yourself and into servant mode. The truth is, most of the people you are nervous about approaching or interacting with are so nervous themselves that they don't have time to worry about how you look, if what you said was stupid, or whether you measure up. So decide before you go that your main mission at the conference will be helping *others* to feel comfortable and encouraged. If you do that, I guarantee you will be well liked and highly thought of, and you will ultimately come away from the conference feeling it was a worthwhile venture.

What are some tangible ways you can serve others at a conference?

- If you see someone standing alone and looking lost, confused, or nervous (or crying!), approach them and introduce yourself. Ask if there's anything you can do to help. You may have to admit that you're a newbie yourself, but between the two of you, you can probably figure out what you both need to know.
- Don't spend too much time talking about yourself. Yes, people want to get to know you, but most people respond best to someone who not only shares their own story but is also interested in what others have to say. Ask leading questions, and be sure to listen to the answers. At a writers' conference, "So, what genre do you write?" and "What are you working on now?" are always valid questions. Or ask people where they are from. Chances are you'll discover you have something in common.
- Make the most of opportunities to help in tangible ways. At

a conference, there is always an elevator door to hold, a box of books to carry, directions to a meeting room to offer, a cell phone to loan, a cup of coffee to buy, a friend to introduce.

- The minute you start concentrating your efforts on helping others feel welcome and at ease, your own nerves will start to untangle. I promise, if you look for ways to serve, the Lord will provide! But you'll never recognize the needs if your eyes

TOP WRITERS' CONFERENCES

Here are some of the top Christian writers' conferences around the country:
- **Writing for the Soul** (Christian Writers Guild); February—Denver, Colorado; www.christianwritersguild.com/conferences/default.asp
- **Florida Christian Writers Conference;** February/March—Leesburg, Florida; www.flwriters.org
- **Mount Hermon Christian Writers Conference;** March/April—Mount Hermon, California; http://mounthermon.org/adult/professionals/writers-conference
- **Blue Ridge Mountains Christian Writers Conference;** May—Asheville, North Carolina; http://snipurl.com/blueridgeconference
- **Colorado Christian Writers Conference;** May—Estes Park, Colorado; www.writehisanswer.com/Colorado/index.htm
- **Gideon Media Arts Festival;** May/June—Ridgecrest, North Carolina; www.gideonfilmfestival.com
- **Write-to-Publish Writers Conference;** June—Wheaton, Illinois; www.writetopublish.com
- **St. Davids Christian Writers' Conference;** June—Grove City, Pennsylvania; www.stdavidswriters.com
- **Write! Canada;** June—Guelph, Ontario; www.writecanada.org
- **Oregon Christian Writers Conference;** July—Portland, Oregon; http://oregonchristianwriters.org

are too focused on how you feel, how you look, or how frightened you are.

- Bathe the conference in prayer. If you go expecting God to work in and through and for you, you can be sure that's just what will happen. Maybe not in exactly the way you expected, but certainly in ways you'll look back on and thank him for down the road.

- **Greater Philadelphia Christian Writers Conference;** August— Philadelphia, Pennsylvania; www.writehisanswer.com/philadelphia/ index.html
- **American Christian Fiction Writers Conference;** September— various cities; http://acfw.com/conference
- **San Diego Christian Writers Guild;** September—San Diego, California; www.sandiegocwg.org
- **Maranatha Christian Writers Conference;** September—Muskegon, Michigan; www.writewithpurpose.org
- **Sandy Cove Christian Communicators' Experience;** September/ October—North East, Maryland; www.sandycove.org/docs/ communicators.php
- **CLASS Christian Writers Conference;** November—Abiquiu, New Mexico; www.classervices.com/CS_Glorieta_Conf.html
- **Blue Ridge Christian Novelist Retreat;** October—Ridgecrest, North Carolina; www.lifeway.com/novelretreat
- **American Christian Writers conferences;** numerous conferences throughout the year—various cities; www.jameswatkins.com/acw/ acwconferences.htm

—Deborah Raney

¶

What to Expect from an Editor
Colleen Coble

Congratulations! An editor has just told you your project is going forward. You have a publishing home for your precious baby. But now you have a new set of worries—What about working with this new person in your life? Exactly what does your editor do? And how do you move forward from this point?

WHAT AN EDITOR DOES

Too many authors make the mistake of sending in their book and thinking it's done. Turning in the manuscript is only the beginning of the process. Your book is a team project.

Edit Manuscripts

When the editor read your book, she loved it, and that's the reason she bought it. The editor saw the potential in the manuscript. But also know this: she saw the flaws as well. And there *will* be flaws. No manuscript is perfect. You know what you intended to say, but until you get input, you don't know if you conveyed your full vision. A good editor is able to see to the heart of the story. She recognizes what's missing and what needs to be more fully developed.

Your editor is going to come back to you with suggestions for how the story can be strengthened and how the characters can be more fully realized. Listen to her! More often than not, you'll find out she's right.

Know the Market

Expect your editor to have the pulse on publishing. If she tells you a certain scene or attitude won't work well for her house's market, she knows what she's talking about. The best editors always tell you that this is your story, but the smartest authors know their editor has seen more and knows more about the market than they do. Only you can know if some suggestions work or not, but learn to listen with your defenses down.

Oversee the Process

Expect your editor to care about everything that goes into turning your manuscript into a book. You might find that your editor isn't in love with your title. Realize that's often changed because the marketing and editorial teams know how important the title is. Be flexible when your editor asks for other title ideas or comes back to you with an idea of her own.

Once the editing is done and you've had time to make revisions, your editor will send the manuscript out for more proofreading. She's also going to oversee back cover copy, the way the cover integrates with the story, and the copy written for the sales catalog. At many houses, the editor is going to want your input on those things, though at some houses, you might not have a choice. If you're not in love with something, take a day and think through what works and what doesn't before coming back with your opinion. The professionals at your publishing house put a lot of thought into how they are marketing the book, so voice any criticism in a positive way. Most of the time, only small tweaks are needed.

Act as an Advocate

Expect your editor to be your advocate with your publishing house. She is your front person for contact with your publishing house, and most questions can be directed to her. Your editor will consult with marketing and publicity people as well and ensure they have a good grasp on what your story is about.

BUILDING PUBLISHING HOUSE RELATIONSHIPS

When the book has been edited and is moving along through the production process, what happens next? You move on to the next story. Your editor is a good ally here too.

Take a deep breath and ask your editor what you need to work on. Characterization? Maybe learning to say less and trust your reader to get it. Maybe you need to work on integrating the setting into the story better, or you need to make your dialogue sing. For the author who is brave enough to ask, the editor will have some suggestions. You never arrive as a writer. With every book you turn in, you should be growing in your craft. Trust your editor to help you.

Your goal as an author is to be someone your editor wants to work with again. You want the people you work with at your publishing house to smile when they see your name pop up in their inbox. You can do that by being encouraging and open to constructive criticism.

Here are some suggestions on building those relationships:

- Plan a visit to your publishing house. Even if it's on *your* dime.
- Learn key people's birthdays and send a card or even a small gift like a Starbucks card.
- Take a picture of you with the group, stick it by your computer, and pray for them.

- Meet your sales rep. When you're going to a different area, contact the rep in that area and let them know you're going to be signing books. The rep will generally turn up, and you can forge a friendship.

- In all areas, be a professional. Your relationship with your editor may become a friendship, but you should still maintain some distance to be able to effectively take the constructive criticism you want from her.

- Don't complain. Have a good attitude even if someone messes up (and everyone does) just as you'd want them to have a good attitude if you mess up.

- Be grateful! This is a big one. I can't tell you how often I see ingratitude. An author feels there's not a big enough promotion budget; someone else got this or that. When someone inside the house does something great—like selling foreign rights or book club rights—send an e-mail saying thank you and follow it up with a card or chocolate. You can get a list of who does what from your editor or publisher.

- Talk up your house! Be proud of these professionals and who they are.

- Recommend other writers to the publisher. It helps the people at your house know you are proud of them.

- Above all, remember you are part of a *team* that wants you to succeed and make money. Your editor wants to be known as the brilliant person who discovered you, the perfect author every house wants to work with because of your great attitude and your growing sales. Put down your defenses and resolve to be a team player. You won't be sorry!

CHAPTER 17

MARKETING

¶

Promoting Your Novel
Melanie Dobson

Now that you've finished writing your novel, it's time to let people know about it. While there are many ways to market a book, one of the most effective and inexpensive ways to promote your work is through free reviews and interviews in newspapers, magazines, e-zines, and blogs, as well as on radio and television shows.

The publicist at your publishing house should coordinate some reviews and interviews for you, but they will probably want you to assist with the process. Where do you start? Call your publicist first and ask specifically what the publisher's team will be doing to promote your book so you can help without duplicating their efforts. Once you have established your role with your publishing house, grab a cup (or pot!) of good coffee and get ready to create your plan.

Every successful publicity plan includes three elements:

- Media hooks to pique the interest of producers and writers
- An overview of the materials to include in your press kit
- A detailed list of media to pitch interviews or reviews for your book

MEDIA HOOKS

Magazines, newspapers, TV shows, and radio programs are all searching for one thing—a great story! It's your job to help them find one. If you develop pertinent and compelling angles based on your personal story as well as your novel, you can pitch these hooks as part of your media campaign.

The best place to find these different angles is to ask a set of questions about yourself and your work. How is your novel different from other novels? What is unique about your personal story? What topics do you address in your novel—topics you could discuss for a twenty- or thirty-minute live radio interview?

My first novel was a story about an adoptive mother who had to give back the baby she loved, days before his adoption was finalized. As I spoke with media about my novel, I shared my family's adoption story, talked about the fears involved with adoption, and then discussed the reason I wrote this book.

Is there an issue you can tie to your novel? Is your book set in an exotic location that you've visited? Do you feature a specific holiday in your novel? Does the story focus on a historical figure or contemporary event?

As you narrow down the different angles you can discuss in an interview, be alert to current topics in the news that relate to your book. Randy Alcorn's novel *Safely Home*, for example, is a powerful story about a twenty-year reunion held in China between two college roommates, one an American businessman and another a Chinese man being persecuted for his faith. While we were working on the PR campaign for the book, Beijing was named as the host city for the 2008 Olympics. As this story was featured in national media, Randy interviewed on radio stations across the country about the persecution of Chinese Christians, and he discussed the true stories he uncovered while researching this novel.

PRESS KIT

Once you have established your media angles, it's time to create a press kit. If your publicist doesn't write a full kit for your book, find sample press kits online that introduce new books to the media as examples in preparing your own. This kit should contain an overview press release about your novel that includes one or more of your media hooks. It should also contain a book description, book reviews, pricing information, a short author biography, your contact information, and your Web site.

As part of this kit, write suggested interview questions for radio and TV producers and, if you'd like, a full-page author profile. Also, some authors include a question-and-answer sheet to answer specific questions about themselves and their book. This Q&A is a great resource for print media—they can pull author quotes and use them in their articles.

When the press kit is complete, it should be uploaded onto your Web site and either placed in a folder or tucked into your book when you mail review copies to media.

MEDIA LISTS

After you finish writing the press kit, the next step is to develop a media list of fifty to one hundred contacts with specific names and updated contact information. This list should be targeted to media who write book reviews, interview novelists, or have done articles or shows about your topic.

Search online for media and contact information. Often both print and electronic media publish the contact names and e-mail addresses as well as their physical address online so you can contact the correct person with your story idea.

To find magazines that may be interested in reviewing your book or setting up an interview, skim through magazines at your local library or bookstore and select those that review similar novels. Sally Stuart's *Christian Writers' Market Guide* is an excellent resource to research the contact information for various magazines targeted to Christian readers.

Once you find your contact information, compile your list into a spreadsheet or another database so you can sort the names and create both mailing labels and contact lists with phone numbers and e-mail addresses.

PITCHING TO THE MEDIA

When you have finished your plan and press kit, it is time to begin sending out review copies of your book to your contact list and pitching media via e-mail and the phone.

The best way to tell media about your book is to send your contact a review copy and a press kit along with a personal letter of introduction. If you don't hear back from your contact in three weeks, e-mail a short follow-up note with the press release included.

After three more weeks, if you still don't have a response, I suggest calling your contact once and leaving a short message that includes your media hook as well as your contact information. At that stage, the producer or writer should contact you if they are interested in coordinating an interview or reviewing your book.

Magazine Articles

While most media will want you to send a final review copy of the book, magazine editors will want to review your manuscript before it is published. Approximately four to six months before publication, you or your publisher should send out an introduction letter along with advance reader copies (or bound galleys) of your novel to both trade magazines (like *Publishers Weekly* and *Christian Retailing*) and consumer magazines for potential book reviews. If this is your first novel, also research which publications feature new novelists and explain in your pitch letter that this is your debut.

Newspaper Articles

Another good place to pitch an article about your book is your hometown weekly or monthly paper. Often, smaller newspapers will feature local authors, and these are excellent clips to include in a press kit. When you mail a review copy of your book to larger daily newspapers in your area, include a personal letter with information about your involvement in the community.

If you have lived in several different areas, e-mail the managing editor or book review editor information about where you grew up or your other connections to the area. Unless you are a well-known author, newspapers outside where you live or have a personal connection are not likely to do an article or review about your book.

Online Articles and Blogs

Thousands of Web sites and blogs review books and interview authors. You can develop a Web site list by contacting the reviewers and bloggers on sites that review novels similar to yours and asking if you can mail them a review copy and kit. When I send out my novels, I target specific, high-traffic blogs and send an e-mail to the blogger to see if they would be interested in doing a review or interview. Offer one or more review copies for giveaways as an added incentive. When a blogger or writer reviews your book or interviews you, add the article link to your author Web site for additional publicity.

Radio Interviews

If your novel has a pertinent news angle, radio hosts across the country may be very interested in interviewing you. My second novel was about a Christian woman addicted to gambling. For my press kit, I compiled a page of statistics about how often Christians gamble and how quickly people fall into addiction. Because of the unique topic and research, I was honored to interview on large and national radio shows across the country to share the stories and facts behind my novel.

Even after your novel has been out for a while, be alert to news stories that might pertain to the topics in your book. You can always send out a press release with your unique perspective on a news topic. Also, if you are able to compile additional facts on an issue relevant to your book, this is a tremendous help for the producers who are prepping their boss (the host) for an interview. The easier you make a producer's job, the more likely they are to set up an interview with you.

TV Interviews

Before you begin contacting national television shows, local shows are the best place to begin pitching and interviewing about your book (and a great place to practice if you haven't done many TV interviews). Once you have interviewed locally, you can mail a clip of the interview to larger and national TV shows.

When you pitch TV, watch the specific show you want to be a guest on and make sure it is a fit for your book. Then contact the station and determine which producer sets up interviews. Send the producer a personal note, press kit, review copy, and ideas for visuals or video clips to include with your interview. If the television station is close to your home, you may want to personally deliver the package—a TV producer will almost always remember a package that has been hand delivered.

The most effective publicity occurs when you develop relationships with media representatives and make yourself available to assist them with creating a lively and interesting story. Because publicity is free placement, there is no guarantee that your book will garner reviews or interviews. However, sending your book and a compelling press kit to a targeted list of producers and writers will help get the word out about your novel.

¶

Shameless Self-Promotion
Patricia Hickman

I'm the least likely candidate to be writing about self-promotion. Most of what I've learned about authors promoting their books through media, I've gleaned through nervous observation followed by the art of stepping out and testing my own promotions.

At the outset, self-promotion seems wrong. I know I'm not the only novelist who gets hives at the thought of thumping my own conga. The reasons not to do it pile up next to that squeaky little player in the back of our heads that is telling us, "If you don't believe in yourself enough to broadcast it, then no one else will either."

Before Karen Kingsbury became an icon of Christian fiction, she and I spent a few book conventions together. Karen and I were each promoting a book we'd written for the same publisher, and that tossed us into the same events and meetings. In the middle of the convention floor, Karen stood smiling with these saddlebags strapped around her. She must have been lugging twenty pounds around that entire week. She wore them into every restaurant and even into a theme park, where she climbed into the log flume with me, those awful bags smashing the two of us into the seat. She had ordered some pens and coffee mugs with her name on them. They clanked against her as we walked from venue to venue. But I would soon realize that they were tools in a marketing expert's pretty little hands.

Karen was an author on a mission. No one had ever heard of her, and she had six children—six reasons to get her name flashing in the black at the top of the best-seller lists. Karen was smelling blood. She told every person we met that they would need a box of tissues when they read her stories. She had her speech down pat. But she did not *hand* the person her promotional pen. No, she held it up as though it were floating in the air waiting to be plucked. And every single time, each person took the bait and reached for the pen. Something about that ritual must have caused these people to go home and reach for her book.

If every author runs to the summer convention and tries this method, though, it will lose its effectiveness, as all good overused ideas do. So please hear me out. I share this story not because it's a formula for sales success. But if we have the good fortune to contract a story and see our name in a byline, then within us, I believe, is also placed the personal aptitude to sell it.

The important thing is not that Karen invested in pens and coffee mugs, or even that she spent her own money doing it—money we all have to eat in Web design and other promotional venues. It's that Karen was good at being Karen. And she was bold enough to be Karen.

My sales background is what helped me recognize Karen's techniques: *Get the buyer to touch and talk about your product. Tell them what it will do for them.* But if I try to give a sales speech, it will come off as false, or worse, forced. So I had to be good at being Patricia. I carry very beautiful bookmarks in my purse, and when someone sees my book cover on one, it takes her eyes off me and onto my book. My goal is not to finish telling them about the story and its hooks but to get them to ask about it. It's that mental reaching that spurs the potential reader to rummage around for my book in the bookstore or online. It becomes relational.

When I released a book that had taken two years to write, I had to remind readers that I had been writing a special book with some extra layers. Over time, the news that my novel had released spread throughout the Carolinas through my simple, personal, grassroots marketing. When the local stores ordered only a few copies, I reminded them that the book was still selling well. After three reorders, the managers finally placed a sizeable order in a middle aisle with a sign that said "New Fiction." That transferred my novel out of the ghetto of faith-based fiction aisles and into the mainstream.

Why all this trouble over a local sales program? In spite of million-dollar advertising campaigns, novels still flounder. Publishers are still dependent on two parts of the big sales equation—the story's ability to sell itself and the author's personal investment in it. You see, in addition to inviting the buyer to both touch and talk about our books, readers need to be excited enough to tell others.

Instead of a bookstore tour, my publisher had invested in what is called a blog tour. A blog tour is time well spent. It costs the authors no traveling expenses because it's done from home at our desks. And often I was sent an advance interview by each blogger so I could answer the questions at my leisure and edit them. Two weeks out, Technorati listed my novel as the most talked-about book on the Internet.

Since then I have chanced upon an idea that worked well in my own blog, Words to Go. I e-mailed our online group of published authors asking if any of them would answer a couple of questions from me on the topic of a memoir I was developing: "On Being Good." I took one friend's responses, then broke our thoughts out into a chat between us and broadcast an invitation to the chat on Facebook, calling it "Mystery Guest Friday." Readers who visited would seemingly eavesdrop on our conversation, and more important, instead of knowing us by those rather dry and dusty biographies tucked into our books, they would know us more authentically.

We were swamped with feedback. So I put together a few more weeks of author chat themes. I lined them up, and Words to Go took on a new nuance and gained a following. I've published blog chat themes like "Lessons Learned Livin' Down South" and "The Pinnacles and Pitfalls of Being in Love." While my author friends and I share personal stories, these are also themes that spin out of my novels.

The reason that Words to Go continues to draw hits is because I've touched a nerve and helped readers connect the ordinary with something extraordinary—novelists' lives are just like theirs.

When I treated the business of writing as something separate from the craft of writing, it was an uncomfortable skin for me. When I integrated my writing and marketing under one purview that draws on who I am as a human being, then I found my voice as an author and a promoter. Now all of my work metrics have found common ground, and that is how my readers find me. Our ordinary lives all somehow intersect, and that is what makes our stories all extraordinary.

¶

Blogging! Who, Me?
Maureen Lang

Mention the word *blogging* to an author, and you'll get either a glimmer of interest or a glazed sort of eye roll.

On one end are those who love blogging. It's another form of social networking, one more way to reach others and to be reached. It's also an instant form of publication, without editing, where the blogger is indeed the boss of every word and all content. If there are any limits, they reach only as far as whatever image the blogger hopes to portray to others.

On the opposite end you have those who are overwhelmed by the notion of maintaining a blog. They neither read nor write blogs and resent the implication that every author ought to have one as a marketing tool. They might agree blogs have a place in this Internet-connected world (thus the resentment felt when a friend or PR person suggests trying one) but barely have time to meet deadlines, let alone host a running dialogue about life or art or the writing industry or any other topic imaginable in order to fill up a blank screen. They realize this is another marketing mouth that must be fed.

If you, like me, are on the side of the scale tipping toward overwhelmed, there are a few options to consider before ignoring the blogging world altogether.

WHY SHOULD I BLOG?

Some of the biggest complaints I hear about blogging are these: What would I talk about? Why commit to something that will demand so much of my time? How would I reach readers? There are already thousands of blogs out there; what could I possibly write that hasn't already been written?

Every blog is unique simply because God made each of us unique. Two people may devote themselves to the same topic but will present their content in totally different ways. Your blog will be uniquely *you*, with your voice, your thought process, your life's filter. And there's no one else like you.

Of the many competitive methods to market your name or your work, blogging is one of the easiest and cheapest. Having a blog is about exposure—connecting with your readers and attracting new ones. Novelists don't tend to have the sort of platform a nonfiction writer brings to a chosen subject, but if readers enjoy your book, chances are they'll check out your Web site, to which your blog can be linked. It's one more avenue through which word-of-mouth advertising can travel.

WHAT SHOULD I BLOG ABOUT?

Your first decision will be regarding the subject matter, and the possibilities are endless. Choosing a blog topic should be fun. It's likely whatever passions you have in life are already showing up on the pages of your books, but a blog offers you an opportunity to expand. Here are a few suggestions to get you going:

- Discuss an issue. Is there a similar, underlying theme in some of your books, some aspect that keeps showing up? Characters that care about the environment or pets? A specialized community? You might find a topic in the layers of your books.
- Talk about things you enjoy like hobbies or movies or music. But keep safety in mind. Realize including a few personal references may encourage readers to feel like they know you far better than they actually do. Careful bloggers should refrain from naming their young children, posting pictures of family members, or revealing too many personal facts.
- Generate "added value" for new releases and take a behind-the-scenes look at your writing process, like a director's cut giving the reader an inside view of how your story went

from an idea to the printed word, including everything from research trips and the sale to critique partners and marketing.

- Let one of your characters "author" a blog to give readers a peek at his or her everyday life.
- List how-to tips on writing or conference preparation or any other subject your authority warrants.
- Review books and conduct author interviews with contests to win free books by the authors.
- Discuss controversial subjects like politics, social values, theology, and so on. But keep in mind that passions run strong on both sides of issues and it's easy to alienate others.
- Do a limited-term blog that focuses on one book or subject, with content written in advance and an appropriate launch and end date (to coincide with a new book release).
- Pair up with other authors to share the content demands and broaden your exposure.

The topic should allow the reader to feel a connection to you and your work. Choose a topic in which you have either unique experience or knowledge or choose something you're passionate enough about to explore and enlighten yourself and then others.

BLOGGING TIPS

Don't be intimidated by the mechanics of blogging. There are a number of free, simple services available that take a short time to set up (just type in a search for "free blogging service"). Make sure you have antivirus software in place, but for the most part blogging is safe and incredibly easy.

Keep It Visually Appealing

Blogs that work best are clean and not cluttered, with easy navigation and easy-to-read fonts that don't compete with background color. Your blog should be free of ads and should not play music. (Even the most appropriate instrumental background can be annoying if your blog is read at the wrong time or place for noise.)

Entries that are visually appealing tend to be shorter rather than longer, with relatively brief paragraphs separated by a double return to give more white space. Length ranges from about five hundred to one thousand words on average per post, although there are no set rules.

Pictures, when they fit the topic, are a visual pleaser. A behind-the-scenes look at your writing career or current project might include research trips, conferences, book signings, and book club visits. It's important that the pictures relate to the topic: how your research trip factored into your story, a landscape captures the mood of your book, or a famous face resembles your character, or how a book signing was a marketing success. Overall such visuals make for great variety and easy, engaging online reading.

Prepare Content in Advance

In the writing business there are often long delays between when we create something and when it's available to an audience (whether it's a book or a presentation at a conference).

For a blog topic that's directly tied to a book release or a conference appearance, it's important to launch within a time frame that best suits the buzz—that word-of-mouth advertising we're told is the most effective. You might want to discuss this with your publisher's marketing or PR staff, but generally speaking, the date should be near enough to the book's release or conference appearance to avoid frustrating readers whose interest will be piqued and who will want immediate access to your topic.

It's key to write content when you're most excited about the topic you've chosen. Writing your blog text in advance helps on at least two levels. First, your content will sparkle with enthusiasm. Your fun will show up in every word. The text you wrote with excitement and passion will appear as fresh and new to your audience as if you'd just written it.

Second, once you launch, you can fit blogging into any busy schedule. Posting a prewritten topic takes only a few minutes of your time. By the time you run out of initial material, you will have given yourself a chance to work blogging into your routine so that, like all of the other demands in your life, it can be juggled and managed.

Post Consistently

Whether you're going to post every day or a few times a month should be decided in advance of your blog launch. Consistency is more important than frequency, both for those who follow your blog and for you to make it part of a regular routine.

Keep in mind that it takes patience to build a loyal blog readership. A successful, long-term blog that is given a chance to build can have payoffs in broader exposure and greater name recognition for better book sales and in expanding influence. Some have gained a source of income by selling (limited) ads and/or products.

Attract Readers

Find ways to let the online world know your blog exists. Start by adding a link to your automatic e-mail signature as an advertisement every time you push Send. If you have an e-newsletter or Web site, include a link for others to subscribe. Do you already belong to a number of online communities? If the list host allows such invitations, send a post to the loops about your blog.

Running a contest for free books or other goodies you can afford to invest in always helps to attract new readers. So does investigating similar blogs and establishing a linking network by writing comments on other blog sites.

Offering an RSS feed (Rich Site Summary) will notify interested readers when you've updated without having to send out e-mails that can either be annoying or easily ignored. Your blog provider can supply you with information on setting up an RSS feed, or you can google "RSS feed" for an in-depth explanation of how they work.

Online search engines like fresh content, so you may want to let blog services like Technorati know when you update. They like relevant, helpful information around keywords that come up often when people search for various topics. You might also consider submitting one of your blog entries as an article to various online magazines or free article sites, which invite you to link back to your blog. Just google "article directory" for a list of free sites such as Article Dashboard.

Since it takes time to establish a blog presence—to increase back links between your blog and others and move up in the search engine rankings—blogs can tease the ambitious blogger or torment those who dabble. So be realistic about what your blog will accomplish. Its purpose is to reach a targeted audience (your readers) as an added value to your latest product.

In testing the blogging world, you may find it easier than you thought to work into your schedule and may want to continue blogging far longer than you originally anticipated—in which case ranking, expanding readership, linking, and RSS feeds will all take on new meaning for you. Or you may find this a path for sharpening your writing skills a reward in itself.

Knowing your topic, preparing content in advance, and using your blog as a tool to connect with readers will make blogging more fun than just another duty that demands your time. It's doable, valuable, costs only the time an author puts into it, and has a freshness date that'll last as long as your books, characters, and blog remain relevant.

¶

The Value of Online Social Networks
Rachel Hauck

One of the biggest debates among writers is how much time to spend in cyberspace. It seems distracting and time-consuming. It appears to invade our lives as well as the lives of those we invite to join us in our cyber world.

But the times are changing. Writers need all the cyber face time we can get. Social media are becoming an industry unto itself.

News organizations such as the *Wall Street Journal* and *Good Morning America* are planting their cyber footprints in places like Twitter.com. Even businesses like Zappo and Thomas Nelson Publishers are joining in.

About five years ago, I joined Xanga when I heard the youth at church talking about this new online community. MySpace soon swept the world, and I joined with the inspired idea that I'd make a bunch of "friends" and tell them about my books. I don't know how ahead of the curve I was—perhaps a stride or two—but soon the notion of having a cyber footprint exploded for everyone.

My philosophy was to make friends with readers in a way that was easy and convenient for all of us. Writing a hundred or a thousand different e-mails or letters announcing my books would be overwhelming. I didn't have enough known readers for a newsletter. Plus, those who became my online friends might have some small interest in who I am and what I write.

After MySpace, I joined myCCM, then ShoutLife. I was ecstatic when Facebook opened up membership beyond college students. Then I discovered Twitter and other cyber communities like BeenUp2 and Fabulously40. There are grand book communities like Shelfari.

Among the larger social communities, my friend total is about four thousand, give or take, including friends that are in common to all cyber houses.

Other online options for reaching new readers include GodTube and YouTube. Anyone can buy a video camera and record a snippet of her writing day, then post it on the Web. A unique book trailer I produced has over 1,600 hits with little promotional effort.

You may say, "Okay, Rachel, you sold me. But how can I manage it? I have deadlines, a day job, ministry, children, obligations."

I'm with you. Here's what I do: *what I can*. Simple as that. If I don't have time to hit all my cyber haunts, I don't. Fortunately many of them are connected to each other, like Twitter and Facebook.

Sometimes I take shortcuts like pasting my husband's blog into multiple sites. I post announcements about friends' book releases. I track random thoughts and ideas and post those. I update my pictures once a year or so.

Once you're set up with a few online sites, they are easy to maintain. Building friendships can take time, however. In the beginning, I'd spend an hour or so on the weekend evenings looking for and adding friends. Now, most of the sites are sophisticated enough to recommend friends in an easy, convenient manner.

Make your cyber house unique. Let it express your personality, your passions, and your life. You can be as open or as private as you want, but however you decorate your cyber house, make it reflect a bit of yourself the reader won't always see in your writing.

THE
WRITER'S
INDISPENSABLE
BOOKSHELF

Tamara Leigh

BOOKS ON THE WRITING CRAFT

The Christian Writer's Manual of Style: Updated and Expanded Edition by Robert Hudson (general editor). This guide focuses on meeting the unique demands of religious publications. It covers grammar, punctuation, usage, book production and design, and written style. ISBN 978-0-310-48771-5.

The Complete Guide to Writing and Selling the Christian Novel by Penelope J. Stokes, PhD. From a Christian perspective, this multi-published author and editor takes readers through the creative process of writing for the inspirational market, from plot development to characterization to revision. ISBN 978-1-58297-268-8.

The Complete Idiot's Guide to Writing Christian Fiction by Ron Benrey. This handy book presents the steps to creating strong stories that deliver Christianity's messages—from answering what Christian fiction is to shaping an intriguing story to integrating Christian themes. ISBN 978-1-59257-681-4.

Creating Character Emotions by Ann Hood. This book consists of lessons that enable a writer to convey thirty-six different emotions, ranging from anger to forgiveness, from longing to worry. ISBN 978-1-884910-33-3.

The Elements of Style: 50th Anniversary Edition by William Strunk Jr. and E. B. White. Here's a classic that presents seven rules of usage, eleven principles of composition, and a guide to style. ISBN 978-0-205-63264-0 (also available free online at www.bartleby.com/141).

Getting into Character: Seven Secrets a Novelist Can Learn from Actors by Brandilyn Collins. This best-selling inspirational author provides proven techniques for creating vivid, believable characters, from determining each character's objectives and motivations to writing natural-sounding dialogue and endowing characters with realistic emotions. ISBN 978-0-471-05894-6.

Goal, Motivation and Conflict: The Building Blocks of Good Fiction by Debra Dixon. "*GMC*" is a jewel of a book that sets out the basics of building a story and creating characters with whom readers can relate. ISBN 978-0-9654371-0-3.

On Becoming a Novelist by John Gardner. This classic informs the writer on what it takes to be a novelist and what one must guard against in the pursuit of a writing career. ISBN 978-0-393-32003-9.

Plot & Structure: Techniques and Exercises for Crafting a Plot that Grips Readers from Start to Finish by James Scott Bell. A best-selling inspirational author, Bell provides clear information on how to create believable and memorable plots and ways to correct common plot problems. ISBN 978-1-58297-294-7.

Revision & Self-Editing by James Scott Bell. This book helps the writer transform a first draft into a polished final draft with emphasis on plot, structure, characters, theme, voice, style, settings, and endings. ISBN 978-1-58297-508-5.

Stein on Writing: A Master Editor of Some of the Most Successful Writers of Our Century Shares His Craft Techniques and Strategies by Sol Stein. Using examples from best-selling authors, Stein explains how to create interesting writing as well as how to fix flawed writing. ISBN 978-0-312-25421-6.

The Writer's Journey: Mythic Structure for Writers by Christopher Vogler. Based on the work of Joseph Campbell, Vogler's book provides insight into using mythic structure to create powerful stories with believable plots and realistic characters. ISBN 978-1-932907-36-0.

Writing for the Soul: Instruction and Advice from an Extraordinary Writing Life by Jerry B. Jenkins. The best-selling author of the Left Behind series offers advice and intimate anecdotes from decades of experience in the writing and publishing world. ISBN 978-1-58297-417-0.

Writing the Christian Romance by Gail Gaymer Martin. This book offers instruction in the creation of stories of romance that meet the Christian market standards, such as how to incorporate personal, romantic, and spiritual growth, and ways of realistically presenting sexuality from a Christian view-point. ISBN 978-1-58297-477-4.

The 3 A.M. Epiphany: Uncommon Writing Exercises that Transform Your Fiction by Brian Kitely. This is a unique book that offers over two hundred fresh writing exercises to help transform stale writing into exciting fiction. ISBN 978-1-58297-351-7.

Write His Answer: A Bible Study for Christian Writers by Marlene Bagnull. This recent find is a Bible study designed to bring Christian writers nearer the source of their inspiration. ISBN 1-892525-12-7.

REFERENCE BOOKS

The Bible. Keep several translations of the Bible on hand, especially when writing contemporary fiction. Whereas one translation may fit an older, Scripture-quoting/pondering character, another translation may better fit a "hip" young character.

The Dimwit's Dictionary by Robert Hartwell Fiske. If clichés riddle your writing, this book presents thousands of overused words and phrases and offers clear and concise alternatives. ISBN 978-0-7858-2356-8.

"Promise" books. Need Scripture dealing with forgiveness? How about sin? loneliness? adultery? Some of these "God's Promises/Bible Promises" books have a hundred categories that will point you to the right Scripture to help your characters deal with whatever messes they have gotten themselves into.

A good dictionary and thesaurus (several available free online). If you don't have access to an online thesaurus, you should get a thesaurus in print. But don't overdo it or your writing will sound more like a thesaurus than a story.

Christian fiction. One of the best ways to learn how to write is to read—lots. Reading books by authors in the genres in which you wish to write will give you an idea of what publishers are buying and, therefore, what sells.

INTERNET SOURCES

Check out writers' Web sites, good places to learn the craft of writing—or at least to begin the process. Many writers are very generous with advice that can assist you on your journey toward publication.

Other Web sites may offer free access to dictionaries, thesauruses, Bible translations, grammar points, and more. This is not an exhaustive list.

Bible translations: www.biblegateway.com

Dictionaries: Dictionary.com (http://dictionary.reference.com) or Merriam-Webster's (www.m-w.com)

The Elements of Style by William Strunk Jr., E. B. White, and Roger Angell: www.bartleby.com/141

Respectfully Quoted: A Dictionary of Quotations Requested from the Congressional Research Service: www.bartleby.com/73

Roget's II: The New Thesaurus: www.bartleby.com/62

Names: There are many sites with lists of names, including www.babynames. com. (Use a search engine like Google to find more sites.)

CONTRIBUTORS

Carolyne Aarsen (*www.carolyneaarsen.com*) lives on a farm in Alberta with her husband and numerous pets. When the four kids and thirteen foster kids moved out, she gained time to write and be involved in her church community.

Rick Acker's most recent books are the legal/biomedical thrillers *Blood Brothers* and *Dead Man's Rule*. When he's not writing, he is a deputy attorney general in the California Department of Justice, where he prosecutes corporate fraud cases. Visit his Web site at *www.rickacker.com*.

Randy Alcorn (*www.epm.org* and *www.randyalcorn.blogspot.com*) is a best-selling author of over thirty books, with 4 million in print. His greatest joy is spending time with his wife and best friend, Nanci, and their family, including his four precious grandsons. He also enjoys reading, research, biking, and tennis.

Hannah Alexander (*www.hannahalexander.com*) is the pen name for the husband-wife collaboration of Dr. Mel and Cheryl Hodde. With generous input from her husband, an emergency room physician, Cheryl writes suspenseful and romantic novels set in the world of medicine. They have published twenty-two novels, and their most recent release is *A Killing Frost*.

Tamera Alexander (*www.tameraalexander.com*) is a best-selling novelist whose deeply drawn characters, thought-provoking plots, and poignant prose resonate with readers. Having lived in Colorado for seventeen years, she and her husband now make their home in Franklin, Tennessee, where they enjoy life with their two college-age children and a silky terrier named Jack.

James Scott Bell (*www.jamesscottbell.com*) is the best-selling author of many thrillers, and also has two titles in the Write Great Fiction series from Writer's Digest Books: *Plot & Structure* and *Revision & Self-Editing*.

Ron Benrey is the author of *The Complete Idiot's Guide to Writing Christian Fiction* and has cowritten three cozy Christian mystery series with his wife, Janet. More recently, he joined Benrey Literary, the literary agency Janet founded in 2006. Visit their Web site at *www.benreyliterary.com*.

Lisa Tawn Bergren is a wife, mom, and author of more than thirty books. Her most recent fiction titles are *The Blessed* and *Breathe*. You can learn more about Lisa and find a listing of all her work at *www.LisaTawnBergren.com*.

Terri Blackstock (*www.terriblackstock.com*) has sold 6 million books worldwide. Her Christian suspense novels are frequently best sellers. Her latest books include *Intervention*, *Double Minds*, and her popular Restoration series (*Last Light*, *Night Light*, *True Light*, and *Dawn's Light*).

Sandra Byrd (*www.sandrabyrd.com*) is the best-selling author of more than four dozen series books for women, teens, and tweens. Her most current projects include the French Twist series with its Christy Award finalist *Let Them Eat Cake* and the forthcoming London Confidential series for teens and tweens.

Robin Caroll loves to spend time at home with her husband, her three beautiful daughters, and their four character-filled pets. To learn more about this author of Deep South mysteries of suspense to inspire the heart, visit Robin's Web site at *www.robincaroll.com*.

Mindy Starns Clark (*www.mindystarnsclark.com*) is the best-selling author of ten novels, including *Shadows of Lancaster County*, and the nonfiction title *The House That Cleans Itself*. A former stand-up comedienne, Mindy is also a popular playwright and inspirational speaker. She lives with her family near Valley Forge, Pennsylvania.

Best-selling author **Colleen Coble** (*www.colleencoble.com*) has won the ACFW Mentor of the Year award twice, and her books have won or been finalists in numerous contests including RWA's RITA Award, the Holt Medallion, the ACFW Book of the Year, Booksellers Best, the Daphne du Maurier, and the National Readers' Choice Award.

Brandilyn Collins (*www.brandilyncollins.com*) is a best-selling novelist known for her trademark Seatbelt Suspense. These harrowing crime thrillers have earned her the tagline "Don't forget to b r e a t h e . . ." She has written more than twenty books. Brandilyn is also known for her distinctive book on fiction-writing techniques, *Getting into Character: Seven Secrets a Novelist Can Learn From Actors* (John Wiley & Sons).

Anne de Graaf (*www.annedegraaf.com*) has written more than eighty books, which have sold over 5 million copies worldwide and been translated into more than fifty languages. Born in San Francisco and a journalism graduate of Stanford University, she has lived the past twenty-five years in the Netherlands with her husband and their two children.

Mary DeMuth helps readers and writers turn their trials to triumph. She writes hope-filled Southern dramas and is a mom of three, pet owner of two, and wife of one, living in Texas. Meet her at *www.marydemuth.com* and improve your writing at *www.thewritingspa.com*.

Athol Dickson's writing has been favorably compared to the work of Octavia Butler (*Publishers Weekly*), Daphne du Maurier (Cindy Crosby, *Christianity Today* fiction critic), and Flannery O'Connor (*New York Times*). His novel *They Shall See God* was a Christy Award finalist, while both *River Rising* and *The Cure* won Christy Awards for best suspense novel. Athol's latest, *Winter Haven*, was a finalist for the 2009 Christy Award in the suspense category, making four novels in a row to receive that honor. Athol lives with his wife, Sue, in Southern California. Visit his Web site at *www.atholdickson.com*.

Melanie Dobson (*www.melaniedobson.com*) is the former corporate publicity manager at Focus on the Family and owner of the publicity firm Dobson Media. Her novels include *Going for Broke*; *Love Finds You in Liberty, Indiana*; and *The Black Cloister*.

Sharon Dunn is the author of five humorous mysteries. *Sassy Cinderella and the Valiant Vigilante*, her second book in the Ruby Taylor mystery series, was voted Book of the Year by American Christian Fiction Writers. You can read more about Sharon's humorous whodunits at *www.sharondunnbooks.com*.

Linda Ford (*www.lindaford.com*) is mother of fourteen—four homemade, ten adopted—now all grown. She shares her life with her one and only husband, an adult son, and a paraplegic client. She makes her home on a farm/ranch in Alberta, Canada, near enough to the Rockies to enjoy them every day.

Robin Jones Gunn (*www.robingunn.com*) has been writing for twenty-five years and is on the board of directors for Media Associates International. Sales of her seventy books have topped 4 million copies with translations in nine languages. A storyteller at heart, Robin loves speaking around the world and encouraging new writers to trust God in deeper ways as they write for him.

Rene Gutteridge (*www.ReneGutteridge.com*) is the author of fifteen novels, including both suspense and comedy, and has been working as a full-time novelist for a decade. She has also been published as a playwright and has studied screenwriting. She lives in Oklahoma with her family.

Award-winning novelist **Linda Hall** reads constantly, both for pleasure and to learn. She has written fifteen mystery and romantic suspense novels and invites readers to visit her Web site at *writerhall.com*.

Robin Lee Hatcher (*www.robinleehatcher.com*) is the best-selling, award-winning author of over sixty novels, including *Wagered Heart* and *A Vote of Confidence*. She finds her greatest joy in sharing her faith through the books she writes and through her relationships with others.

Award-winning, best-selling author **Rachel Hauck** lives in central Florida with her husband and ornery pets. Visit her at *www.rachelhauck.com*.

Patricia Hickman is the author of more than sixteen books including *The Pirate Queen*. She earned an MFA in creative writing from Queens University and speaks around the country at women's conferences and places where fellow storytellers gather. You may find more about Patricia's novels at her Web site, *www.patriciahickman.com*.

Patti Hill (*www.pattihillauthor.com*) writes women's fiction from her home in Colorado. Her first book, *Like a Watered Garden*, was a 2006 Christy Award finalist. Since then, she has added four more novels to her portfolio, including *The Queen of Sleepy Eye* and *Seeing Things*.

Sharon Hinck (*www.sharonhinck.com*) writes "stories for the hero in all of us"— novels about ordinary people experiencing God's grace in unexpected ways. When she's not wrestling with words, she enjoys speaking to various groups and spending time with her family in Minnesota.

Christy Award winner Dr. **Angela Hunt** writes novels for those who have come to expect the unexpected. One of her novels, *The Note*, was made into a popular movie for the Hallmark Channel. She and her husband live in Florida with their two mastiffs. Visit her at *www.angelahuntbooks.com*.

Jerry B. Jenkins's novels have sold more than 63 million copies since 1995, including the phenomenal mega-best-selling Left Behind series. His books can be found regularly on the *New York Times* best-seller lists. He and his wife, Dianna, live in Colorado and have three grown sons and four grandchildren. Visit his Web site at *www.jerryjenkins.com*.

New York Times best-selling author **Karen Kingsbury** is the author of more than forty titles, including the Redemption series, the Above the Line series, and the 9/11 series. She has nearly 15 million copies of her books in print and a dynamic Web site where more than 6 million people keep in touch with her work each month. You can find out more about Karen and her tips for writers at her Web site, *www.KarenKingsbury.com*.

Jane Kirkpatrick is a Wisconsin native and winner of the Wrangler Award from the Western Heritage and National Cowboy Museum and the WILLA Literary Award from Women Writing the West. Her fourteen other best-selling historical novels were short-listed for several awards, including the Christy Award for the best in Christian fiction. You can visit her at *www.jkbooks.com* and *www.janekirkpatrick.blogspot.com*, as well as on ShoutLife and Facebook.

Maureen Lang (*www.maureenlang.com*) considers herself a reader who learned to write the stories she'd like to be reading. Her books are full of romance, a touch of adventure, plenty of angst, and always, but always, a happy ending.

Tamara Leigh (*www.tamaraleigh.com*) is the best-selling author of eleven novels, including *Splitting Harriet*, *Faking Grace*, and *Leaving Carolina*. A former speech and language pathologist, Tamara lives with her husband and their two sons in Tennessee.

Multi-award-winning novelist **Gail Gaymer Martin** is the author of forty-two novels with 3 million books in print. She writes for Steeple Hill and Barbour Publishing and is the author of *Writing the Christian Romance* from Writer's Digest. Gail is a cofounder of American Christian Fiction Writers and a popular keynote speaker and workshop presenter at conferences across the U.S. Visit her online at *www.gailmartin.com*.

Nancy Mehl (*www.nancymehlbooks.com*) began writing cozy mysteries in 2006. Her Ivy Towers mystery series was released in 2008. She is currently at work on a new series that should debut in 2010. She lives in Wichita, Kansas, where she loves to spend the winter writing and reading cozy mysteries.

Susan Meissner (*www.susanmeissner.com*) is the multi-published author of contemporary fiction with historical threads, books such as *The Shape of Mercy*, named as one of the Best Books of 2008 by *Publishers Weekly*. She and her husband are the parents of four young adults and make their home in Southern California.

Siri Mitchell (*www.sirimitchell.com*) has written eight novels, two of which— *Chateau of Echoes* and *The Cubicle Next Door*—were named Christy Award finalists. A graduate of the University of Washington's business school, she has worked in many levels of government and lived on three continents.

Jill Elizabeth Nelson is an award-winning author of mystery and suspense. She writes what she likes to read—tales of adventure seasoned with romance, humor, and faith, earning her the tagline "*Endless Adventure, Timeless Truth.*" For excerpts from her novels and book giveaways, visit her on the Web at *www.jillelizabethnelson.com*.

After an early retirement from teaching, **Donita K. Paul** dove into a second career of writing. She has written three Christian romances, four novellas, two picture books, and six Christian fantasies, plus short stories and magazine articles. Her DragonKeeper Chronicles have sold almost a half-million copies. Visit her Web site at *www.donitakpaul.com*.

Cara Putman is a wife, mother, author, attorney, and all-around crazy woman. She loves writing historical romances set during World War II and romantic suspense. Learn more about Cara and her books at *www.caraputman.com*.

Deborah Raney (*www.deborahraney.com*) is best known for *A Vow to Cherish*, which inspired the World Wide Pictures film. She is now at work on her eighteenth novel and enjoying her career as a writer. However, her most cherished calling is as wife to Ken and mother to their four children. She loves small-town life in Kansas and being "Mimi" to two little grandsons, who live much too far away.

Francine Rivers (*www.francinerivers.com*) has enjoyed a successful writing career for more than twenty-five years. Her best-selling novels have been awarded or nominated for numerous prizes including the RITA Award, the Christy Award, and the ECPA Gold Medallion. Francine and her husband, Rick, live in northern California and enjoy spending time with their three grown children and taking every opportunity to spoil their grandchildren.

Gayle Roper (*www.gayleroper.com*) has authored more than forty-five books, most recently *Fatal Deduction* (Multnomah). She is a RITA winner and a multiple Christy finalist, has twice won Book of the Year, and is the winner of three Holt Medallions, a Reviewers Choice Award, and a Lifetime Achievement Award.

Nancy Rue (*www.nancyrue.com*) is an award-winning author of fiction for women ages eight to eighty. Her novel *Healing Waters*, written with Stephen Arterburn, was selected as the Women of Faith Novel of the Year for 2009. She lives in Lebanon, Tennessee, with her husband, Jim.

Kim Vogel Sawyer (*www.kimvogelsawyer.com*) is the best-selling, award-winning author of thirteen novels including *Waiting for Summer's Return*. One of Christian fiction's newest writers, her compelling stories provide not only entertainment but also life lessons her readers can use on their Christian walk.

Janelle Clare Schneider has been writing for more than twenty-five years and has had six novels and four novellas published. When she's not writing, she keeps busy as a military wife, mother of two creative children, and house-servant to two dogs.

Randy Singer (*www.randysinger.net*) is a critically acclaimed, award-winning author and veteran trial attorney. He and his wife, Rhonda, have two grown children and live in Virginia Beach.

Virginia Smith (*www.virginiasmith.org*) is the author of eight novels, including *Stuck in the Middle* and *Murder by Mushroom*. She and her husband, Ted, divide their time between Kentucky and Utah and escape as often as they can to scuba dive in the warm waters of the Caribbean.

Camy Tang (*www.camytang.com*) writes romance with a kick of wasabi. A former biologist, she now works with her church youth group and leads a worship team for Sunday service.

Before her writing career took off, **Carol Umberger** spent twelve years in the Air Force. When her sons were born, she became a stay-at-home mom. Carol is a mentor for the Jerry B. Jenkins Christian Writers Guild, working with teenage writers as well as adults. She lives with her husband of twenty-eight years and two Jack Russell terriers. For more information please visit *www.carolumberger.com*.

Amy Wallace (*www.amywallace.com*) is a wife, homeschool mom, author, speaker, and avid chocoholic. She loves crafting high-action suspense and delving deep into heart issues, but who she really is can be summarized easily: Amy is a daughter of the King learning to live and love with laughter.

Elizabeth White (*www.elizabethwhite.net*) writes inspirational romance for Zondervan and Steeple Hill. She lives in the Deep South with her husband, an executive pastor at a Baptist church, and has two children. Her upcoming release, *Tour de Force*, is a love story set in the world of contemporary professional ballet.

Brad Whittington (*www.fredtexas.com*) is the author of the Fred trilogy, coauthor of *Hell in a Briefcase*, and is always writing something.